Social Adaptation to Food Stress

PREHISTORIC ARCHEOLOGY AND ECOLOGY

A Series Edited by Karl W. Butzer and Leslie G. Freeman

Social Adaptation to Food Stress

A Prehistoric Southwestern Example

Paul E. Minnis

University of Chicago Press

Chicago and London

The University of Chicago Press, Chicago, 60637
The University of Chicago Press, Ltd., London
Ⓒ 1985 by the University of Chicago
All rights reserved. Published in 1985
Printed in the United States of America

94 93 92 91 90 89 88 87 86 85   54321

Library of Congress Cataloging in Publication Data

Minnis, Paul E.
    Social adaptation to food stress.

    (Prehistoric archeology and ecology)
    Bibliography: p.
    Includes index.
    1. Mogollon culture. 2. Indians of North America--
New Mexico--Food. 3. Food supply--Social aspects.
I. Title.   II. Series.
E99.M76M56   1985   306.3   84-28103
ISBN   0-226-53022-1
ISBN   0-226-53024-8 (pbk.)

Paul E. Minnis, an archeologist and ethno-
botanist, is assistant professor of anthropology at the University of Oklahoma at
Norman.

For My Parents

Jean Reynolds Minnis

Roy B. Minnis

Contents

Series Editors' Foreword

Food stress has become a major issue in the contemporary world. The 1970s drought in the Sahel and Ethiopia first drew significant attention to famine as a recurrent social and ecological process. This impression has been reinforced by the agonizing media coverage of yet another catastrophic famine in Ethiopia since 1984. Less attention has been accorded to equally important scholarly exploration of historical case studies of periodic environmental stress and its feedback interlinkages, both positive and negative, with social processes. Such examples range from Pharaonic Egypt to the European harvest crisis of 1816 and the Great Plains dust bowl of the 1930s. Stressful events have considerable evolutionary significance, and contemporary situations offer "laboratory" opportunities for anthropologists to frame and test hypotheses about environmental change and human behavior. One is reminded of the earth sciences' rediscovery that recurring "catastrophes" may have a greater explanatory value for observed configurations than the cumulative impact of innumerable moderate-magnitude events.

Periodic famine is but one type of food stress. The other is a matter of chronic environmental constraints, "overpopulation," and limited or unequal access to resources. The grim UNESCO data on increasing global mortality due directly or indirectly to massive malnutrition in many less developed countries provide a current example that continues to defy resolution. Studying such occurrences in the archeological record poses major problems of identification and interpretation. Paul Minnis' Social Adaptation to Food Stress: A Prehistoric Southwestern Example uses archeological data from prehistoric New Mexico to test a theory about the nature of human organizational responses to food stress. He argues that, faced with food stress of increasing magnitude, human groups will employ a graded hierarchy of responses that are both increasingly effective and increasingly costly, and perhaps increasingly permanent.

Minnis' approach is predicated on anthropological theory,

archeological method, and a combination of paleoethnobotanical and resource data rather than on physical anthropological studies, which are all too often unavailable for this type of investigation. He develops a method of quantifying food stress, combining estimates of prehistoric population and the productive capacity of various resources with estimates of changes in the critical, limiting factors. On this basis he identifies a period when high population density and limited effective moisture should have created food stress, and then examines the archeological record for evidence of economic and sociopolitical responses.

The study is of particular interest because it explicates archeological criteria to identify food stress, emphasizes the variability of environmental parameters, and examines the interaction of the component parts within a complex system that includes the environment, population, technology, subsistence choices, sociopolitical organization, and exchange. The resulting model of cultural adaptation to food stress is applied to a sophisticated interpretation of the twelfth-century abandonment of the Mimbres area. Minnis concludes that the population had outrun the productivity of the regional environment, given the technology available and the socially imposed limitations to alternative solutions.

Whether or not the reader is completely satisfied with the adequacy of this case study for testing the theory, this volume provides much material for thought, and its importance transcends the region or even the prehistoric context. The process of adaptation to stress, the problematics of starvation, and the experience provided by case studies are all pertinent if we are to deal more successfully with contemporary famines or with the impending global food shortage. Cultural ecologists and human geographers should therefore also be able to derive a wealth of ideas, methods, and data from Minnis' work. His study represents an exemplary effort to chart new understanding on the exciting frontiers of the social sciences.

Karl W. Butzer
Leslie G. Freeman

Preface

The genesis of this work can be traced back to 1976 when I first read Waddell's description of Mae Enga responses to crop-killing frosts and a number of articles by Slobodkin on adaptive strategies. Work with the Mimbres Foundation from 1974 through 1980 provided me an opportunity to adapt some of Slobodkin's ideas to an archeological case study of human behavior. The primary purpose of this book, then, is to explore the role of food stress in culture change and in the prehistory of the Rio Mimbres drainage of southwestern New Mexico.

To address this problem I must sidetrack the discussion from the specific study area. The first part of this work (chaps. 1 and 2) provides a broad background for the case study. Chapter 1 introduces several concepts central to this work, discusses the research limitations, and outlines previous anthropological and archeological research on food stress. Chapter 2 elaborates a model of responses to food stress and considers special facets of it when dealing with human behavior, then compares this model with ethnographic examples of human groups under food stress.

The second part, chapters 3-6, is devoted to the specific study area. Chapter 3 outlines the prehistory of the region. Chapter 4 presents information on the natural environment, particularly variation in factors critical to the prehistoric economy. Chapter 5 discusses evidence of the prehistoric Mimbreño subsistence economy, considers the various factors limiting this economic structure, and then makes estimates of the frequency and magnitude of food shortages faced by the prehistoric inhabitants of the study area. Chapter 6 considers what responses might be expected and in what order they would occur, based upon the model presented in chapter 2. Finally, chapter 7 summarizes this analysis, puts it in a regional perspective, and suggests further implications of this work and the perspective from which it originates.

This book focuses on nonstratified societies that are not

extensively involved in a market economy and are not part of a colonial polity. Yet I believe that with modifications the theoretical perspective outlined here may be useful for understanding responses to food stress in all human groups. In fact, it may be applied to responses to a wide range of material scarcities. For example, Rudel's (1980) study of the responses in New York and Atlanta to the gasoline shortage of 1973-74 is consistent with my theoretical perspective.

This volume is a modification of my dissertation (Minnis 1981b). I owe an unpayable debt to Richard Ford, my doctoral committee chairman, for his advice, patience, standards of scholarship, and friendship. I thank the other members of my committee, Kent Flannery, John Speth, and Robert Miller, for their insightful comments on this work.

I owe another unpayable debt to Steven LeBlanc, who by offering his friendship, directing research, and raising funds for the Mimbres Foundation provided the opportunity for me to do this research. He does not agree with all that I have written, but he made it possible. Other Mimbres Foundation staff members provided intellectual stimulation and camaraderie; Ben Nelson, Margaret Nelson, Patricia Gilman, Roger Anyon, Michael Blake, Susan Blake, and Robert Kelly helped in more ways than they realize.

I extend special thanks to Douglas Schwartz and his staff, who provided time and a congenial working atmosphere at the School of American Research in Santa Fe for the final completion of my dissertation. The Weatherhead Foundation provided support in the form of a Weatherhead Scholarship.

I thank several poor souls for giving their editorial assistance, an onerous task if there ever was one: Patricia Gilman, Jean Minnis, and Mary Jane Berman. Darlene Thornton typed this manuscript in masterly fashion and managed an Apple that is more intelligent than I am. Joe Grissom of the University of Oklahoma Computer Center helped in computer editing. The staff of the University of Chicago Press showed grace under fire when dealing with an author who took too long to produce too little.

Numerous individuals provided insightful suggestions during the revision of the original manuscript. These include Frank Bayham, Karl Butzer, Mark Nathan Cohen, Martin Etter, Chet Lancaster, Jane Lancaster, John Moore, Stephen Plog, Stephen Thompson, and Susan Vehik.

My wife, Patricia Gilman, helped in innumerable ways, such as offering critiques, but I never could get her to type anything. I

could not get her to do much cooking either, but this book could
not have been finished without her patience.

This research constitutes Contribution 29 of the Mimbres Foundation.

1

Introduction

All people must eat, but the quantity and quality of the human diet may become inadequate for varying periods of time, from days and weeks to years and decades. This book focuses on the economic and organizational responses human groups make to food shortages or to a food supply perceived as inadequate.

Famines have been conspicuous events in recent history, but food shortages are not just a modern phenomenon. As Braudel (1967:38) has commented, "famine recurred so insistently for centuries on end that it became incorporated into man's biological regime and built into his daily life." Dando (1976) estimated that there was one famine or hunger year out of every five in Russia from A.D. 971 to 1970, and Cox (1978:209) concluded: "in some regions, such as China and India, it would be safe to say that prior to the development of modern transportation systems, famine somewhere within the region was a nearly annual occurrence." Perhaps the ultimate indication of food shortages in our biological past is the large number of physiological and behavioral strategies the human body uses when faced with periods of nutritional inadequacy.

Most research on food shortages focuses on massive famines in present-day Third World countries. For the most part, this research concentrates on emergency assistance (Mayer 1975). Unfortunately, little is systematically known about prehistoric food shortages or responses by traditional groups ("traditional" denoting nonindustrial societies). Researchers who have recognized the frequent periods of severe food shortages among modern peasants have too often also created a fiction of ecologically stable traditional populations. This myth has only recently been confronted with a more realistic picture of the nutritional needs of small populations and the ability of their production systems to supply these needs. That little is known about the responses of traditional groups to periods of food shortage is due to a lack of reporting, not to the absence of food stresses. Perhaps the greatest contribution that archeology can make to the study of food shortages is to provide an evolutionary background from which to view the current problem of providing for the nutritional needs of the world's population.

The perspective used here is derived from evolutionary theory, which views the relationships between organisms and their environment (defining "environment" broadly to include the natural, social, and cultural contexts in which organisms exist) as adaptation—the processes by which organisms cope with a changing world.

In this book, any type of food shortage or perceived food shortage, regardless of severity, that invokes a reaction by the human group will be considered a stress. Obviously there are degrees in the magnitude of the stress, and these will be discussed in the next section. Conversely, an overabundance of food can also create problems that must be dealt with, but that consideration is outside the scope of this work.

Dimensions of Food Stress

Although widespread famines attract the greatest academic and humanitarian attention, there are a number of types of food stress. These vary on several dimensions, including magnitude, frequency, duration, areal extent, speed of onset, spatial dispersion, and temporal spacing (Burton, Kates, and White 1978). There are significant qualitative differences in food stress, which can involve caloric, protein, or other nutrient deficiencies or a combination of these. Furthermore, the effects of food stresses will vary for different groups and for individuals as opposed to populations (Segraves 1977). Subsistence strategies, sociopolitical organization, and population density are three major dimensions that influence population vulnerability and the type of responses to food stresses employed. These three factors are critical for determining the capacity of a group's production system and the total nutritional needs of the population. From this diversity of food stresses, we can identify two general types of stress—acute events and chronic malnutrition. The effects of these two types of food stress on human groups range from tolerable nuisance to devastating catastrophe.

A crucial aspect of the study of human responses to food stress is the perception of stress. This characteristic is defined by Bennett (1976a,b) as "anticipation" in adaptation. Obviously, reactions to a problem begin only when a problem is recognized. Studies have shown that there is often a marked divergence in the perception of a problem and its danger (Slovic, Fischoff, and Lichtenstein 1979; Burton, Kates, and White 1978). It would be convenient to believe that food provisioning problems can be objectively defined; but studies have demonstrated that this is incorrect and obscures important relationships in human coping strategies. Schneider's (1957) research, for example, illustrates this point by showing that the cultural threshold for defining a food shortage is more sensitive than are physiological triggers. That is, the Yap considered themselves faced with a problem before there were actual nutritional shortages. In fact, there should be strong selective pressure for cultural systems to develop a lower threshold to stress than the human physiological system. Individual activity is adversely affected by starvation (Keys et al. 1950). Therefore, lower cultural thresholds of stress may trigger responses before physiological impairment occurs.

Acute food shortages are relatively short term events in human groups that are otherwise able to acquire adequate nutrition. Along a continuum of severity, the two extremes are famines and hunger seasons. Famines are severe acute shortages. They have received attention because of widespread loss of life and temporary social disruption. In famine stricken nations, it is not uncommon for millions to perish.

The occurrence of famine is not necessarily a direct catalyst for social change; as Lessa (1964:44) emphasized:

> The function of disaster as a catalyst of change is not a newly recognized role, having been emphasized by Price, Carr, Sorokin, and to a lesser extent Spillius; but perhaps specific recognition of it has seldom been given for a tribal society. Catastrophe does not, however, always lead to permanent social change, for in any system that is virtually closed, a great impact in the form of a disaster will simply mean that after a recovery there will be more or less of a complete return to the old pattern without enduring change.

A particularly important indirect link between severe food shortages and social change is through radical demographic change due to the relationship between inadequate nutrition and disease (Bang 1978; McNeill 1976). Nutritionally weakened populations are unusually susceptible to disease, so that epidemics take a particularly high toll. With widespread death, the demographic profile and population size may change to such a degree that previous social and food production organizations cannot be retained. Widespread famines often can be dealt with in stratified societies without structural changes by concentrating the effects of the famine on a particular class (Segraves 1977). Even in nonstratified societies, severe famines may have no direct relation to lasting social structural change. By the time the problem becomes pronounced and severe, malnutrition sets in, and the physiological ability of individuals is impaired (Keys et al. 1950). Faced with the immediate concern for procuring food under these conditions, it is difficult to organize collective action beyond the level of the household (Jelliffe and Jelliffe 1971). Thus, though conspicuous, acute shortages are not as important as they may first seem in generating sociocultural change.

If famines are not necessarily responsible for lasting social change, then hunger seasons are even less important. Hunger seasons are short periods of the year when food resources are low. People may simply decrease their consumption by doing without their normal ration, substitute less-preferred foods for the unavailable staples (Jelliffe and Jelliffe 1971), modify food preparation techniques, or borrow food from others for a limited time (Richards 1939; Donald 1970). I doubt that these responses have much of a direct role in changing social fabric.

The case of chronic shortage is in contrast to acute shortage. Here, insufficient food is "normal" rather than an unusual event within a generally adequate diet. Chronic shortages can involve specific nutrients (e.g., protein or various vitamins), energy, or both. The human body is quite flexible in terms of specific nutritional needs, and there are examples of populations apparently surviving with what was thought to be inadequate consumption (Robson and Wadsworth 1977), so that definition of chronic malnutrition is not always clear-cut. Chronic and acute shortages can occur together, and acute shortages tend to have devastating consequences on chronically malnourished populations or segments of populations (Dando 1976; Woodham-Smith 1962).

Chronic shortages, like acute shortages, do not necessarily have a direct role in culture change. Often the causal relation is reversed; culture change adversely affects nutritional adequacy. To understand the relation between food stress and culture change, it is necessary to specify the linkages between the two. In addition, situations where food stress appears to associate with sociocultural stasis must be studied.

As mentioned earlier, individuals and groups may take action in anticipation of their vulnerability to food shortages, regardless of whether a physiological stress develops. Individuals and populations faced with a probable food shortage may be in a position to alter their food procurement strategies. They can also widen their social relationships and alliances to ensure themselves a more secure and equal food supply. An example that will be discussed in greater detail later is the Gwembe Tonga (Scudder 1962). Here strategies involved with the location of fields changed because through population growth and inheritance practices primary fields were divided to the point that households did not consider themselves adequately secure. Therefore farmers began opening up fields in the hills above the river valley, until nearly half the fields were in these locations. This process was initiated not by immediate devastating famines, but rather by the farmers' realization that they were becoming increasingly vulnerable to food shortages. Food stress, then, should be defined by sociocultural criteria, not just physiological responses.

In summary, two types of food shortages have been defined--acute, episodic events and chronic, recurring problems. As we have seen, both these types vary widely in their severity. Further, a distinction was made between actual and perceived problems of nutritional adequacy. Contrary to popular opinion, actual severe food shortages do not necessarily lead to obvious change in social structure. Changes, in fact, may result from perception of increasing vulnerability rather than from the shortages themselves.

Research Limitations

Clearly this research cannot deal with all aspects of food shortages in human groups. Specific psychological, physiological, and fecundity/mortality consequences of severe malnutrition are not considered in detail. These topics have been discussed elsewhere (e.g., Keys et al. 1950; Schneider 1957; Burton, Kates, and White 1978; Sorokin 1975; Dirks 1980; Stein and Susser 1975). In addition, not all human groups will be considered. Interest will be focused on nonstratified groups and populations not heavily involved in a market economy or closely tied to a colonial administrative system. Finally, research limitations include the types of responses. Economic and social organizational responses will be primarily considered.

Social and Economic Limitations

Two socioeconomic characteristics will be used to limit the types of human societies considered. These will be discussed in detail to provide a better explanation of how this research relates to modern food provisioning problems.

Stratification

The presence of social stratification represents significant change in a cultural system's responses to food shortages and is therefore a convenient analytic dividing point. A stratified society is "one in which members of the same sex and age status do not have an equal access to the basic resources that sustain life" (Fried 1970:186). By definition, a stratified society exhibits class variation in access to food. During times of normal food acquisition this differential access may manifest itself as a more luxurious or more varied diet for elites, but during times of stress the unequal access may be the cutting edge between death and survival. Wilson (1932:52) graphically illustrates this point:

> In the bazaar of Kermanshah sat the traders, sad-eyed but imperturbable, behind their stalls on which were displayed dates, bread, and food grains. A few yards away lay some poor Lazarus; flies swarming about his head, filling his nose and mouth; from his mouth oozed a black liquid yet he was not dead.

More dispassionately, Segraves (1977:209) expresses the same point: "the poor, then, are ultimately the expendable, a relatively cheap price for the system to pay for self-regulation."

The relation between social inequity and food availability is not just a simple matter of the upper classes being able to respond better to food shortages than the lower classes. Prindle (1979) provides an illustrative case study from Nepal. He documents how wealthy upper caste Brahmin families fare better during food crises than lower caste Bhujels. However, the upper-caste Brahmins who are poor have a harder time than the Bhujels, because they are tabooed from many economic activities that the Bhujels can use as an alternative economic base. That is, Bhujels have a more generalized economy than poor Brahmin families.

The security of having a more stable food supply during food shortages does not necessarily occur, even in societies with a belief system that emphasizes differential access to resources. For example, Firth (1959) records that Tikopian chiefs do not necessarily fare better than others during food shortages, even though they are supposed to be "the last to die." Stealing from the chief's gardens was a common occurrence, as was theft from commoners' fields.

Generally, in nonstratified societies the effects of food shortages are more evenly distributed throughout the population by means of reciprocal obligations (Sahlins 1972). Even during times of extreme deprivation, the form, if not the substance, of fulfilling one's obligations is often maintained (Firth 1959). This is not to say that all suffer equally. Some nutritionally sensitive cohorts such as weaned infants may experience a high incidence of ill health and death during food shortages (Wetterstrom 1976). Turnbull (1972, 1978) describes graphically how certain segments of the Ik population (infants, the weak, young children, and the old) suffer more than the young and middle aged adults during times of food shortages.

Colonialism and Market Economies

Colonial disruption of traditional economies has altered patterns of food shortages by introducing a profit efficient market economy, an economy geared toward the benefit of the colonial administration and local elite. In these cases, famines or severe food shortages are often more a function of the organization of production and distribution than a result of natural factors influencing crop maturation (Young 1978; Robbins 1975; De Castro 1952; Dando 1976; Derman 1978; Bhatia 1963). Food shortages in underdeveloped countries are often the result of "improper distribution of consumer goods" (De Castro 1952:281) or "a lack of purchasing power" (Bhatia 1963:9) on the part of the nonelite. Dando (1976), in a study of Russian famines during the past millennium, stresses the role of inefficient and inadequate transportation and market systems as important factors contributing to the occurrence of famines.

The similarities between famines in Ireland (Woodham-Smith 1962), India (Bhatia 1963; Singh 1975), and China (De Castro 1952; Snow 1961) illustrate the disruptive effects of a colonial system on the native economy. First, colonial economies are geared toward generating profit for the colonizing country. Hence Indian goods faced heavy tariffs in the English market, whereas English goods flowed freely into the Indian economy (De Castro 1952). Second, these economies are organized toward maximizing profit in the administered area. Large landlords are encouraged to raise high-profit crops which often make many farm tenants a liability. When this happens, the tenants become a displaced, landless class, dependent upon the most marginal and vulnerable segments of the economy. Profit also encourages planting of cash crops rather than subsistence crops. Thus, during shortages, the organization and technology of production are directed to nonfood crops (such as tea, rubber, or coffee), so that it is difficult to alter basic production to increase food production. Profit efficiency also tends to maximize dense single crop production, inherently a locally unstable and vulnerable strategy. For example, because of their marginal position, Irish peasants were forced to rely on the potato, which could produce a sufficient crop on what little land they were able to farm. But infestation by a single fungus type devastated the potato monoculture and therefore the base of peasant sustenance. All this was aggravated by taxation systems that were notoriously insensitive to fluctuations in the economy. Thus we are given a picture of starving Irish peasants placing priority on paying taxes over buying food (Woodham-Smith 1962). The most vulgar expression of the profit orientation is the commonly documented practice of price speculation and export of basic foods from famine-stricken regions (Woodham-Smith 1952; Bhatia 1963).

An indirect, and often intentional, result of colonial administration is the strengthening of local elites or the creation of a new elite class, and this weakens the reciprocal obligations of these elites to other segments of the population. In Ireland, British policies made it virtually impossible for landlords to aid their charges during famines if they were so inclined (Woodham-Smith 1962).

Another factor influencing the responses to food shortages in market systems is government aid. Government, private, and international aid has become a standard relief approach, one that some believe has obscured and is insensitive to indigenous responses (Waddell 1977).

Incorporation into a market economy also provides income options to farming. Wage labor becomes available, and often there is a large migration from rural areas to urban centers, resulting in the common tin-roofed shantytowns in cities. Often only the men leave for part of the year to work for wages. This can affect local food production by reducing available workers, particularly when labor requirements reach a peak, such as during planting or harvest. For example, Scudder (1962) reports that a large percentage of the Gwembe Tonga households did not cultivate enough land because men were not there during the agricultural cycle. Because of these changes due to colonial policy, groups extensively involved with colonial administrations are excluded from this research.

Traditional Economies and Food Stress

Now that the areas excluded have been outlined, let me briefly discuss the types of human societies that will be studied here. Basically, I will be concerned with groups having mechanisms that ideally or actually distribute wealth and institutionalized power throughout the community. Service (1962) and Sahlins (1968) characterize those groups as bands, tribes, or simple chiefdoms; Fried (1970), using different criteria, terms them egalitarian. Production in these economies is generally oriented toward a subsistence goal--the domestic mode of production (Sahlins 1972). Economic activities are embedded in social/kin relationships. In the absence of effective long-distance transportation, livelihoods are closely tied to the local region. Usually these economies are more geared toward local food production than to a regionally extensive exchange of goods. Most of these populations are agriculturalist to some degree.

Previous Anthropological Research on Food Stress

Organizational and economic responses to food stress by traditional societies have been investigated from two perspectives, defined by the type of stress studied. On one hand are short term studies of acute events or chronic malnutrition. On the other hand is the study of long term trends of food production in relation to population requirements. Rarely do these two perspectives merge.

Short Term Studies

Most anthropological descriptions and analyses of relatively short term stress derive from the "fortuitous" residence of an ethnographer in a group experiencing problems feeding itself. Some of the better examples of this type of study include Prindle's (1979) work, Firth's (1959) studies on Tikopia, Waddell's (1972, 1975) work among the Fringe Enga, Turnbull's (1972, 1978) research with the Ik, Cawte's (1978) investigations among the Kaidilt, Scudder's (1962) and Colson's (1960, 1979) research among the Gwembe Tonga, Cove's (1978) studies among the Tsimshian, Newman's (1970, 1975) work among the Sandawe, and research on Yap (Schneider 1957), on the Trobriand Islands (Malinowski 1935), and in various areas of West Africa (Horowitz 1976). Firth's, Scudder's, and Waddell's studies are particularly noteworthy because they document a range of responses and place their descriptions within a theoretical perspective.

In contrast to these types of studies, some explicit, comparative, anthropological works on food stress also exist. Some of the earliest modern work was concerned with a wide range of "disasters" (Demerath 1957; Demerath and Wallace 1957; Rayner 1957), where food stresses were only one type of short term catastrophe. More recently the "natural hazards" school in geography has systematically studied natural environment perturbations as they affect human groups (e.g., White 1974; Burton, Kates, and White 1978). Again, the focus of these works is on short term problems caused by natural hazards such as flood, drought, and earthquakes.

Recently, ecological anthropologists have begun to study responses to perturbations and risk avoidance strategies (e.g., Vayda and McCay 1975), but no synthetic work has yet emerged. Similarly, applied anthropologists have looked at variation in subsistence strategies and environmental-social conditions (Hitchcock 1978; Barlett 1980; Horowitz 1976).

While there are numerous studies of acute and chronic shortages among traditional peoples, little synthetic or theoretical work concerning responses to food stress has developed (for exceptions see the excellent work by Dirks 1980; Laughlin and Brady 1978; Torry 1979). Dirks (1980) proposes a cross-cultural model of sequential changes in cultural systems under acute food stress. Using Seyles' (1956) general stress model, Dirk outlines three stages to human food stress responses—alarm, resistance, and exhaustion.

These largely ethnological studies are most useful for understanding specific mechanisms of adaptation to food provisioning problems, because they provide a very detailed record of interrelations between critical phenomena. However, they cannot directly, or easily, be used to document the patterns of evolution of food stress adaptation; comparative ethnological taxonomies do not necessarily reflect evolutionary patterns. Neither can these synchronic studies observe the long term consequences of responses. Archeological data are necessary to study these aspects. Hence the complementary relationship between ethnology and archeology in the study of human food stress.

Long Term Studies

Long term trends in potential food provisioning problems have been studied under the rubrics of "carrying capacity" and "population pressure" (e.g., Boserup 1965; Binford 1968, Zubrow 1971; Glassow 1978; Spooner 1972; Cohen 1977). The concept of carrying capacity is concerned with the effects of increasing population on the adequacy of food procurement systems. The use of these ideas has been criticized (e.g., Hayden 1975; Cowgill 1975; Street 1969), but these concepts remain viable for anthropological purposes (Glassow 1978). There are production constraints imposed by environmental, technical, economic, and social factors. The concept of carrying capacity recognizes these constraints. Archeologists have been particularly active in using these concepts, primarily because of the time depths under investigation. By their nature, however, these types of studies tend to ignore the patterning of specific responses to food stresses.

Food stress is a common explanation for a change in prehistoric human behavior (e.g., intensification of subsistence activities, regional abandonment or other settlement pattern shifts, increased warfare). Too often these explanations are simply correlations between some changes in an environmental parameter and roughly contemporary culture change. These explanations have become more sophisticated in modeling the environmental change, largely because of a wealth of new paleoenvironmental techniques. However, we still lack sufficient theory and systematic cross-cultural studies of the links between environmental change and the dynamics of sociocultural change. We need to generate cross-cultural models of food stress response patterns. Although the specific economic and organizational responses employed by different groups may well be dissimilar, there should be common characteristics in the way humans respond to food stresses. A model of the sequence of responses is proposed in the next chapter. Other common characteristics of economic and organizational responses may also be identified. In addition to improved models, we as archeologists must be better able to identify prehistoric human behavior change in the archeological record--"middle-range studies" as termed by Binford (1977). This book adds little to this requirement.

Because archeologists have explained much of human social evolution and history as a result of environmental changes, I will not discuss this further. Rather, I will consider this topic in chapter 7 and focus on the prehistory of the Greater Southwest of North America.

2

A Model of Economic
and Organizational Responses
to Food Stress

Here I adopt an evolutionary/ecological perspective to propose
cross-cultural generalizations about individual and group responses
to food stress. After a general discussion of the concept of
adaptation, I present a model that considers the sequence of
responses to food stress, then discuss ethnographic data illustrating economic and organizational responses by traditional
human societies. This last step includes a consideration of three
case studies of responses to food stress, as well as a brief
catalog of various responses employed.

Human Adaptation

"The concept of adaptation lies at the intersection point
between evolutionary and ecological theory" (Kirsch 1980:102). As
such, the study of human adaptation has the potential to be a
unifying paradigm within anthropology. Adaptation refers to adjustments that individuals and groups of individuals make to
changes in their context of existence, including their natural,
social, and cultural environments.

An ecological focus, both in biology and in anthropology, tends
to be synchronic and concerned with the interrelation between
components of systems. These studies provide necessary system
descriptions and are useful for developing and testing models of
the mechanisms of adaptation. Obviously, ethnological data is well
suited to an ecological perspective.

Evolutionary studies focus on the differential persistence of
variability through time and the selective and stochastic causes of
change in variability. Both in anthropology and in biology, an
evolutionary perspective provides documentation of the processes of
adaptation, particularly the causes of change. Since archeological
analysis is best suited to a diachronic framework, it is uniquely

useful for understanding the evolution of human society.

Kirsch (1980:103) enumerates three definitions of adaptation.

1. In reference to a particular structure or feature of an organism; that is, a wing is an adaptation to flight
2. As a state of being, of fitness in a particular environment
3. As a process of change, of modification so as to achieve a better fit between organism and environment.

The first two definitions tend to emphasize the static result of adaptation, are best used with ethnological data, and are susceptible to tautological interpretation. Not only is the third approach the one in which evolutionary and ecological theory intersect, as Kirsch points out, but this perspective treats adaptation processually. Therefore archeological analysis can best make use of this third definition.

The term "better fit" in the third definition should not be interpreted to mean that adaptation necessarily results, proximally or ultimately, in increased "efficiency" or "maximization." As Lewontin (1978:215) points out, "natural selection over the long run does not seem to improve a species' survival but simply enables it to 'track' or keep up with the constantly changing environment." Or "selection promotes what is immediately useful, even though it may be fatal in the long run" (Dobzhansky 1958:1098). Therefore, the archeological study of the evolution of human sociopolitical organization should decrease emphasis on static typological models of general cultural evolution (band-tribe-chiefdom-state) and increase emphasis on developing a theory of the processes of human adaptation that result in organizational changes. This book is a step, I hope, in this direction. Following Slobodkin (1964, 1968; Slobodkin and Rapoport 1974), I will consider a predictive model of the ordering of responses to system perturbations. The emphasis on ordering of responses rather that on specific responses allows this model to be applied cross-culturally. Because it deals with a sequence (which must include the dimension of time), the logic of this model is uniquely well suited to archeological research. Specific adaptive behaviors will depend on the particular historical, environmental, social, and cultural context of each group, and these behaviors can be novel and unexpected (Gould 1977). System perturbations are considered here because all environments change, in the short term as well as in the long run. Therefore a major feature of any living system, including human sociopolitical organization, is a repertoire of strategies for dealing with change.   Because the adequacy of food supply directly affects individual health and reproductive success, responses to food stress must have been under strong selective pressure.

The basis of Slobodkin's model and that presented here is that:

> "successful evolution requires the maintenance of flexi-
> bility in the response to environmental perturbations and
> that this flexibility must be maintained in the most parsi-
> monious way. The parsimony argument is that organisms must
> not make an excessive or unnecessary commitment in
> responding to perturbations, but at the same time the deeper
> responses must be ready to take over to the degree that
> superficial responses are ineffective" (Slobodkin and
> Rapoport 1974:198).

Thus Slobodkin and Rapoport suggest that selection for response ordering results in a hierarchy of responses from "superficial" to "deeper."   They propose three criteria for classifying responses: the speed of the response activation, the degree of the resource commitment, and the reversibility of the response.   They suggest that these three criteria are correlated in such a way that more slowly activated responses are less reversible and are also the most inclusive.   Slobodkin and Rapoport (1974,Fig. 1) isolate six classes of responses of increasing "depth"--behavior, physiology, physiological acclimatization, death rate changes, selective mortality and fecundity, and genetic changes.

An example will illustrate this model.   Take a hypothetical case of a small mammal population such as cottontail rabbits faced with the introduction of a new predator (a type of perturbation). The most quickly activated response might be for the prey simply to outrun the predator whenever they encountered each other.   Assuming that this low level behavioral response is not adequate, deeper responses may become important.   These could include other be-havioral responses such as changing the pattern of browsing to lessen contact with the predator.   If a certain part of the prey population exhibits markings or coloration that lessen the chance that these individuals will be spotted and caught by the predator, and if the lower-level responses are not successful, then lower mortality rates of the marked individuals may increase their pro-portion in the population.   Assuming all things equal, a genetic change in the population then takes place.   The genetic response is less reversible than simply running away from a predator, and this genetic change can have wider ranging consequences for the survival of the prey population.

An example of Slobodkin and Rapoport's model extended to human behavior might be organizational responses to various disaster levels. Imagine a severe storm somewhere in the Midwest. Minor crop damage to one field might be handled by the farmer's taking out a small loan or absorbing the loss. If a whole county is affected, then the financial resources within the county might be taxed beyond capacity, and state or federal agencies might take action to underwrite loans for the affected area. If the whole state and some adjacent states are hit with widespread crop damage and destruction of transportation and communication facilities, still wider-ranging responses, such as declaring a disaster area and mobilizing the National Guard, may become necessary. How necessary would these two responses be for managing the single-field damage? In short, then, <u>the magnitude of responses should match the severity of the perturbation</u>. To do otherwise creates situations where adaptive flexibility is lost, with the result that other perturbations may not be addressed effectively.

The perspective briefly outlined here presents adaptive behavior as a sequence of responses to environmental problems. These responses are ordered from low level responses, which are quickly activated and commit few resources, to stronger responses, which require a greater resource commitment, are more slowly activated, and are less reversible. This perspective further emphasizes that adaptive behavior encompasses a wide range of responses, including, but not limited to, genetic changes.

How does this perspective relate to transgenerational change, the type of change most easily studied with archeological data? The concern with homeostasis has been extensively criticized (e.g., Whyte 1977; Burnham 1973; Wood and Matson 1973). For example, Waddington (1974:35) suggests that "we should think not in terms of homeostasis, but rather of homeorhesis, the stabilization not of a steady state, but of a pathway of change in time." Homeostatic maintenance is not homeostasis. Romer (1933) recognized this in regard to paleontological evolution, when he suggested that the primary purpose of a favorable innovation is to allow the continuation of the status quo. Thus, there is the apparent paradox that by trying to stay within traditional bounds, organisms and populations usually irreversibly change their conditions of living. The basic reason this occurs is that few factors important to biological groups are static. Therefore, similarity between changes in the organization of different societies reflects the continuance of similar responses to various perturbations.

Furthermore, the principle of equifinality holds in this case. Similar organizational and economic responses may have been used for different selective problems.

The general direction of transgenerational change in evolution is another level of analysis that is not directly considered here. It must be emphasized that there is no intrinsic directionality in evolutionary change within a single phylogeny (Slobodkin 1968; Sahlins and Service 1960). Inherent directionality assumes the presence of an evolutionary goal. Therefore we cannot posit an evolutionary teleology beyond that of survival, as early evolutionary social scientists assumed (e.g., Spencer 1871; Morgan 1877).

The Model

From the perspective discussed in the previous section, it was concluded that adaptation can be analyzed as a sequence of responses to problems faced by living systems. The sequence of responses is hierarchically ordered in such a way that more permanent responses will become important after more ephemeral responses fail to cope with the problem. I propose several criteria for ranking responses according to their depth. As developed here, the model of responses to food stress by nonstratified groups will differ from the biological perspective in two ways. The first departure is that I will be concerned only with economic and social organizational responses. This is predicated on the assumption that the most human adaptive behavior is cultural, and that, particularly in nonstratified societies, economy and social organizations are closely interdependent (Sahlins 1972; Dalton 1971). The second departure from the biological perspective concerns the criteria used to order responses. In fact, only one criterion will be used to rank economic and social organizational responses, the social inclusiveness of the response. That is, the greater the number of social units involved in a single response type, the deeper the response. We would then expect that these more inclusive responses would occur after more superficial, less inclusive responses had been attempted. The criterion of greater inclusiveness is based largely on the assumption that in the absence of unrestricted mobility, social groups faced with food provisioning problems will have to enlarge their social/economic network so as to have access to a more reliable food supply.

Ceteris paribus, the greater the provisioning problem, the wider the social network necessary. Social inclusiveness can be measured on two axes, vertical (hierarchical) and horizontal (spatial). Responses organized at a higher level of sociopolitical integration are clearly more inclusive because a larger number of groups are involved. Spatial inclusiveness is more variable and does not necessarily reflect the involvement of social groups. Trading partners or kin who reside long distances from each other may have no higher level of organization than the interaction between adjacent households. However, using longer-distance relationships may require greater commitments because of increased transportation and logistics costs. To explain and partially justify the use of this assumption, the economic structure of non stratified societies will be discussed.

Sahlins (1968, 1972) discusses the familial or domestic mode of production (DMP) in traditional societies. Rarely is the individual a viable economic unit. The most elementary decision-making economic group is the household (a nuclear or extended family). The household exhibits a surprising degree of economic autonomy, since the "family is entitled and empowered to act autonomously in its access to the resources of production" (Sahlins 1968:76). Each household not only is autonomous in its access to resources but also has a great deal of freedom to determine its level of production. This autonomy creates a situation in which each household can gear its economic activities toward the one self-centered goal of its own survival and reproduction.

However, as Sahlins points out, households are not always self-sufficient:

> The DMP has to be counteracted and transcended. This is not simply for technical reasons of cooperation, but because the domestic economy is as unreliable as it is functional, a private nuisance and a public menace. The greater kinship system is one important way it is counteracted. (Sahlins 1972:129)

Sahlins believes that providing for others during times of scarcity is a primary force undermining household autonomy. That no households are economically autonomous is a partial function, I believe, of the fact that there are no environments that provide constant and absolute resource abundance.

Enlarging the social network creates opportunities for access to resources that normally are outside the use rights of a house-

hold. This increases the resource diversity available to households, and subsistence diversity is a hallmark of system stability
(Segraves 1974; Margalef 1968). Wiessner (1982) provides an excellent example of this strategy as employed by the !Kung San of
Botswana and Namibia. A structured system of rules provides a
network of allies who can be called upon for assistance or refuge.
This institution, hxaro, provides a support network based upon
mutual obligations. Although most hxaro partners are relatives,
nonkin can be involved. This network creates alliances between
participants who have use rights to environments with diverse
resource structures and between partners separated by long
distances: "there are very few which do not have at least one
partner between 150 and 200 km away in an area which is likely to
have sufficient resources when /Xai/xai does not" (Wiessner
1982:76).

Braun and Plog (1982) apply a similar logic for understanding
the evolution of nonhierarchical ("tribal") social networks.
Specifically, they postulate that networks that act as effective
strategies for coping with unpredictability ("risk-reducing
strategies") have a selective advantage.

There are two other common ways to increase the diversity of a
household's resource base. One way is for each household to have
primary access to a wide catchment area. Generally this requires a
great deal of mobility and is effective only with relatively low
human population densities and/or where there is great natural
environmental heterogeneity. The second approach for increasing
diversity is to utilize a wide variety of secondary resources such
as famine foods. As I will discuss later in this chapter, there
are serious constraints on the effectiveness of this option for
coping with severe periods of food scarcity. For most modern
populations and the prehistoric one considered here, enlarging
social networks is the most effective option available for increasing the diversity of their food supply.

There is good reason for households to resist the involvement
of others in their economic pursuits. Under the system of reciprocity, goods and services obtained from others come with the
expectation that they will be returned in some form and at some
time. These expectations reduce the household's freedom to be
concerned solely with its own survival. Therefore, increasing
one's social/economic network is accomplished by increased risk to
each household and is likely to be considered principally as a
result of necessity. Wiessner (1982) clearly shows that the !Kung

San carefully consider the advantages and disadvantage of taking on a new hxaro partner.

One should not conclude that food provisioning problems are the only cause of social bonds beyond the household. The necessity for maintaining a sufficient breeding population, and the need for cooperative efforts in defense, warfare, and construction, will also bind social groups together. What I am stating is that with greater and greater food provisioning problems, we would expect greater and greater involvement of others in responses.

Figure 1 illustrates a model of the ordering of responses to periods of food stress. Consistent with the expectations just outlined, we see that responses that involve greater numbers of social groups will become more frequent after less inclusive responses are tried. In this model, four levels of responses are designated: household, kin group, community, and extracommunity. These are not absolute states, but convenient points along a continuum of more inclusive social groups. These categories will not be found in all situations, and in some, one category may be subsumed under another. For example, a community may simply be a kin group of some sort such as a lineage. Nevertheless, these points are adequate for illustration.

As shown in figure 1, I propose that more inclusive responses will be used to a greater degree after less inclusive responses

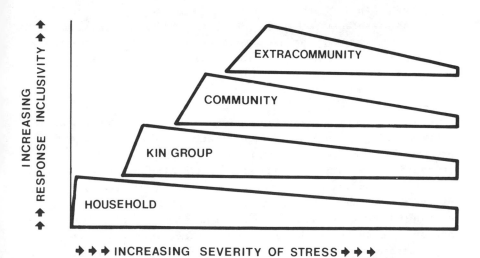

Figure 1. Sequence of responses to food stress. The primary logic of this model is that with increasing stress severity, there should be increasing social inclusivity of the responses used.

have proved ineffective. There is no independent criterion to measure the effectiveness of responses except continued existence (although the relative effectiveness of various responses is discussed later in this chapter), because effectiveness must be considered in regard to the specific conditions of particular cultural systems.

Various levels of responses can occur simultaneously, as shown in figure 1. This is also evident in the discussion of ethnographic cases of responses to periods of food stress, considered later in this chapter. The situation is different in the biological model, where some levels of responses can occur only after more ephemeral responses; genetic selection cannot happen without the "failure" of lower-level responses. According to the logic discussed in this chapter, there should be a relative ordering of responses. If the model is applicable, more inclusive responses will become more frequent after less inclusive responses have been used.

As a predictive model about human behavior during food stress, we can use it to deduce concrete expectations. With increased food stress, where more inclusive responses are used, we would expect increased probability of the survival of a cultural system. The corollary is that with increased food stress, where more inclusive responses are not employed, we would expect an increased probability of cultural system dissolution. Remember that cultural survival and dissolution must be considered in terms of the immediate selective pressure, not as a long term state. More inclusive responses, although successful for dealing with an immediate food stress, may prove maladaptive for other environmental or organizational problems.

There are two analytic approaches that can be used for testing propositions derived from this model. One could take a specific response category such as storage strategies and see if there is a progression from less to more inclusive responses of this type with increasing severity of the food stress. Although simplistic, a change from family to centralized storage would fit the expectation of the model. Another example of this approach would be changes in exchange between groups, such as from reciprocity to redistribution. Increased exchange between more distant social groups might also be interpreted as supporting the expectations from this model. The second analytic approach would be to examine a number of different response categories such as storage, exchange, use of low preference foods, and selling of surplus goods to buy foods. One could then look for increasingly inclusive use of these different response types. For example, if one found that asking assistance from trading partners occurred after the household collected and used low preference foods, then this is consistent with the model because assistance from trading partners involves greater inclusivity than the household-centered response of low preference food use. Both approaches will be used here. In the next section I discuss three ethnographic cases. In this chapter I will consider a wide variety of responses because the ethnographic description is not detailed enough for analyzing changes in individual response categories. In the archeological example from the Rio Mimbres Valley discussed in chapter 6, I will use changes in the inclusiveness of responses within single categories of responses, because it is easier to consider only a few response types in archeological research.

Ethnographic Examples of Responses to Food Stress

There are few ethnographic descriptions of the range and timing of traditional group responses to food stress. Most ethnographic descriptions are anecdotal, describing only isolated, highly visible responses with no consideration of the severity of the stress. Even the more detailed analyses consider only short periods of adjustment and rarely discuss in detail the long term trends in food procurement. However, the three best analyses I know in the ethnographic literature will be considered here in relation to the model outlined above. These cases are the Tikopia (Firth 1959), the Fringe Enga (Waddell 1975), and the Gwembe Tonga (Scudder 1962, 1971, Colson 1979). I will then consider potential responses to food shortages described ethnographically in order to catalog common responses to food stress by traditional societies. Let me emphasize that in all the cases discussed here only relatively short periods of adjustment to food shortages have been documented, with little consideration of long term trends in food production patterns.

Tikopia

Firth (1959) records Tikopian responses to a period of food

stress when food production was interrupted by hurricanes and a drought in 1952 and 1953. According to Tikopian informants, this famine was as severe as any in the past. However, some government relief supplies were distributed, so that the actual shortage was not as severe as it could have been.

Tikopia is a small (under 10 km^2), remote island in the western Pacific studied by Firth (1936, 1939, 1959). In 1952 the human population was 1,700, up from 1,300 in 1929, a 24 percent increase. The population density in 1952 approached 207 per square kilometer. Tikopia is a classic chiefdom. In the production of food, the chief acts primarily as an organizer and regulator. Ideally, a chief should be the last to die during a famine and generally has control of a wider economic base than commoners. In actuality, some chiefs are poorer than commoners, and theft from the chief's fields during the food shortage of 1952 and 1953 was common.

Tikopians have a diverse economy that centers on the cultivation of many crops, taro being the most important. In addition to plant husbandry, Tikopians also use a variety of seafoods and naturally available resources. According to Firth, the population has increased to the point that most cultivable land was under production by 1952.

The severity of the famine in 1952 and 1953 is not clear. On the one hand, only 17 percent of the households faced starvation, and the social structure of Tikopia was not permanently affected. On the other hand, the death rate increased at times, particularly among the very young and very old. Necessary organizational responses to the shortage were undertaken. Although the shortage appears to have been as bad as any the Tikopia remembered, it did not seem to permanently change Tikopian society.

The first responses to the famine were initiated by and involved only the individual household. Most of these efforts consisted of conserving food supplies and later increasing agricultural production to meet immediate needs. After the initial destruction of the crops, the Tikopia salvaged, processed, and stored what they could and used resources that were damaged but not storable. After stored commodities had been eaten, lower preference foods were gathered from the bush, and when necessary, immature crops were eaten, although this ultimately lowered the crop yield.

As the severity of the shortage increased, more costly responses were undertaken. To increase food production, fallow time was shortened, new areas, where available, were opened up for additional fields, and access to fields previously open to others was restricted to members of the family. All these actions were initiated at the household level and did not involve decision making by other households. During this period, normal reciprocal obligations beyond the household generally were met.

As the famine continued and became more severe, wide-ranging responses were taken. Theft from other households and the chief's fields became rampant. In addition, concerning the numerous ritual obligations, Firth concludes:

> To sum up, the famine thus resulted in, and was regarded as morally justifying, a range of modification in ceremonial funeral behavior; reduction in the size and in general the quantity of food transactions; merging of phases of ceremony; lopping off of "extras" as status indices; dropping of structural differences in taskwork; curtailment of obligation period. (1959:88)

In other words, "the skeleton of the social order was preserved, however attenuated the content" (ibid.:88). In addition to ritual obligations, Firth (ibid.:93) found "widespread evasion or rather omission of obligation but there was no radical denial of obligation." Like thievery, subtle evasion of responsibilities does not necessarily challenge the social order.

These changes in the content of obligations often involved more than a single household. For example, during the famine, more work parties were called to repair communal property; this always required labor and never the scarce commodity food. This increase in ad hoc, famine-specific work parties is in contrast to the decrease in ritual activity. Firth notes that strictly social occasions that did not require an outlay of food (e.g., dances) increased in frequency with the famine and sustained social interaction that normally required food transactions.

It is interesting to examine some potential responses not used by the Tikopia. According to Firth, tabooed foods were not eaten, although we do not know what these potential foods were or how nutritionally significant they may have been. The colonial administration suggested that part of the population migrate to another island, but as Firth concludes, this was too costly in that Tikopian society is highly integrated and it would have been too difficult to break off a segment of the group. Although a Tikopian village was later settled on another island, this settlement was intended only as a part-time residence, thus retaining this group's integrated ritual position on Tikopia.

From this example of Tikopian responses to a prolonged food shortage, we can see a not necessarily orderly progression of responses, increasing in their inclusivity. The first responses involved only the household. As the threat of the famine increased, wider responses were undertaken such as restricting obligations, creating ad hoc work groups, and committing antisocial acts (theft). Had the food stress on Tikopia increased and been more prolonged and more inclusive, wider-ranging responses might have been undertaken.

Fringe Enga

Waddell (1975) describes and analyzes the responses by the Fringe Enga of New Guinea to frosts that kill their crops, resulting in periods of food shortage. The Enga of the western New Guinea Highlands, who number approximately 150,000, inhabit mountain valleys with a heterogeneous pattern of microenvironments. The Fringe Enga live in the higher mountain valleys, and the Valley (Central) Enga reside in the larger, lower-elevation valleys. The basic social unit for subsistence decision making is the composite family (a "household" in Waddell's terminology). These families are in turn organized into clans and phratries. However, the "ultimate authority in matters of food production, consumption, and distribution and in membership of the household is vested in a single person, the husband or 'household' head" (Waddell 1972:21).

The Enga population lives in permanent villages of dispersed households. The people are sedentary in that there is little seasonal variation in residence, although there is a surprising "turnover" in the population within a village. Population density in Waddell's study area averaged about 71 per square kilometer.

The Enga are heavily agricultural, and they also raise pigs. The sweet potato is the single most important crop although Waddell lists a total of forty-three plants cultivated (1972,appendix 3). In the lower-elevation valleys, among the Valley Enga, the sweet potato is less important and there is a more diversified crop assemblage. This, combined with the fact that the Fringe Enga fields are more vulnerable to frost damage, gives the Valley Enga more secure food production. The Fringe Enga do practice agricultural mounding, which minimizes the effects of most frosts.

The unusually severe frosts of 1972 were met by several re-

sponses, including government aid. Waddell divides these responses
into three categories, local, interregional, and extraregional, and
concludes that:

> These mechanisms may be conceptualized as a three phased
> series built into the structure of adaptation. Of these the
> lowest (local) level is in constant operation, whereas the
> other two become progressively operational as the intensity
> of the climatic perturbation (frosts) increases. (1975:267)

At the local level, the Fringe Enga employ several agricultural
techniques that mitigate the effects of moderate frosts. These
include planting sweet potatoes on mounds to raise the plants above
the cold air, which settles in the low spots between the them.
They also use green manure extensively in the mounds, and its
decomposition increases the temperature of the mounds and helps
guard against frost. The Fringe Enga also plant crops in two
separate locations--the bottoms of the slopes and in the valley
bottom. By doing this, they spread their risk. Frost may damage
only one field location and leave the others untouched. Recently,
the Fringe Enga have begun planting Irish potatoes, which are more
frost tolerant than their indigenous sweet potato.

If a frost kills the crops in one field despite their horti-
cultural efforts, a household will move temporarily to the other
field location and stay there until the affected fields have been
replanted. If a frost is severe enough to kill all the plants in
all fields, the Enga have a month or two before the tubers become
inedible. During this time they slaughter pigs, reducing the
consumption of crops the pigs eat and increasing the human food
available from pork. All the actions are at the household level.

During the hiatus between the time the crops are killed and the
time food availability is severely restricted, males visit kin and
friends in unaffected areas, primarily among the Valley Enga, to
arrange hosts for when the Fringe Enga move out of the mountains
and into the lower valleys. Many of these friends are trading
partners with whom relationships are continued during times of
normal food availability by trade in salt, stone axes, tree oil,
pigs, and shells. Despite the high population densities among the
Valley Enga, immigrants are usually welcome because they help
minimize the effects of ongoing raiding among the Valley Enga.

When the tubers are all gone, a massive migration to the Valley
Enga takes place. Up to three-quarters of the Fringe Enga emi-
grate, and the remaining population can usually subsist on

naturally available resources such as pandanus nuts. The Fringe Enga reside with their hosts from six months to three years, and many never return to their home territory. During this exile, they will periodically visit the mountains to replant crops and collect wild resources.

Although the timing of these responses is not well detailed, it is clear that as the frost damage become greater, more drastic responses are initiated. Early responses such as killing pigs are primarily the responsibility of the households alone. As the situation worsens, the actions taken involve more inclusive levels than the household, such as approaching distant trading partners and relatives. Finally, a substantial portion of the population emigrates, which certainly changes, at least for a short period, the organization and interaction among the Fringe Enga. As in the example of the Tikopians, the severity of the perturbation affecting the Fringe Enga seems to be matched by the magnitude of the response.

Gwembe Tonga

Scudder (1962, 1971) and Colson (1979) examined the responses the Gwembe Tonga of Zambia made to the threat of widespread famine. Their studies were begun in order to document the effects of massive population relocation owing to the flooding of the Tonga homelands by the construction of the Zambezi Dam in 1957-58.

The Gwembe Tonga originally inhabited the middle Zambezi River Valley around the Kariba Lake basin on what is now the Zambia-Zimbabwe border. The topography consists of a fertile alluvium along the river valley and upland hills away from the river floodplain. When studied by Colson and Scudder in 1956, 57,000 Gwembe Tonga lived in the Gwembe Valley. This population was organized into numerous permanent or semipermanent villages:

> Two to seven villages are drawn together into neighbourhood communities called cisi. In practice nearly endogamous and formerly self-sufficient except when crops failed, these cisi or neighbourhoods are the largest indigenous political units within the Valley. Varying in size from under 300 to over 1,500 residents, and with population densities of under 100 to 350 per square mile, neighbourhoods in the same vicinage may be adjacent (in which case their boundaries are well defined) or separated by several miles of uninhabited scrub. (Scudder 1962:25-6)

Within in each cisi, one clan took ritual priority, and that clan's leader functioned as a ritual coordinator but not as a political authority.

The Gwembe Tonga were agriculturalists who cultivated numerous crops, particularly cereals (e.g., millet, maize, and finger millet) and some cash crops such as tobacco, maize, and peanuts. They used several field locations, and two crops were harvested each year, a rainy-season crop and a dry-season crop. They practiced some animal husbandry. Therefore the Gwembe Tonga had a wide variety of strategic options in their agricultural complex with which to match complex climatic and edaphic conditions.

Both Scudder and Colson discussed the Gwembe Tonga's responses to famines. Several factors caused food shortages, and Scudder listed irregular rain, devastating floods, and pests as the most important. Initial responses the Tonga made to food shortages included conservation efforts such as processing foods in different ways and eating less. In addition, they gathered low preference foods from the bush. Furthermore, eating became a less conspicuous and social occasion, with meals taken in the house so that other households could not gauge the provisions available.

As the shortage became more severe, household goods and livestock were bartered for food, if a buyer could be found. Craft production increased as families manufactured goods to sell.

With even greater hunger, theft increased, and before colonial administration, intervillage raiding also increased. Villages might be abandoned, and the inhabitants might break up into temporary foraging groups scouring the bush for anything edible. Some households sought refuge with unaffected kin and friends. As Scudder (1962) pointed out, these relationships were continually maintained by visits and by trade in various goods. In addition, during the nineteenth century, children were occasionally sold. Colson (1979) reported that she could find little genealogical evidence of widespread death from starvation, suggesting that these coping mechanisms were largely successful. However, the genealogies reveal significant migration as a result of problems in obtaining enough food locally.

Like the Tikopian and Fringe Enga examples, the Tonga case shows that the first responses are conservation efforts and responses that basically involve only the household. With greater stress, more inclusive responses are activated, such as avoiding social obligations and selling one of the most important assets for agricultural peoples, children. In all these cases, it is clear that the responses are based on rational decision making, with some lead time from the recognition that a problem will occur to the actual impact of the shortage.

The Gwembe Tonga example is particularly interesting because these responses to relatively short-term problems are set within a well-documented trend of increasing population density. Scudder described this in some detail. With increased population, many of the prime field locations along the Zambezi floodplain were so subdivided by inheritance that they offered inadequate subsistence security for households. Also, many fields were eroded and had lost much of their fertility. Hence the best farming locations were inadequate to meet the needs of the growing population. Furthermore, the plateau that had been a center of refuge and migration during earlier famines had become overpopulated itself, thus closing off a safety valve for the expanding valley population. The colonial administration had enforced a Pax Britannica that stopped intervillage raiding. These changes increased the vulnerability of the Tonga to the effects of crop destruction by eliminating several important responses. On the other hand, the Gwembe Tonga added new potential responses. First, there was a dramatic increase in the use of fields away from the floodplain. These temwa fields increased in importance so that by 1956 a large percentage of the Tonga fields were in the uplands away from the Zambezi floodplain. In addition, the Tonga constructed communal granaries, and some households began to grow cassava, which is more drought resistant than their traditional crops. How long these adjustments would have been adequate is unclear.

A Catalog of Some Common Responses to Food Shortages

There are numerous studies reporting on the incidence of famine or hunger periods among traditional populations. Unfortunately, most of these reports describe responses in isolation from the magnitude of the problem and from other responses. Nevertheless, responses to food shortages commonly cited in the ethnographic literature are discussed to document the range of the common responses.

Colson classifies most responses to food shortages into five "devices" used to lessen the risk of food stresses:

1) diversification of activities rather than specialization

or reliance on a few plants or animals, 2) storage of foodstuffs, 3) storage and transmission of information on what
we can call famine foods, 4) conversion of surplus into
durable valuables which could be stored and traded for food
in an emergency, and 5) cultivation of social relationships
to allow one to tap resources of other regions. (Colson
1979:21)

I will discuss Colson's five categories and then consider other
responses.

Economic Diversification

Nearly all traditional agriculturalists recognize the local
vulnerability of monoculture. Typically, they diversify by
planting several different crops, often using many different locations or agricultural techniques. As we have seen, this is the
case with all three groups discussed in detail here. There are
many other ethnographic examples of diversity of agricultural
practices and cultigens among traditional peoples (e.g., Werge
1979; Ford 1972a; Hack 1942; Brush 1977). Both Kirkby (1973, 1978)
and Cancian (1972), in detailed analyses of Indian and mestizo
farming in Mexico, show the rational planning involved in manipulating differences in hydrologic factors, edaphic conditions, crop
genotype, and timing to minimize economic risk. Similarly, one can
diversify by planting many crops together. Wilkes (1977) points
out that some mestizos in Mexico may plant three different maize
varieties in the same location, thus helping ensure that under
adverse conditions at least one type will bear fruit.

Some crops have been adopted as standby security in the event
that the main crops fail. Cassava among the Gwembe Tonga and other
tropical groups is one example (Newman 1970). The sweet potato and
papaya in the Trobriand Islands (Malinowski 1935) and the Irish
potato among the Fringe Enga are other examples.

The diversification of agricultural strategies can be effective
at the local level. However, if the perturbation, such as a severe
drought, affects a wide area, then the diversification may not be
very effective in preventing sustained crop loss. Like the other
responses restricted to small regions, diversification of the agricultural base is effective for all but the most widespread
problems.

The diversification of prehistoric agriculture can be detected in the archeological record if field facilities were relatively permanent or if the remains of various crops are preserved. For example, from the distribution of field houses, irrigation works, or terraced fields we can infer spatial diversity of farming locations. Similarly, analysis of cultigen remains can show varietal differences in the crop assemblage or the presence of numerous crop types. However, it is quite likely that some prehistoric agricultural diversity in a given region will be ephemeral, leaving very subtle archeological remains or none. Brush irrigation dams are an example of this.

Storage of Foods

Annegars (1973) found a correlation between storage and the absence of hunger periods in some parts of Africa. However, storage of food supplies is only a partial solution to food stress. While stored goods may allow a group to survive a brief shortage, storage is not particularly effective in guarding against a prolonged shortage. In some areas, particularly in humid regions, it is difficult to store plant foods for extended periods because resources with a high water content, such as tubers, will decompose, and an increasing share of the stores will be eaten by pests such as rodents, insects, and fungi. Stored goods are also vulnerable to raiding and reciprocal obligations, although they can be hidden within a village (Wilson 1934) or in the bush (Buskirk 1949). Furthermore, basic foods tend to be bulky, and the resources necessary for several years would require enormous space. Nevertheless, food storage can be a significant buffer for short term shortages and can lessen the effects of long term shortages. In the absence of effective storage technology, organization, and transportation, its value as a hedge against long term shortages is questionable.

Prehistoric storage can be a most difficult response to deal with archeologically. In many cases food was stored in permanent features (e.g., storerooms, granaries, or extramural pits), which are frequently found at archeological sites. In many other cases food may have been stored in locations and facilities that are not so easily recovered. If foods were stored in space used for a number of purposes, it is difficult to determine the pattern of prehistoric food storage. Granaries made of perishable material, such as those of the Pima (Castetter and Bell 1942), may not leave

obvious archeological remains. Because of this marked diversity of
storage behavior available to prehistoric peoples, archaeologists
need to be cautious in discussing prehistoric storage practices.
An example of this is the hypothesis that southwestern great kivas
with attached rooms were used for the storage of foods to be redis-
tributed (Lightfoot 1979). Even if these were storage rooms, they
may have stored materials other than food, such as ritual parapher-
nalia.

Low Preference Foods

The most widely documented response to food stress is the use
of low preference foods. The most common low preference foods are
famine foods or "queer foods" (Kagwa 1934). These are resources
that are known to be edible but are not consumed in any quantity
during times of normal food availability. A short reconnaissance
of the Human Relations Area Files revealed that the use of famine
foods was the most commonly cited response to food shortages. An
example of the ubiquity of famine food use is that between 1385 and
1400 Chou Wang Tsaio cataloged over four hundred famine foods used
in Hunan Province, China (Reed 1942). It would be safe to assume
that the knowledge of famine foods is universal. Even modern North
Americans are familiar with stories of hobo shoe-sole soup, a
famine food of sorts. Myths and legends of previous food shortages
are critical for transmitting the knowledge of famine foods across
generations (Cove 1978; Colson 1979; Cushing 1920; Reining 1970;
Galt and Galt 1979). Tabooed foods are sometimes eaten during food
shortages (e.g., Cerulli 1964; Honigmann 1954), probably more commonly than is reported ethnographically.

Another type of low preference food is seed or tubers set aside
for future planting. Although they recognize that eating these
reduces future yields, it is not infrequent for people faced with
starvation to consume their seed stock (Faron 1964; Malinowski
1935; Bouroncle Carreon 1964). Likewise, immature crops may be
eaten, and again this lowers future yields.

Because of the widespread reports of the use of famine foods,
it is easy to overestimate their value in alleviating the effects
of food shortages. It is true that many of these foods are less
adversely affected than other foods by many environmental perturbations. Malinowski (1935:16) describes how during drought in a
molu (hunger year) most of the preferred wild and cultivated foods

do not produce, so that the Trobriand Islanders "have to fall back on the despised fruit of the <u>noku</u> tree, which is hardly edible but hardly ever fails." However, many of these resources have low nutritional value and high bulk, produce adverse effects with prolonged use, or require tedious processing to make them edible. Calculating the efficacy of using low preference foods is complex and certainly involves a number of factors, the most important being human population density. In other words, Can the natural edible biomass furnish enough food to support a given population density? I agree with Scudder that:

> while I believe that a number of these reports are overly optimistic about the ability of wild produce alone to support an agricultural population for extended periods of time without widespread malnutrition and starvation, it cannot be denied that time and again crop failure has led to intensive exploitation of the rich flora of the Valley. (1962:211)

The use of low preference foods can be one of the most difficult responses to detect in the archeological record. Many of these resources have a high water content and therefore are unlikely to be preserved. Furthermore, during times of food stress, food will be curated more carefully, and this may well lower the number of times that foods are accidentally preserved. If the use of famine foods is a short term event in an otherwise normal dietary regime, then the use of famine foods may be analytically "masked" by the more frequent use of normal foods. The interpretation of prehistoric famine food use is complicated because resources known ethnographically as low preference foods may have been normal dietary items in prehistory. Therefore one cannot ascribe a prehistoric food as a famine food only on the basis of ethnographic analogy.

Surplus Conversion

Colson's fourth "device" is the conversion of surpluses, such as household goods and valuables, into foods. Selling valuables, "asset depletion," is a very common response (Bohannon and Bohannon 1953; Merker 1910; Rahaman 1978; Jodha 1978; Evans-Pritchard 1940). Children may be considered a potential disposal "durable" that can be sold to acquire food. Selling children occurs in market economies during food shortages, particularly in Africa (Dim

Delobsom 1932). This action not only reduces household consumption and provides for one's children, but it also brings in exchange value (Newman 1970).

There are, however, several important constraints in selling valuables and other goods to purchase food. First there must be a buyer, either within the village or outside it. Unless there is a pronounced differential in wealth within a community, it is unlikely that a household would further risk its position by accepting goods in exchange for food. This is the reason Firth cites for the lack of barter among the Tikopia during times of food stress. For a buyer to be available outside the community requires at least one of two conditions. Either the factors that account for the shortage must be localized so that there are unaffected people in the region, as in the case with the Tonga area, where there is an active barter system, or if the shortage is widespread there must be a buyer outside the region. With modern transportation it is now possible to move basic foodstuffs over very long distances. If these conditions are not met, then the conversion of goods into food is not a particularly effective strategy.

Another problem with selling goods to obtain food is pricing. During food shortages, the value of goods drops and the value of food increases. This process is most evident in market economies (Macfarlane 1976; Redfield 1950; Cone and Lipscomb 1972), but it probably occurs in nonmarket economies.

The conversion of goods into foods is a very difficult process to detect archeologically. As discussed here, this conversion is a short term event, and it would be hard to obtain fine enough temporal divisions in the archeological record to detect this process. Even if this conversion was one-way—that is, one social group accumulated goods by selling food resources—the resultant pattern would be similar to other economic processes, such as simple wealth differential between groups.

Social-Economic Interactions

Cultivating social relationships that allow one to tap the resources of others is a very common response and probably is the most effective given the conditions under which most traditional peoples live and their limited transportation. We have seen this with the Gwembe Tonga and the Fringe Enga. It is not as true for the Tikopia, who live on a small island and have limited contact

with people living on other islands.   Similarly, Faulkingham and
Thorbahn (1975) argue that inhabitants of a parent village in Niger
could not use this strategy because they lacked ties with people
in outside villages.   The common mechanisms used to ensure outside
contacts are to cultivate trading partners, create fictive kinship
ties, and encourage exogamy.   With these contacts one not only can
obtain food but can also find points of refuge and relief during
times of food stress (e.g., Bennett and Zingg 1935; Stevenson 1904;
Talayesva 1942; Nino 1912; McKim 1947; Castetter and Bell 1942).
Often when transportation depends on human backs, it is easier and
more effective to go to the food supplies than to move the supplies
to the affected population.

Sharing within a community can be different from exchange
between groups living in different areas.   Sahlins (1972) offers a
model of intragroup sharing during times of food stress (fig. 2).
He suggests that sharing increases during times of minor shortages,
but that with increased provisioning problems the sharing decreases.   Laughlin (1974) extended Sahlins's discussion of sharing
during times of scarcity.   He studied the effects of seasonal food
supply shortages among the So of East Africa.   During a time of

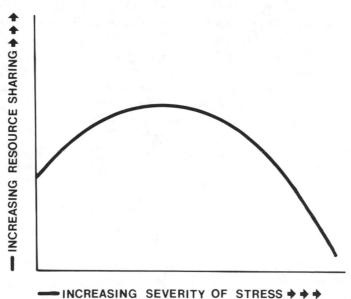

Figure 2. "Sahlins's curve."   Sahlins and others have suggested
that intragroup sharing increases with initial stress and then
decreases within increasing stress severity.

food scarcity, the sphere of generalized and balanced reciprocity decreased. This "accordion" affect means that more generalized reciprocity is increasingly restricted during food shortage seasons. Ford (1972a) has shown how normal ritual mechanisms for food distribution within a Tewa community increases when the stored resources are the lowest.

Like the conversion of goods into foods, using established social relationships to acquire food during a shortage is a viable strategy only if the shortage is more localized than the social network. Generally, the distribution of food within a community will not be as effective as distribution of food within a wider region because of the localized nature of a community's resource base. Regions of environmental heterogeneity are particularly well suited for this strategy since there are often striking differences in food production techniques over short distances. The Fringe Enga region and much of the Puebloan Southwest (Dozier 1970) are examples of this heterogeneity.

Many archeologists have attempted to describe prehistoric social and economic systems. This has proved more difficult than originally thought, but it remains a valuable pursuit. It is difficult to analyze how prehistoric social and economic interactions operated during times of food stress. Generally the most productive approach is to use ethnographic models of how these interactions are used as responses to food stress.

Other Common Responses to Food Shortages

Numerous other types of responses to food shortages have been recorded ethnographically. One that is useful only for very short periods is the conservation of food supplies. People can either fast, reduce their intake, or change the preparation of foods (e.g., Hallowell 1955; Faulkingham and Thorbahn 1975; Silva 1962). Obviously this cannot be carried on long without seriously reducing the labor capacity of the affected group or making it more vulnerable to disease and illness. It is almost impossible to detect these conservation strategies in archeological studies. Not only are they short term events, but they also do not leave enduring remains.

Under some conditions it is possible for population aggregates to break up into small temporary foraging groups, a common response for the Hopi (Thomas 1932) and the Goba (Lancaster 1981). This response is also a characteristic of hunter/gatherer groups (Hitchcock 1978). Under relatively high population densities, low natural biomass, or both, this strategy may not be very effective. Like conservation, this response is difficult to discuss archeologically because it is difficult to detect the presence of small mobile groups in the archaeological record.

Probably one of the most common responses, and one that can be difficult to observe with the largely synchronic data of ethnology, is the intensification of food-acquiring activities. This process is the basis for Cohen's (1977) and others' explanation for the development of agriculture. Maclachlan (1983) suggest that Yaava-halli (a village in southern India) was able to avoid the devastating effects of drought that affected neighboring villages owing to their intensification of food production and well drilling. Where intensification results in environmental alteration and permanent facilities, this strategy should be one of the easiest to observe archeologically.

In some groups, certain cohorts such as the very young and the very old absorb the greatest impact of the food stress. One of the best known examples is old Eskimos floating away on ice floes (Hara 1976; Stefansson 1913), but this response is also used by other groups (Turnbull 1972, 1978; Aginsky 1939; Faulkingham and Thorbahn 1975; Simmons 1954). Through the analysis of osteological remains, it is possible to determine differential mortality between various population cohorts in prehistoric studies.

A response to food production problems can involve economic specialization within a regional economy. As we have seen with the Gwembe Tonga, craft specialization increased with increased severity of food stress. In some cases, communities poorly situated for self-sufficiency in food production may specialize in craft production or trading. Picuris Pueblo in New Mexico (Ford 1972b) and Chamula in southern Mexico (Collier 1975) are two examples of this. This approach is viable during times of food stress if a portion of the exchange system is unaffected by the shortage. This is a most effective strategy for coping with low food production in specific locations when the rest of the region produces normal food supplies. Economic specialization can be detected in the archeological record. Specialized manufacturing facilities or marketplaces imply regional exchange and economic specialization.

Raiding and warfare may increase during times of food stress, but this is not as effective a strategy as it might appear (Drucker

1951; Talayesva 1942; Dundas 1908). An attacking party can carry back only so much food and still defend itself. In addition, raiding invites retribution. The reverse situation also is a response to food stress. For example, the Kikuyu call a truce during times of food stress in order to concentrate on food acquisition (Leakey 1953). Under some conditions it is possible to detect raiding and warfare in the archeological record, perhaps by the presence of defensive structures or of wound marks on bones. However, these are not universal characteristics of raiding and warfare, so not all incidents will leave archeological remains.

The most highly publicized and overestimated response to food shortages is cannibalism. In some extreme circumstances, human flesh can be a source of food. However, as Garn and Block (1970) suggest, there are serious constraints on the efficiency of cannibalism as a food acquisition strategy. Like raiding and warfare, cannibalism may leave archeological remains.

Scattered throughout the ethnographic literature on food stress are mention of changes in ritual and ceremonial activities (Morgan 1901; Faron 1964; Reichel-Dolmatoff 1949–50; Wilson 1959; Dempsey 1955; Skinner 1964). Most traditional people consider the social environment a causal part of the natural environment, so that problems in the natural environment indicate social problems (e.g., Nash 1970). For example, the Ngonde consider food scarcity the result of either senility of the chiefs or neglect of ritual duties (Wilson 1959). It is therefore not unexpected that groups attempt to correct a natural environmental problem by correcting imbalances in social relationships. The increase in witchcraft accusations in southwestern societies during periods of food stress is an example of this (Smith and Roberts 1954; Leighton and Adair 1963; Cushing 1920).

It is often thought that ritual activity increases during times of food stress. This is only partially correct. Rappaport (1971) divides ritual activities into two categories, time-dependent (calendrical) and variable-dependent. Time-dependent rituals have set schedules of observance and tend to be insensitive to events. Ford (1972a) has documented this for the Tewa of New Mexico. In contrast, variable-dependent rituals are event-dependent. The Tsembaga ritual system is an example of this type (Rappaport 1968). By definition calendrical rituals do not increase during times of food stress, and it is not clear whether they decrease. The form of a calendrical ritual may continue during food stresses, but any material obligations may become attenuated, particularly if the stress is severe and food is involved in the ritual.

The situation with variable-dependent rituals is different. The intensity and frequency of these rituals are sensitive to variables such as food security. Jodha (1978) documents the post-ponement of "social consumption," such as marriages in India during times of economic insecurity. Alternatively, some variable-dependent rituals seem to increase during times of food stress, as was the case with the Tikopia. In fact, some rituals may occur only under extreme food shortages.

In addition to rituals, other "communication events" are variable-dependent. The ad hoc work parties, dances, and meetings on Tikopia during the famine are examples of this. Similarly, the Iroquois call special meetings during times of food stress (Morgan 1901). These events, as well as variable-dependent rituals, in-crease during periods of food stress and are primary methods of information exchange, consensus building, and social bond re-inforcement during times that tend to strain social and organi-zational relationships. The archeological implications of social interactions as responses to food stress are discussed in chapter 6.

Summary

Based on an evolutionary/ecological perspective outlined in the first section of this chapter, I offered a model of economic and organizational responses to periods of food stress by nonstratified societies. Briefly, this model suggested that there is a hierarchy of responses that involves the inclusiveness of the response--the number of social groups involved. I proposed that more inclusive responses will become more frequent and important after less in-clusive responses have been found to be ineffective for coping with the stress. I compared this model with three ethnographic examples of groups faced with food stresses. In each of these cases there seems to have been a progression from less inclusive to more in-clusive responses, although the time reference and ethnographic description were not as clear as one could wish. In none of these three examples were the stresses very severe, so that we would not see a wide range of responses. These examples would miss the more inclusive response if the model is correct.

The enumeration and discussion of commonly recorded responses to food stress were given in order to "flesh out" the framework of the model. This discussion also considered the effectiveness of these responses, the conditions under which these responses would be adequate for coping with a food stress.

3

Archeology of the Rio Mimbres Region

The form of argument must now shift from the general, theoretical, and ethnological to the specific archeological case study. The next five chapters present a detailed discussion of the case study and could not be shortened without omitting critical data or interpretive links. If you are unfamiliar or uncomfortable with archeological analysis and interpretation, you may want to read just the chapter summaries and the final chapter. In this way you will be able to follow the logic of my arguments, although you will not be able to judge the soundness of my interpretations.

A brief note about the general nature of this archeological research is necessary. I am not conducting prehistoric ethnography. Archeology is not well suited to describing the state of cultural systems. Archeologists can best investigate changes through time in selected aspects of human behavior--in other words, take an evolutionary perspective (Dunnell 1982). This form of research divides the range of human behavior into analytic parts--divisions that are not necessarily those used in sociocultural anthropology. For example, I avoid social organization terminology (e.g., lineage, clan, moiety) when discussing level of behavioral interaction. Instead these types of activities are phrased in spatial terms.

Research by the Mimbres Foundation

The Rio Mimbres region comprises approximately 6,500 square kilometers in southwestern New Mexico. The specific Mimbres Foundation study area in Grant and Luna counties, New Mexico, encompasses approximately 4,300 square kilometers. Figure 3 shows the study area in relation to the "international four corners" (Arizona, New Mexico, Sonora, and Chihuahua), and figure 4 illustrates the study area topography.

The Mimbres Foundation conducted three years of survey and five

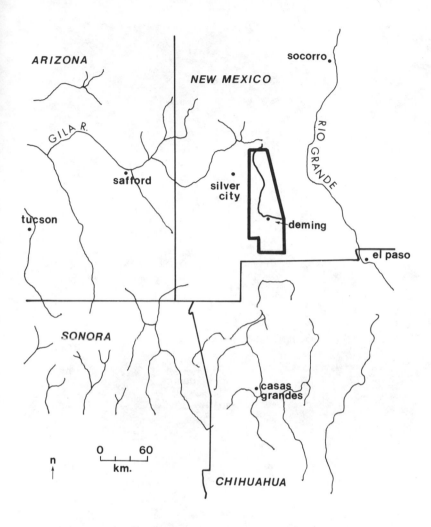

Figure 3.   International four corners.   The rectangular area within the heavy lines is the Mimbres Foundation study area.

years of excavation in the Mimbres area.   The first survey season concentrated on the major river valley--the Rio Mimbres.   The second season of survey focused on the desert area around Deming.   During the third survey season the mountains surrounding the Rio Mimbres and the secondary drainages were sampled.   In all, approximately five hundred sites have been recorded.   The majority of the Foundation excavations were on sites along the Rio Mimbres floodplain,

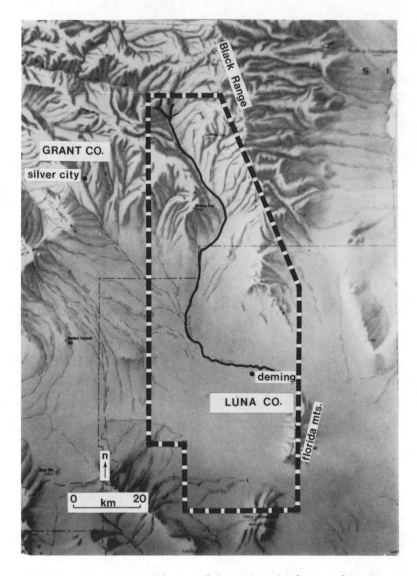

Figure 4. Topography of the Mimbres Foundation study area.

although some sites in other locations were excavated or tested. Mimbres Foundation field crews have excavated or tested twenty-six sites. Table 1 lists these sites and gives pertinent information on them. Figure 5 shows their location.

The Mimbres Foundation survey set out to accomplish two goals. First, we wanted to locate sites that appeared to have been relatively untouched by pothunters. Since at least 95 percent of the

Table 1

Sites Excavated by the Mimbres Foundation

Site	Excavation[a]	Time Period[b]	Drainage Location[c]
Old Town (Z:5:14)	t	CM (+)	1
McAnally (LA 12110)	m	EP	1
Thompson (Z:5:35)	m	EP	1
Beaugard (Z:1:27)	m	LP	1
Galaz (LA 635)	M	LP/CM (+)	1
Wheaton-Smith (Z:1:46)	M	LP/CM	2
Mattocks (LA 676)	M	LP/CM	1
Bradsby (Y:4:35)	M	LP/CM	3
Montezuma (Z:1:30)	M	LP/CM	1
Mitchell (LA 12076)	M	LP/CM	1
Martin (Z:1:6)	m	CM/A	1
LA 12109	M	CM	1
Hadji Baba (Z:1:126)	m	CM	2
Ernestine (Z:1:203)	m	CM	2
Walsh (Z:5:80)	m	A	1
Montoya (Z:5:112)	m	A	1
Dike (Z:5:42)	m	A	1
Janss (LA 12077)	M	S	1
Stailey (Z:1:78)	M	S	1
Disert (Z:5:10)	M	S	1
Z:9:19	t	A	1
Z:13:1	t	CM	4
Z:14:3	t	CM	4
Z:14:6	t	LP	4
Z:14:7	t	?	4
Z:14:31	t	CM	4

a. t = test; m = minor; M = major.
b. EP = Early Pithouse; LP = Late Pithouse; CM = Classic Mimbres; A = Animas; S = Salado; ( ) = additional component.
c. 1 = along Rio Mimbres; 2 = side drainage; 3 = higher elevation; 4 = desert regions.

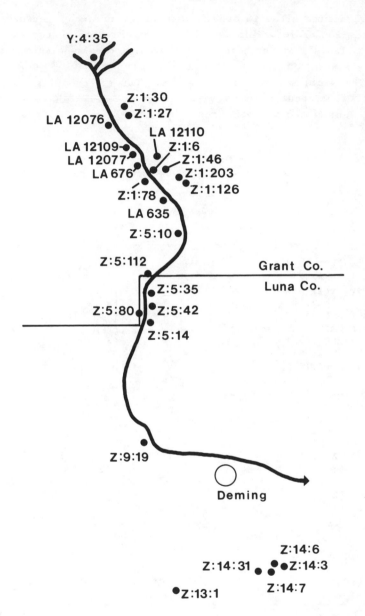

Figure 5.   Location of sites excavated by the Mimbres Foundation.

Classic Mimbres sites in the Rio Mimbres region had been vandalized (Minnis and LeBlanc 1979; Graybill 1974), it was important to find and identify sites that held the potential for containing relatively undisturbed archeological information. The second objective of the survey was to obtain a data base from which we could make reasonable estimates of the settlement patterns and population sizes in the valley and adjacent drainages.

A nonrandom, stratified, opportunistic sampling strategy was used. The survey area was stratified by topography and hydrology, and the actual areas surveyed were selected from the areas that fulfilled the stratification criteria. Because some landowners would not grant permission for the foundation to survey their land, the survey was not strictly random. Every effort was made to sample the range of environmental diversity within the study area. Approximately 11 percent of the study area in the mountainous area around the Rio Mimbres was intensively surveyed. In the desert regions around Deming, nearly 6 percent of the total study area was surveyed. The proportion of each stratum surveyed varied, but in general the strata with the greatest site density were surveyed the most. For example, in the Rio Mimbres Valley proper, almost 40 percent of the area was intensively surveyed. This "biasing" helped ensure that estimates of prehistoric population size were more accurate. While we cannot estimate the error involved with this procedure, we have confidence that we did everything possible to minimize it in these circumstances (Blake and Narod 1977).

Given limited budgets and a very large research area, a major problem with excavation was to devise a strategy that would allow us to make regionwide comparisons. The excavation strategy consisted of excavating "clusters" of sites. A "cluster" consisted of a number of sites near each other. Clusters were situated in different environmental settings within the study area. Therefore we have samples that maximize environmental and spatial diversity. Similarly, within each cluster, sites of different time periods were excavated so that we could have some control for temporal as well as spatial changes. In some cases it was not possible to have access to sites of a particular time period in a particular cluster. Perhaps the greatest deficiency in this method of choosing sites was our lack of excavated materials from Animas period sites in the upper end of the Rio Mimbres Valley. Permission to excavate on the few sites that fit this category was not forthcoming until the summer of 1979. With this research design, however, it was possible to have relatively good control for spatial and temporal patterns within the budgetary and personnel limitations faced by the Mimbres Foundation. The advantages of employing this excavation strategy have been most evident in the chipped stone artifact analysis (Nelson 1981).

Although archeological work by the Mimbres Foundation is restricted to the area bordering the Rio Mimbres, the patterns of settlement location and prehistoric population size made apparent by the foundation's work are similar to patterns for a much larger area (LeBlanc and Whalen 1980). For example, Mogollon population size reached a zenith during the Classic Mimbres period in the study area. This is mirrored throughout the mountainous areas of southern New Mexico (Minnis 1980b; Berman 1979).

Culture History Outline

Humans have occupied southern New Mexico for the past twelve thousand years. I will employ nine analytic periods in this discussion: Paleo-Indian, Archaic, Early Pithouse, Late Pithouse, Classic Mimbres, Animas, Salado, Protohistoric, and Historic. Table 2 correlates these analytic units with the traditional temporal taxonomy (see LeBlanc and Whalen 1980). Several of these periods, such as the Paleo-Indian, the Archaic, and the Protohistoric, are poorly represented in the archeological record. Because of an increase in recent archeological work in southwestern New Mexico, major syntheses available for the Mogollon (e.g., Wheat 1955) are rapidly becoming obsolete. For more detailed discussion of the archeology of the study area, one should consult a recent review and synthesis (LeBlanc and Whalen 1980) and shorter considerations by Brody (1977) and LeBlanc (1983). The research in this volume concentrates on the Late Pithouse, Classic Mimbres, and Animas periods.

Estimating Prehistoric Population Size

Estimates were made of the prehistoric population in the study area (Blake 1979; Blake, LeBlanc, and Minnis 1983). I will summarize the methodology used and present estimates. These population estimates and the discussion in chapters 5 and 7 exclude the desert regions of the study area. Except during the Animas period, this region was sparsely inhabited.

Table 2

Chonological Divisions

Traditional Divisions	Divisions Used Here
Paleo-Indian	**Paleo-Indian**
Archaic	**Archaic**
Pine Lawn (Hilltop)	**Early Pithouse**
Georgetown San Francisco Three Circle	**Late Pithouse**
Classic Mimbres	**Classic Mimbres**
Animas	**Animas** (Black Mountain)
Salado	**Salado** (Cliff)
Early Contact (Jano/Manso/Jocomes/Jumano)	**Protohistoric**
Historic (Apache/Hispanic/Anglo)	**Historic**

Twenty-nine distinct transects ranging in size from 8 ha to 1,579 ha were intensively surveyed by crews walking 10 to 20 m apart, depending on the topography. All prehistoric sites found were recorded, and a sample collection of surface artifacts was taken from each site. A site was defined as an area having archi-tecture or an artifact scatter with at least ten artifacts within 10 m^2.

The survey area was divided into nine strata, and a total of a little over 10,000 ha out of the total survey universe of 90,000 ha was investigated. Approximately 11 percent of the study area was intensively surveyed. However, the mean surveyed sample fraction was 45 percent and the mode was between 30 percent and 40 percent.

Largely on the basis of architecture and diagnostic ceramics, sites were divided into six time periods: probable Archaic, Early Pithouse, Late Pithouse, Classic Mimbres, Animas, and Salado. Some sites could not be placed temporally. One such example is a multi-component site for which it is difficult to estimate the size of the early occupation. This can be corrected to a certain degree with data derived from excavated multicomponent sites. Furthermore, there is reason to believe that very small Classic Mimbres sites were occupied only seasonally, perhaps as field houses. Therefore, based partly on excavation (Nelson, Rugge, and LeBlanc 1979) and partly on intuition, Classic Mimbres sites of seven rooms or less were not considered permanent habitations and were excluded from this analysis.

From the surveyed data, we estimated the number of "rooms" for each time period by calculating area of room block rubble for pueblos for each site and by dividing the mean room size for each period as determined from excavation data. Pithouse depressions were noted when present. The raw room counts are presented in table 3. These figures assume that all rooms were occupied for the same length of time, and any intraperiod population growth is ignored. These figures could be used to estimate the population size by simply assuming a population estimate for each number of rooms and an estimate of the number of rooms occupied at any one time.

Table 3

Room Estimates for the Study Area[a]

Period[b]	Time Span	Estimated Room Area (m^2)	Standardized Room Area for Seventy-five Year Period (m^2)	Change between Periods
EP	400	12,807	2,433	1.00
LP	400	26,401	5,015	2.06
CM	150	60,783	30,392	6.06
A	125	30,818	18,491	0.61
S	75	4,800	4,800	0.26

Source: Adapted from Blake, LeBlanc, and Minnis (1983)
a. Excluding the desert regions.
b. EP = Early Pithouse; LP = Late Pithouse; CM = Classic Mimbres; A = Animas; S = Salado.

Population estimates are made by estimating a growth rate for each period and the use life for each room. For this analysis it was assumed that pithouses were used for seventy-five years and that surface pueblo rooms were used for either thirty, forty, or seventy-five years. Growth rates based on the data in table 3 are: Early Pithouse, 0.18 percent; Late Pithouse, 0.25 percent; Classic Mimbres, 0.83 percent and 1.00 percent; and Animas, 0.25 percent. Since all known Salado sites in the valley have been excavated, the population size estimates were calculated differently for the Salado than for the other periods: we assumed a growth rate of 1.00 percent, contemporaneity of all Salado sites, and a population maximum fifty years after the beginning of this period.

The estimated population size maxima derived for these assumptions of growth rate and room use life are presented in table 4. Obviously, many of the assumptions used to compute these population sizes are at best crude approximations. Nevertheless, the generated estimates do not appear to be outlandish, and they may well be

Table 4

Estimates of Human Population Size in the Study Area[a]

Period[b]	Estimated Growth Rate (%)	Estimated Room Use Life (years)	Maximum Population Size[c]
EP	0.18	75	478
LP	0.25	75	1,205
CM	0.83	30	3,187
	1.00	40	4,021
A	0.25	40	1,221
	0.25	75	2,404
S	1.00	All contemporary	680

Source: Adapted from LeBlanc (1979).
a. Excluding the desert regions.
b. EP = Early Pithouse; LP = Late Pithouse; CM = Classic Mimbres; A = Animas; S = Salado.
c. Using Casselberry's (1974) formulas.

conservative estimates. Most of the assumptions used in the next chapter to construct indexes of crop failure and food stress are purposely conservative so that any overestimation of population size will be minimized.

Paleo-Indian Period

Few Paleo-Indian period remains have been found in southwestern New Mexico, and no Paleo-Indian period sites have been recorded in the study area (Nelson 1980). Two Paleo-Indian period sites reported by Fitting and Price (1968) and a few other isolated finds of Paleo-Indian period projectile points are the only documentation of the Paleo-Indian period occupation in southwestern New Mexico (Wendorf 1959). The absence of remains in the study area is very likely a result of unfavorable geological processes creating conditions of low archeological visibility for the material culture remains of the Paleo-Indian period. It does not reflect a lack of occupation of the region. But this paucity of remains does preclude any detailed analysis of the Paleo-Indian period use of the study area. Assuming that the Paleo-Indian period occupation in the study area was similar to that in better-documented regions (e.g., Judge 1973; Wilmsen 1970), this period is most probably characterized by a small hunting and gathering population with very friable patterns of aggregation and dispersal.

Archaic Period

Compared with the Paleo-Indian period, the Archaic period is represented by a larger number of sites in the study area, but there is still a severe problem with biasing owing to differential archeological visibility. Most Archaic period sites have been exposed by the deflation of sand dunes or by arroyo cutting, processes found in only a few areas. Therefore it is uncertain whether there are Archaic period remains in the areas where such geological processes are not active.

The basic definition of the southwestern Archaic, the Cochise, was based upon work in southeastern Arizona (Sayles and Antevs 1941). The original phase designations conceived more that forty years ago still form the basis of Cochise chronology. Sayles and Antevs (1941) proposed a three-stage scheme, and Whalen (1971) has revised the dating of the divisions: Sulphur Springs (7000-3500 B.C.), Chiracahua (3500-1500 B.C.), and San Pedro (1500-200 B.C.). Given the long time depth of the Archaic period and the paucity of material remains, it is necessary to consider this chronological framework very general.

The origins of the Archaic are in doubt.   Irwin-Williams (1967) suggests that the early Archaic period represents a migration into the Southwest concomitant with climatic changes detrimental to the Paleo-Indian economy.   On the other hand, the Archaic phenomenon may represent shifts in exploitative activities of Paleo-Indian descendants.   Similarly, the relationship between the Cochise and other named Archaic period traditions in the Southwest is unclear.   I see little difference between the Cochise and such archeological manifestations as Oshara and Atrisco.

Whatever the "cultural" relationships between Archaic groups, the population was low.   Using Steward's (1938) average Great Basin population density as an analogue (one person per 4,040 ha), the Archaic period population in the Mimbres Foundation study area would have been about 100 individuals.   The meager evidence best supports a hypothesis that the Archaic population was slowly expanding. The Archaic period people were foragers reliant on plant food and small game, although there are two ambiguous records of Archaic period remains in association with extinct megafauna.   Most likely the Archaic period population was organized into small, mobile bands with flexible periods of aggregation and dispersal often controlled by resource availability.   One of the most interesting aspects of Archaic subsistence is the presence of cultigens.   A few examples of cultigens at about 2000 B.C. have been reported, but these are poorly dated.   The first reliable cultigen remains are found dating from about 1000 B.C. (Minnis 1980c; Berry 1982).   Maize and squash are the earliest cultigens; evidence suggests that beans were introduced later.   While the dating of the earliest presence of domesticates is open to chronological revision, the early cultigens probably composed a small portion of the Archaic diet, and consequently harvest failure probably was not a significant event to the Archaic livelihood (Minnis 1980c).

Toward the end of the Archaic period, structures and features were built that have left remains.   Archaic period pithouses are small (2-3 m in diameter), and it has been assumed that these structures were used as domiciles.   In addition to pithouses, numerous extramural pits were used, presumably for storage and resource processing.

Within the study area, there is a marked tendency for Archaic period sites to be concentrated in the desert areas. As I stated previously, this may simply be because geologic processes favorable for site exposure are most often found in the desert area. Outside this study area, Archaic period sites are found in mountainous areas such as Cienega Creek in Arizona (Haury 1957) and in the Pine Lawn Valley and other portions of the upper Gila drainage (Berman 1979).

During the Archaic period, then, we see a small, mobile population of hunter/gatherers. Toward the end of the period this population began to cultivate domesticates and build pithouses and pits.

Early Pithouse Period (Cumbre Phase)

Beginning with the Early Pithouse period about A.D. 1-200, the archeological record becomes more visible with the introduction of durable and obvious material remains such as pottery and large pithouses. On the basis of early excavations in the Mimbres and Gila valleys (Haury 1936) and Pine Lawn Valley (Martin, Rinaldo, and Antevs 1949), four pithouse phases were proposed: Pine Lawn (Hilltop), Georgetown, San Francisco, and Three Circle. These phases cover a period from about A.D. 1-200 to A.D. 950-1000. These designations were based on ceramic, architectural, and site-location information. As used here, the Early Pithouse period is analogous to the Pine Lawn (Hilltop) phase, with a chronology of A.D. 1-200 to A.D. 500-600. For the Rio Mimbres drainage, LeBlanc (1980a) has named the Early Pithouse period the Cumbre phase.

While there are numerous similarities between the Archaic and Early Pithouse periods (Minnis 1980a), there are some important differences in site location and degree of sedentation. Early Pithouse period sites are concentrated along the major river valleys in the Upper Chihuahuan zone. Few sites are found in either the deserts or the mountains. Most Early Pithouse period sites are found on isolated ridges or knolltops that have restricted access. Numerous suggestions have been made to account for this pattern— that pithouse residents used hilltop microenvironments (Rice 1975), that exposed knolls were warmer in winter, that these locations exhibit good drainage, or that residents "liked the view." The two most viable explanations are defense and avoidance of locations where game would concentrate. Like LeBlanc (1980a), I suspect that defense is the most reasonable explanation.

Another difference between the Archaic and Early Pithouse periods is the degree to which the population was sedentary. Unlike the Archaic period (Whalen 1971), there is little direct evidence for a pronounced seasonal settlement shift during the Early Pithouse period. The evidence for the Early Pithouse period is more indicative of a relatively sedentary pattern with only isolated or low visibility movement (LeBlanc 1980a). However, Gilman (1983) suggests that pithouse villages may have been winter settlements, and that there probably was greater seasonal movement than traditionally assumed. If this position is correct, the presence of substantial pithouses may indicate a more regular seasonal movement than occurred during the Archaic period.

These attributes may be related to the increasing dependency on cultivated products. Remains of maize have been recovered from Early Pithouse period contexts in the study area. Contrary to Cutler's (1952) suggestion that there might be a drop in the quantity of maize from Tularosa Cave during the Georgetown phase, there is in fact an increase (LeBlanc 1980a; Heller 1976) when the length of each period is considered. Although the evidence is weak, it points toward an increasing dependency on maize cultivation. Early maize in the Southwest is found at high elevations in the Upper Chihuahuan zone between 1,770 m and 2,100 m (Minnis 1980a). The clustering of Early Pithouse period sites in this zone may well be related to an increase in the use of the zone best suited for dry farming of maize.

One can suggest a relationship between increasing agriculture and the location of sites in defensive locations. Perhaps mechanisms for regulating the scarce commodity of the best arable land created occasional tension among competing communities, thus necessitating defensive site locations. A major problem with this suggestion is the low population density in the study area during the Early Pithouse period. LeBlanc (1980a:127) suggests that Early Pithouse period sites were "quite large, with upwards of 100 people," and that there were few contemporary sites; thus, there would have been little competition for arable land between communities. However, the evidence for the contemporaneity of pithouses within a village is not good, so that the size of the Early Pithouse period population at any one time is difficult to assess.

During this period some structures appear to have had at least two major functions. All pithouses are round with rampways and seem to be domestic structures. Some also appear to have a religious-ceremonial function (Anyon and LeBlanc 1980). This is the first evidence of ceremonial structures. They continue to occur through the Late Pithouse period and culminate in special nondomicile kivas of the Classic Mimbres period.

Because of the difficulty in defining site contemporaneity and population size changes as well as the basic lack of burial data, it is difficult to describe the population organization during this time period. Most likely, the Early Pithouse period occupation consisted of small groups of up to about 100 people, living in apparently unplanned villages. There is no evidence of site hierarchy or status differentiation. In all probability, the Early Pithouse period people were egalitarian as defined by Fried (1970).

Additionally, there is little evidence of an extensive trade in durable goods during this time. There is no reason to believe that pottery or other material culture items were extensively traded, although the presence of shell artifacts whose source is outside the Southwest is documented. Although exchange among groups existed, one cannot assume that it was a particularly well organized or important economic activity.

Compared with the Archaic groups, the Early Pithouse period people were more sedentary and used domesticates more extensively. They lived in larger, more permanent villages in high locations with difficult access overlooking major river valleys in the Upper Chihuahuan zone.

Late Pithouse Period

The Late Pithouse period occurred between A.D. 500 and A.D. 1000 (Anyon, Gilman, and LeBlanc 1981). It has traditionally been divided into three phases: Georgetown, San Francisco, and Three Circle. A major problem with Late Pithouse period site visibility is that later pithouse structures and pueblos often are superimposed on earlier pithouse structures, obscuring the evidence of the earlier occupation. This may be the reason for the supposed population drop during the Georgetown phase in the Pine Lawn Valley (Bluhm 1960).

In relation to the Early Pithouse period, this period exhibits several differences. In addition to the early recognized changes in architectural form and ceramic assemblages, changes in site location, site size, and population size occur. The traditionally cited changes between the Early Pithouse and Late Pithouse periods are a progression from round or D-shaped pithouses to rectangular ones. Some of these have subterranean cobble walls. Also, the ceramic assemblages change from Alma Plain and San Francisco Red to Three Circle Red-on-White during the early part of the Late Pithouse period. Toward the end of this period, Boldface Black-on-White ware is common. This last type is a "prototype" of the well known Classic Black-on-White. Also, a neck-corrugated ware is found in Late Pithouse period contexts.

The Late Pithouse period population is larger than that in the Early Pithouse period, although it is difficult to determine the amount of the difference between the two periods. Not only are Late Pithouse period sites generally larger than Early Pithouse period sites, but there are more of them. This increase seems to represent an indigenous population increase rather than an in-migration, since this increase is panregional (Minnis 1980b). In addition, during the Late Pithouse period one begins to find small, scattered sites in the desert areas and the mountains. In the mountainous terrain, Late Pithouse period villages are found in "parks"--locations with wider floodplains, lower, more rolling topography, and usually a dependable source of water nearby. The mountainous Late Pithouse period sites appear to be similar to the sites in the Rio Mimbres Valley proper. The Late Pithouse period manifestation in the desert areas is harder to define. The Mimbres Foundation and the University of Oklahoma tested a Late Pithouse site (Z:14:6) on the alluvial fan of the Florida Mountains near Deming (Minnis and Wormser 1982). Although no pithouse structures were located, the large amount of midden and the presence of burials suggest that the site was a repeatedly occupied camp and that a wide range of activities were performed there. Some non-durable aboveground structures were constructed in these locations, but I doubt that they were year-round habitations.

Unlike Early Pithouse period sites, Late Pithouse period sites are found on the first bench directly above the floodplain, a location of easy access. Classic Mimbres period, Animas period, and Salado period occupations are also generally in similar topographic locations.

Agriculture was important to the Late Pithouse period population, perhaps as important as during the following Classic Mimbres period. Not only are macroplant remains of maize common (Minnis 1978), but nearly all Late Pithouse period sites are near the best agricultural land (Anyon 1980; Minnis 1980b).

Other economic activities besides basic subsistence become more visible, if not more common. There is an increase in nonlocal exchange items such as shell during the later segment of the Late Pithouse period.

The social organization of the Late Pithouse period populations is not well known. Anyon and LeBlanc (1980) suggest that the basic social unit was a nuclear family, perhaps with community-wide ceremonial interaction as evidenced by a single large "communal" structure for each village. There is no burial evidence of a formal differential status hierarchy.

During this period the population was increasing, and groups expanded into areas away from the main river valley. Similarly, sites were usually on the first bench above the channel. There was no apparent planning to the village layout, and it would be fair to suggest that each village was composed of households knit together by communitywide sodalities. The Late Pithouse period population was heavily agricultural, and it appears that during the later part of this period, extensive field clearing may have begun to affect the floodplain vegetation.

Classic Mimbres Period

The Classic Mimbres period lasted from A.D. 1000 to A.D. 1130 or 1150 and represents a continuation from the Late Pithouse period (Anyon, Gilman, and LeBlanc 1981).

The Classic Mimbres has been investigated more than any other time period in the study area. Several large Classic Mimbres period sites have been excavated and reported on in the past: the Swarts Ruin (Cosgrove and Cosgrove 1932), Cameron Creek (Bradfield 1929), and the Mattocks site (Nesbitt 1931). From the time of these excavations until the mid-1970s, little work was undertaken in the Mimbres area, except for unremitting vandalization. Since the 1970s there has been and continues to be a large amount of archeological work in the study area by such institutions as the Mimbres Foundation, Texas A&M University (Shafer 1982a,b, Shafer, Taylor, and Usrey 1979), the University of Arizona (Graybill 1973, 1975), New Mexico State University, and the University of Texas (Herrington 1979).

Classic Mimbres period sites are highly visible archeologically because of cobble wall rubble and because of the distinctive pottery found at such sites. Although their visibility is high, most Classic Mimbres period sites have been ravaged by pothunters. Graybill (1974) estimated that 95 percent of the Classic Mimbres period sites in the mountains north of the Mimbres Foundation study area have been potted, as have 95 percent of the Classic Mimbres period sites in the foundation's study area (Minnis and LeBlanc 1979). Much valuable information is lost because of hand digging by pothunters. Unfortunately, within the past decade the larger sites have been bulldozed by commercial pothunters, an incredibly destructive technique (Green and LeBlanc 1979). Locations of Classic Mimbres period sites are easy to determine because of their visibility. Determination of some site characteristics is hard to accomplish because of pothunting, and in many cases bulldozing obliterates even rudimentary parameters such as site size. Despite these problems, the Classic Mimbres period is the best known and most reliable part of the Mogollon sequence in the study area.

The Classic Mimbres period population was larger than that of the Late Pithouse period, and this seems to be due to local growth rather than immigration from outside the study area. Most large Classic Mimbres period sites are superimposed on large Late Pithouse period villages, indicating a continuity of settlement location. Most large Classic Mimbres period sites (about 100–150 rooms) are along the Rio Mimbres, but unlike the other periods, there is a significant Classic Mimbres period population in the mountainous regions at higher elevations.

Most of the sites recorded from the mountainous area north of the Mimbres Foundation study area were Classic Mimbres period (Graybill 1973, 1975). Similarly, the mountains away from the Rio Mimbres Valley in the study area have numerous Classic Mimbres period sites. The largest sites in these areas (40–50 rooms) are smaller than the large sites in the valley, but like the valley sites, the large upland sites are superimposed on Late Pithouse period sites. These sites are usually in mountain parks. In the mountainous secondary drainages are smaller sites (about 25 rooms) that we believe were occupied year-round but probably not throughout the entire Classic Mimbres period. Additionally, there are numerous small sites (1–10 rooms) that were probably field houses and that were only seasonally occupied (Nelson, Rugge, and LeBlanc 1979).

During the Classic Mimbres period, there is the first evidence for agricultural structures. These consist of small linear borders or check dams on gentle (5–7 degree) south-facing slopes in the mountains (Sandor 1983). Generally, a small, 1–4 room Classic

Mimbres period pueblo is found with these structures. These agricultural systems are similar to those reported for the Point of Pines area (Woodbury 1961) and in Chihuahua (Donkin 1979; Herold 1965; Howard and Griffiths 1966) but are not as extensive.

Classic Mimbres period sites are also found on the desert plains, although in smaller numbers than those lying in other areas. These sites are sometimes found in hydrologically advantageous areas, near dependable springs or areas of high water table. Unfortunately, the nature of this desert occupation is unclear. Fitting (1971) excavated a small site in the desert with a Classic Mimbres period component and found no evidence of structures, although it is conceivable that his limited testing missed features constructed of adobe. The Mimbres Foundation tested several Classic Mimbres period sites in the desert and also found no evidence of architecture. Whether these sites were occupied throughout the year is unclear. The location of some sites near the best agricultural land in the desert may indicate agricultural activity. The presence of tepary beans, common beans, cotton seeds, and maize from a bulldozed Classic Mimbres period site near Deming supports this hypothesis. However, the location of some Classic Mimbres period sites on settings such as alluvial fans would have made agriculture unlikely. At one site that had been bulldozed, there was an enormous amount of bird bone on the surface, perhaps an indication of a specialized fowl hunting camp.

As is discussed in the next chapter, it is clear that the Classic Mimbres people were very dependent on agriculture, and that with increased population the Classic Mimbreños extensively cleared the the floodplain for fields. Because of historic activity in the valley, evidence of irrigation during the Classic Mimbres period is not clearly present. Herrington (1977, 1979) reported a small irrigation system near Cameron Creek that she believes to be Classic Mimbres period.

It has been argued that there was little change in social organization from the Late Pithouse to the Classic Mimbres period (Gilman 1980; Anyon 1980; Anyon, Gilman, and LeBlanc 1979). This argument contradicts Martin and Rinaldo's argument (1950) for the Pine Lawn region. Those stating no change conclude that each Late Pithouse period pithouse probably housed a nuclear family and that the room size and the construction of contiguous rooms of Classic Mimbres period pueblos also indicate a nuclear family. In contrast, Martin and Rinaldo argued that pithouses were occupied by extended families and surface pueblo units by nuclear families.

Although family organization may have remained the same, there is a change in ceremonial structures during the Classic Mimbres period. Almost universally, there was one large ceremonial structure for each Late Pithouse period village, whereas during the Classic Mimbres period there was an average of one "kiva" per block. Further, the Classic Mimbres period kiva is small, probably serving only a segment of the village population. Anyon and LeBlanc (1980) speculate that villagewide public ceremonies took place in plazas. This dual, public/private nature of ritual space is similar to that in modern pueblos in the Southwest; thus there is some evidence for changes in village integration. The specific mechanisms are not enumerated, however.

In contrast, there is little evidence for site differentiation, except for a distinction between habitation and special-purpose sites. There is no evidence that there was any political, economic, or ritual hierarchy between habitation sites. It appears that larger sites were simply larger aggregates of people. The three best-known Classic Mimbres period sites (Mattocks, Swarts, and Galaz) appear to have started with two or more small (2-4 room) room blocks. Expansion consisted of rather haphazard additions of rooms onto these room block cores (S. LeBlanc, personal communication, 1981). Perhaps some sites may have had some sentimental/ritual status, but if so there is no archeological evidence of this, or we have no way of testing for it.

One of the most interesting aspects of the Classic Mimbres period is its position in a far-reaching regional exchange network that existed in other parts of the Southwest at this time. It has been noted that the Mimbres area is nearly halfway between Casas Grandes and Chaco Canyon (DiPeso 1974). It has also been suggested that the Classic Mimbres period population was heavily involved in extraregional trade (DiPeso 1974) and that this is important for understanding this period (LeBlanc 1976). It is true that extraregional exchange is present during the Classic Mimbres period, but the economic importance of the exchange for the Classic Mimbreños is not clearly documented. Evidence for prehistoric exchange in the study area is discussed in chapter 6.

Animas Period (Black Mountain Phase)

Perhaps one of the most interesting aspects of southwestern prehistory is the Animas period. If it were not for the Gadsden

Purchase, the Animas period would have been considered wholly a "Mexican" phenomenon, because most Animas period sites in the United States are in the area of the Purchase. As it is, south-western archeologists are not well aware of the prehistory outside of Hohokam and northern Mogollon-Anasazi areas. So why is the Animas period so interesting?

Approximately 160 km south of Mimbres is the site of Casas Grandes. DiPeso (1974) estimated that the site covered 36 ha and had an intrasite organizational complexity equal to any archeological site in the Southwest. While the regional complexity is not well understood, it appears that Casas Grandes may have been the hub of a complex regional political and economic system. The nature of this system is not well known. Hence, any discussion of a Casas Grandes system is only a general recognition that within it there is a hierarchy in site size and complexity. The Animas period sites in our study area have strong similarities to the material culture of the Casas Grandes area and therefore may have been a part of the Casas Grandes system. Yet DeAtley (1980) argues that Animas sites were generally independent of Casas Grandes political and economic influence.

In the study area, the Animas period dates from A.D. 1175 to A.D. 1300–1325, which is similar to the dating of the Medio phase at Casas Grandes (LeBlanc 1980c). The archeological manifestations of the Animas period in the study area consist of puddled adobe pueblos with an entirely different ceramic assemblage than the preceding Mogollon tradition. Many aspects of material culture are strikingly different.

The Animas period settlement pattern is much different from that of the preceding Classic Mimbres period. Most Animas period sites are concentrated in more desert regions; there is a decreasing number of sites higher up in the main river valleys, like the Rio Mimbres. In striking contrast to the Classic Mimbres period, no Animas period sites are found in the mountain areas (Minnis 1980b; Graybill 1973, 1975). The largest Animas period sites are along the southern section of the Rio Mimbres channel where the water table is high. Two such concentrations are present (Minnis and LeBlanc 1979). Animas period sites are also near other hydrologically advantageous desert areas such as springs.

The Animas period people were agriculturalists, and remains of maize, beans, and cotton have been recovered from excavated Animas period sites in the study area (Minnis, n.d.). Mesquite appears to have been an important wild food. Excavated Animas period sites in

Hidalgo County have yielded similar assemblages of macroplant remains (Cutler 1965).

While both the Classic Mimbres period and Animas period
peoples heavily exploited domesticates, they probably practiced
different agricultural strategies, as is suggested by the different
site locations between the two periods. This variability may be
only a local phenomenon, however. In Hidalgo County, for example,
Findlow (1979) suggests that there was little difference in subsistence strategies between the Classic Mimbres and Animas periods.

There appears to be a slightly increased mean site size for
the Animas period compared with the Classic Mimbres period (Minnis
1980b), but this may be more apparent than real. The low mean
Classic Mimbres period site size is depressed by the presence of
small, probably seasonally occupied sites that do not represent
true habitation sites.

Because of the paucity of controlled excavations of Animas
period sites, it is difficult to draw a more meaningful description
of Animas period culture history. However, enough data are available to make general comparisons between Animas period sites and
other similar archeological remains. There are several sites in
the study area with material remains similar to those of the Animas
period. The previously discussed Casas Grandes region is one.
Also, many sites in Hidalgo County, southwest of the study area,
have a heavy Animas period occupation. The better known El Paso
phase remains of the Jornada Branch of the Mogollon from the Las
Cruces-El Paso area are another similar tradition.

All these areas have Animas-like remains but with some differences. For example, the ceramic assemblages are different (Le-
Blanc and Rugge 1980). Northern Chihuahuan pottery is more similar
to that of the Hidalgo County Animas period materials than to
either the study area Animas period remains or the El Paso Animas
period material. The variety of burial practices is greater for
the Mimbres Animas period than for Casas Grandes.

Similarly, there are chronological differences between these
areas. The Mimbres Animas period seems to end about the time of
the end of the Medio period at Casas Grandes, whereas the El Paso
and Hidalgo Animas periods persist longer. Therefore, in the study
area there is a distinct hiatus between the Animas period and the
following occupation, the Salado period.

An interesting but poorly understood aspect of the Animas
period is the relationship, if any, between the Classic Mimbres
period and the Animas period. The Classic Mimbres period seems to

end about A.D. 1130 to 1150, and the Animas period begins about A.D. 1175. There may be some overlap in occupation, but the chronology is not refined enough to let me discuss this point further. LeBlanc and Rugge (1980) have suggested that the rise of Casas Grandes exerted pressure on the Classic Mimbres period population, resulting in its absorption into the Animas period system, an explanation I do not agree with.

While only the barest outline of the Animas period is now available, it appears that the Mimbres Animas is a local manifestation of a desert dwelling tradition with some ties to the complex system of northern Chihuahua. Compared with the preceding Mogollon tradition, the Animas period occupation in the study area represents a striking change in material culture and specific economic strategies. It may represent a population discontinuity as well.

Salado Period (Cliff Phase)

The Salado period has been characterized by large adobe pueblos surrounded by compound walls and by Gila and Tonto Polychromes. What this all means is unclear and subject to differing interpretations (Doyel and Haury 1976). Restricting the geographic focus to the study area, the Salado period represents the last puebloan occupation of the valley. It occurred from A.D. 1300 to 1425 and perhaps lasted even longer (LeBlanc and Nelson 1976; LeBlanc 1980b). It is the smallest puebloan population in the study area. Only four sites are known, and there is good reason to believe that these represent the totality of Salado period sites in the study area. However, there is a large, dense Saladoan occupation in the adjacent Gila Valley around Cliff, and it has been suggested that the Rio Mimbres Salado period population represents a geographically peripheral expansion of the Cliff Salado period groups (LeBlanc and Nelson 1976). There is also a Salado period occupation in Hidalgo County.

Salado period sites are larger than sites of other periods (up to 300 rooms in the Cliff Valley), but the largest site in the Mimbres Valley, Z:5:10, is 70-80 rooms. Three of the Mimbres Salado period sites are situated along the Rio Mimbres in the Upper Chihuahuan zone, and one site (Z:9:17) is in the desert (Minnis and LeBlanc 1979). No Salado period sites are found in the mountainous area.

Like the earlier puebloan populations, the Salado people were agriculturalists. We have macroplant evidence of maize, squash, and cotton. In fact, the greatest concentration of cottonseeds in the study area is from the largest excavated Salado period site, and no cotton has been recovered from other Rio Mimbres Salado period sites. The smaller Salado population did not seem to drastically affect the floodplain vegetation as did the earlier Classic Mimbres period population.

The Mimbres Foundation has excavated the three Salado period sites in the piñon-juniper-oak woodland. The largest appears to be the earliest and was abandoned with some planning, since the pueblo was cleared out before abandonment. The two later Salado period sites are smaller, 12 and 30 rooms, and these may have been the final location of the occupants who abandoned Z:5:10. They may, however, represent different microoccupations. All sites appear to have been occupied for a short time, since the trash deposits are thin, there is a lack of remodeling, and no rooms were abandoned during the occupation of the site (LeBlanc 1980b). Either the two later sites were abandoned with haste or the occupants moved farther away, because numerous household items were left behind. The abandonment of household items is a common pattern for the Salado period sites around Cliff.

In the study area, the Salado period appears to be a short and small occupation unrelated to the Animas period. This may not be the case for other areas such as Hidalgo County. The reasons for final abandonment are not understood.

Protohistoric Period

Early Spanish chroniclers (about A.D. 1680-1750) make reference to numerous groups (Jano, Suma, Apache, Jacome, and Manso) in the international four corners area. The Jacome and Jano apparently were situated around the Chiricahua Mountains of south-eastern Arizona, whereas the Manso and Suma were in central and eastern Chihuahua, extending up the Rio Grande as far north as Las Cruces, New Mexico. The Apache, much to the consternation of Spanish, Mexican, and Anglo settlers, roamed over southern New Mexico and Arizona, northern Chihuahua, and extreme western Texas. Except for the Apache, there is no good historical evidence that these protohistoric groups inhabited the study area, but it is quite likely that they occasionally traversed the region.

Early historical records are very unreliable; thus the lifestyle and ethnic/linguistic relationships between these groups are not well known. Most were small-band hunter/gatherers, though some were cultivators residing in rancherias. Sauer (1934) believes that the non-Apache protohistoric groups were Uto-Aztecan speakers. In opposition, Forbes (1957) points to what little evidence there is on protohistoric peoples in southern New Mexico and concludes that they were Athapaskan speakers who, after A.D. 1750, either merged with the Apache or were included with them by the Spanish. Naylor (1969) sides with Forbes and further suggests that with the prehistoric collapse of Casas Grandes, the spatial void (if there was one) was filled by hunter/gatherers moving west from Texas.

Given the nonexistent archeological remains and poor historical evidence, any conclusions concerning the protohistoric populations should be viewed with extreme caution. However, it is likely that at least temporary protohistoric occupation of the study area occurred.

Historic Period

There was a long Apache occupation in the study area, A.D. 1650-1890 and probably longer. This presence is extensively documented by historical records, but there is a marked lack of material remains. Out of over one thousand archeological sites recorded by the five largest surveys of southwestern New Mexico, only four sites have been claimed to be Apache, but these designations are not certain (Minnis 1980b). This points to the general problem of the lack of diagnostic archeological remains of small, highly mobile groups, a bias that also extends to the Paleo-Indian and Archaic periods and to limited-activity loci for all prehistoric periods.

The extensive Spanish, Mexican, and Anglo occupation is outside the scope of this research.

Summary

Evidence for at least twelve thousand years of human occupation of the study area is present. The Mogollon tradition from A.D. 1-200 to 1150 is of greatest interest for this research. During this time period, the human population increased substantially with resultant changes in human settlement patterns.

The largest increase occurred during the Classic Mimbres period and perhaps the later part of the Late Pithouse period. This population increase set in motion processes central to this research.

In order to understand temporal and spatial changes in Rio Mimbres drainage prehistory, the Mimbres Foundation surveyed an environmentally diverse sample of land and excavated or tested twenty-six sites. By making comparisons between assemblages from these sites and survey data, we were able to document clear prehistoric changes. Despite the extensive site vandalization, our data sets provide an adequate base from initial discussion of the relations between natural environmental conditions, economic strategies, and social formations.

4

The Natural Environment
of the Rio Mimbres Region

The analysis of the possible food provisioning problems faced by prehistoric subsistence farmers in a study area requires a detailed description of that environment. This chapter describes the Rio Mimbres natural environment, emphasizing factors important for successful cultivation of crops grown by aboriginal techniques. The natural resource structure available to the prehistoric occupants of the area is then sketched. In order to understand the prehistoric environment as fully as possible, differences between the prehistoric and modern environment are investigated.

General Topography

As Bartlett characterized the environment of southwestern New Mexico, "one becomes sickened and disgusted with the ever recurring sameness of plain and mountain, plant and living thing" (1854:247-48). Contrary to Bartlett's description, the environment of the study area is diverse and complex. This diversity is based upon the often abrupt changes in topography. Within the study area are two broad topographic zones, desert and mountains. The desert area consists of wide, level plains with a base elevation of about 1,200 m and occasional isolated mountain ranges, such as the Florida Mountains, towering to 900 m above the plains. Areas of sand dune drift are found but are not extensive. Watercourses are generally ephemeral, and it is unusually difficult to pinpoint a single "channel." In addition to the mountain ranges, low ridges or hills are frequent; rarely do these rise more than 120 m above the plains.

The mountain zone is widespread. Most of the mountainous study area is below 2,280 m, although occasional peaks up to 2,900 m are present. To the north, in the Gila Wilderness, higher elevations are common. The mountains are dissected by often steep and narrow

drainages. Only the Rio Mimbres and several small drainages flow
year-round, and fertile floodplain alluvium is restricted to these
watercourses, most notably the Rio Mimbres. Small drainages high
up in the mountains occasionally converge, forming mountain "parks"
with wider floodplains, more rolling that the surrounding
mountainous terrain.

Climate

As the topographic relief and elevation vary widely within the
study area, so also do numerous climatic conditions. The most
critical climatic factors for agriculture, precipitation and frost-
free period, will be outlined here. When necessary, more exact
climatic data are presented. Unless stated to the contrary, all
climatic data are from Tuan et al. (1973).

The general scarcity of moisture qualifies southwestern New
Mexico as being arid to semiarid. Deming, at approximately 1,280 m
elevation in the broad desert plains, receives an average annual
precipitation of 230 mm, and Silver City (1,800 m) averages 420 mm
of precipitation per year for a modern thirty-year average (1930-
60). It should be noted that median precipitation is lower than
the mean: "this means that for any month in a given year the rain
that comes is more likely to be below than above the arithmetic
mean" (Tuan et al. 1973:50). Variation in yearly precipitation is
higher at lower elevations, and as noted by Tuan et al. (1973:50),
"in the semi-aridity of New Mexico, the difference in precipitation
from year to year is usually less than that in humid climates, but
this small difference is of far greater importance to agriculture."

Most important is the seasonal patterning of precipitation,
since uneven distribution has critical implications for the
moisture needs of growing plants. Precipitation is bimodally distributed. Figure 6 shows the monthly precipitation as a percentage
of the yearly average. These data are for Silver City, which is
analogous to the main part of the Mimbres Valley. Winter moisture
comes from widespread cyclonic storms, which are most frequent in
February. The summer precipitation period of July through
September contributes about 40 percent of the total annual
moisture. This precipitation generally falls in localized down-
pours, which can miss adjacent fields. The implications of this
localized precipitation for field ownership and intracommunity
sharing has been noted by Ford (1968).

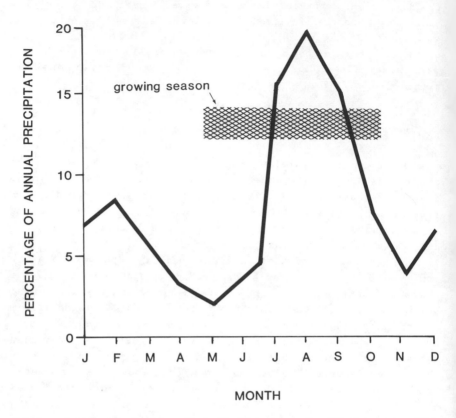

Figure 6. Precipitation distribution near the study area. Note the close relation between the growing season and the precipitation peak.

A characteristic of southwestern New Mexico is that May is the driest month and June is also dry. Because dependable rains do not begin until July, germination and early growth of young cultigens can be uncertain. The importance of moisture to plant growth should be considered in relation to factors affecting plant transpiration. The precipitation effectiveness index (P-E) developed by Thornthwaite (1933) calculates precipitation in relation to evaporation; this measure can then be related to actual rainfall and stored soil moisture to calculate an average annual moisture deficit. The deficit is for Deming 0.5 m and 0.36 m for Silver City. Dregne (1959) devised a crop moisture index (CM). This index is a variation on Thornthwaite's P-E index but is weighted for the modern agricultural growth period of April, May, and June.

The annual P-E ratio is multiplied by the P-E ratio for these three months. The scale ranges from 0 to 850 or more, and the range of the 117 reporting stations in New Mexico is 14 to 740.   Fort Bayard, near Silver City, has a value of 55 and Deming has a value of 16, further illustrating the aridity of the study area.   However, this index is not completely applicable to prehistoric conditions because the prehistoric growing season in the study area probably was not as early as the weighted growing season used by Dregne.   Nevertheless, this index is more appropriate for general comparison between areas than the P-E ratio.

A second important climatic parameter for agriculture is frost-free period.   The meteorological determination of frost-free period is very liberal in relation to agriculture, since below-freezing temperatures are measured at 1.8 m above the ground, whereas damaging frost will develop first at ground level.   Nevertheless, the published data are useful in assessing the importance of frost-free period to prehistoric agriculture.   The frost-free period values are a reversal of precipitation values.   Although the desert areas around Deming are low in moisture, the average frost-free period is 220 days, a period that allows flexibiltiy in planting and harvest timing.   In contrast, Silver City has 181 frost-free days, still a relatively long period.   Higher in the mountains, the frost-free period drops to about 100-120 days, which allows little or no flexibility in planting.   The frost-free period is further shortened in relatively narrow mountain valleys because of the cold air drainage effect, by which cold air collects in low spots.   Compounding the problem of shorter growing seasons at higher elevations is the fact that "the shorter the average length of the frost-free season, the greater the variation in the length from year to year" (Tuan et al. 1973:80).

Other climatic factors are important to agriculture.   For example, high winds are common during the spring in the study area. These dry winds create problems for crops by increasing evapotranspiration, causing potential mechanical damage to the young plants, and removing topsoil or depositing a layer of windborne particulate matter over the topsoil (Skidmore and Woodruff 1968).

In considering precipitation and frost-free period it is clear we have two contrasting limiting factors on agriculture.   Because of low precipitation, high potential evapotranspiration, and high winds during the critical planting months of May and June, and because of the localized nature of summer storms, agriculture is more uncertain in lower southern regions than at higher elevations.

Conversely, at higher elevations and in narrow river valleys the frost-free period may become too short to allow adequate leeway in the timing of planting and harvesting crops.

Prehistoric agriculture was practiced in restricted regions in the desert areas around Deming, as is documented by remains of maize, common beans, tepary beans, and cotton from archeological sites in the desert. It appears that prehistoric agriculture in the desert plains was limited to a few selected areas of high water table, where there was groundwater or surface water or both readily available for crops. No crops are now dry farmed around Deming, and two experimental maize plots I planted in 1976 using drought resistant Papago seed "burned up" even though they were watered weekly. Clearly, without the infusion of water generally unavailable through prehistoric agricultural technology, crop production in the desert regions would have been difficult.

Similarly, no modern agriculture other than scattered home gardens is practiced in the populated valleys above about 2,130 m, but we have evidence of prehistoric agriculture in high altitude regions where it is not now present (Minnis 1978; Sandor 1983). By manipulating patterns of topographic variation such as planting on midslopes of warmer south-facing slopes, prehistoric peoples were able to grow cultigens in a region with a short growing season. Most modern agriculture, using technology available to prehistoric peoples, is practiced in the major river valleys (e.g., Gila and Mimbres) between 1,520 and 1,980 m in elevation. In Grant County, approximately 3,642 ha are now irrigated from perennially flowing streams (Maker, Neher, and Anderson 1971:7), most of which were presumably available to prehistoric populations.

Hydrology

Lack of water is the basic defining characteristic of arid areas. As a prime limiting factor and a human necessity, the distribution of water is critical for understanding prehistoric population settlement locations and economic activities. Water resources were important to agriculturalists in the study area for two primary uses, domestic consumption and crop growth. Surface flow such as rivers, seeps, springs, and areas of high water table suitable for shallow-well construction were the points of water collection for prehistoric human consumption. These are also water resource points for crop growth, but also important for successful harvest is the soil moisture and chemical structure to be discussed in the following section. I will first discuss the characteristics of surface flow, then consider strategies of agricultural water use.

The most conspicuous surface flow is the Rio Mimbres channel, the only large, perennially flowing river in the study area. Generally, the Rio Mimbres flows aboveground from just above the Mitchell site (LA 12076) to south of Old Town (Z:5:14), it then moves underground (fig. 5). Only after severe storms does the Rio Mimbres flow aboveground as far south as Deming. A few times in the past hundred years, the Mimbres has flowed as far south as the international border southeast of the Florida Mountains. During the dry season, certain segments of the normally perennial channel may go dry, with the aboveground flow resurfacing at geological dikes. Variation in the Rio Mimbres flow is illustrated by data from 1931 through 1959, when the average daily flow ranged from 27.45 to 311.3 m^3 per sec (United States Geological Survey 1974). For one specific year (1916) monthly discharge rates varied from 233,131.5 m^3 in July to a high of 8,387,800 m^3 in September (French 1917).

The smaller secondary drainages flow only after heavy storms and remain dry throughout most of the year. Other sources of surface flow are springs or seeps. We do not know the distribution and frequency of all springs and seeps, but where they occur there usually is, not unexpectedly, some evidence of prehistoric occupation. In addition, there are numerous small springs and small pools of water along mountain drainages. Hence, for the mountainous area small amounts of water for domestic uses can usually be found, even during the dry season. In the desert, water availability is a different matter. There are vast regions in the desert where domestic water may not have been available, particularly during the dry season (Darton 1916, 1917). Therefore, it is likely that water would have been a prime limiting factor for most human occupation in the desert but less so in the mountainous areas.

Three strategies of agricultural water use are available: irrigation, modified dry farming, and dry farming. Irrigation in the absence of pumping is restricted to zones with surface flow along the Rio Mimbres and major seasonal drainages. Dry farming is primarily dependent upon the water-retention characteristics of the soil. There is evidence that the first bench above the Rio Mimbres was historically farmed, but dry farming is not practiced there at present. Lower precipitation during the 1940s and 1950s, along with the modern availability of well water, may have ended this practice of dry farming the first bench. It is not clear how successful dry farming would have been prehistorically, but most likely during periods of above average growing season precipitation prehistoric Mimbreños would have been able to successfully dry farm fields that were not situated on the floodplain. Modified dry farming (water conservation) involves changing soil and runoff to increase the efficiency of precipitation for crops (Herold 1965; Sandor 1983; Woodbury 1961). There are some examples of pre-historic check dams and terraces in the study area that were undoubtedly used for fields. These will be discussed in greater detail later.

Soils

Eleven classes of soil have been categorized for the study area (Maker, Neher, and Anderson 1971; Maker, Bailey, and Anderson 1970). These were then generally classified as to suitability for modern irrigation agriculture (including surface flow and ground-water utilization). These classes do not correspond exactly with locations for prehistoric farming for two reasons. First, these classes are plotted onto general soil maps, and small, isolated areas of favorable arability may be overlooked. Second, some areas of good modern agricultural potential, such as around Deming, can be fully used only with deep well pumping. Nevertheless, this soil classification offers a useful baseline from which to view prehistoric agricultural soil, moisture, and plant relationships.

Three soil associations are particularly suitable for agri-culture. The San Mateo-Shanta association consists of nearly level floodplain with deep silty loam, moderate water permeability, and a high-waterholding capacity. This association is found in the Rio Mimbres floodplain north of the Desert site (Z:5:10) and is the best agricultural soil. The Mimbres-Verhalen association is found in the lower Rio Mimbres floodplain. These soils are deep silty clay loam with slow water permeability and a high water-retention capacity. Maker, Bailey, and Anderson state that for this as-sociation "the fine-textured and very slowly permeable soils, although suitable for irrigation, will require a high level of management to prevent accumulation of salts and development of unfavorable drainage condition" (1970:12). However, the Rio Mimbres water is low in soluble minerals, and there is no other evidence of potential saline accumulation in the lower Rio Mimbres Valley (J. McLean, personal communication, 1979). Further, a common grass of this segment of the floodplain, alkali sacaton, thrives in soils of moderate to low salinity (Meinzer 1927). Therefore it seems probable that salinity from repeated irrigation may not have been a problem prehistorically. The third agriculturally important soil, Mimbres, is a deep silty clay loam with high water-retention capacity. This association is found in the area around Deming. Much of this association would not have been available to prehistoric agriculturalists because the water table is so low as to necessitate deep-well pumping. However, the two areas of high water table along the Rio Mimbres around Deming where prehistoric (Classic Mimbres and Animas periods) agriculturalists lived and presumably farmed are in this soil zone (Blake and Narod 1977).

The other eight soil associations in the study area are generally on steep slopes or have a very thin soil mantle with low water-retention capacity, thus limiting their crop production potential. However, in some small areas having these soils there are prehistoric terrace systems attesting to their suitability for agriculture under some conditions. For example, Maker, Neher, and Anderson (1971:26) characterize the Rockland-Luzena-Santana association in the following way: "Although the soils are usually shallow, small areas of moderately deep soils do occur interspersed with shallow soils, rock outcrops, and rock ledges." They suggest that about 1 percent of this zone can support crop production. It is these small areas of deep soils that were often used by the prehistoric agriculturalists. In addition to gross categories of soils suitable for agriculture, attention must be paid to the fertility of these potentially arable soils. This factor is discussed in Chapter 5.

The soils, like hydrology in the study area, demarcate a small, exceptionally fertile floodplain contrasted with the greater part of the region, which is generally unsuitable for agriculture unless more water is made available, either through human manipulation (e.g., pumping or terracing) or through higher precipitation.

Vegetation

The diversity in climatic, edaphic, and hydrological factors within the study area is mirrored by the floral diversity. General plant distributions are largely determined by elevation and its partially dependent variable, precipitation. Specific plant distributions are influenced by other factors such as slope orientation and angle, soil and mineral composition, and local hydrological conditions. The intersection of these factors within the study area can be seen in the diversity of plant associations. Out of this specific diversity, major "life zones" can be described, each of which exhibits great variation and that probably has little relation to the prehistoric "conceptual environment" (Bates 1962:8). Three broad zones will be described: Lower Chihuahuan, Upper Chihuahuan, and Transitional. These are roughly the same as the analytic divisions drawn by Bailey (1913). Several references are available that present more detailed descriptions of vegetation in the study area and surrounding regions (see Castetter 1956; Dick-Peddie 1975; Lowe 1964; Boles and Dick-Peddie 1983). Latin binomials for the common plant names used here are found in the Appendix.

Lower Chihuahuan Zone (1,220 m to 1,680 m Elevation)

This zone is characterized by Basin and Range topography, with isolated mountain ranges surrounded by extensive desert plains. Figures 7 and 8 illustrate the Lower Chihuahuan environment. Except for the Rio Mimbres and the smaller Seventy-six Draw near Deming, drainage patterns are ephemeral, with temporary pools available for up to a week after torrential rains. Desert shrubs interspersed with stands of grass dominate the vegetation. Mormon tea, creosote bush, yucca, littleleaf sumac, and crucifixion thorn are the dominant shrubs on rocky or well-drained soils. Mesquite, often in nearly pure stands, is common on poorly drained soils. Common grasses are grama and tobosa. Water channels are usually marked by desert willow, often with rabbit brush, desert hackberry, and mesquite. A rare cottonwood can be found where there is an unusually dependable high water table, an infrequent occurrence in the desert areas. The large alluvial fans radiating from the bases of the desert mountains are characterized by vertical vegetation banding, from the plains vegetation, through shrub stands, to low density oak and juniper assemblages at the highest elevations. At present, there are no areas of permanently ponded water in the Deming bolson, as are frequent in the narrow valleys to the west of

Figure 7. Lower Chihuahuan life zone. The Florida Mountains shown in this photograph are the largest desert mountians in the study area.

Deming and the northern plains of Chihuahua where playas are present.

Upper Chihuahuan Zone (1,515 m to 2,290 m)

The Upper Chihuahuan vegetation is primarily an oak, juniper, and piñon pigmy woodland. Figures 9 and 10 show the Rio Mimbres in the Upper Chihuahuan zone. It rises out of the desert plains into large mountainous areas with relatively narrow river valleys. Junipers and oak predominate in xeric habitats such as lower elevations or south-facing slopes, whereas piñon is most abundant on the more mesic north-facing slopes and at higher elevations. In addition to the trees, there are many shrubs (e.g., rose, mountain mahogany, apache plume, and cliff rose), agavaceous plants and succulents (e.g., sotol, bear grass, yucca, agave, prickly pear, and cholla), grasses (primarily grama), and numerous herbaceous plants.

The floodplain vegetation in the Upper Chihuahuan zone is distinctive. Along watercourses with a high water table and

Figure 8. Lower Chihuahuan life zone in the Florida Mountains near site Z:4:3.

fertile alluvium is found a well-developed canopy dominated by large cottonwoods with alder, walnut, willow, ash, and box elder. The understory is a robust assemblage of herbaceous plants such as giant ragweed, sunflower, pigweed, grasses, and goosefoot. Side drainages may be marked by occasional cottonwoods but more commonly bear a dense concentration of oak, juniper, and piñon.

Transitional Zone (2,135 m to 2,750 m)

This zone is topographically similar to the Upper Chihuahuan zone, but the higher elevation, shorter growing season, and greater precipitation are responsible for changes in vegetation patterning. Figures 11 and 12 illustrate the mountainous Transitional zone. The dominant woody vegetation consists of ponderosa pine, Gambel oak, and junipers, often with an open grass-covered understory. Ponderosa pine is found at lower elevations in valley bottoms because of the cold air drainage effect. For the most part, little of the study area is in the Transitional life zone.

At higher elevations are coniferous forests dominated by

Figure 9. Upper Chihuahuan life zone in the Rio Mimbres Valley near site LA 12076. Note the distinctive floodplain vegetation.

spruce, Douglas fir, and fir. Generally these high elevation forests are outside the study area. When necessary their importance will be discussed.

Fauna

Although the international four corners is "surely one of the most fascinating regions of the world for the field zoologist" (Findley et al. 1975:4), the animal life of the area is not central to this research. In the desert plains, numerous animals are available for hunting, particularly antelope, jackrabbit, cotton-tail, and coyote. Also, there is a variety of mice, rats, ground

Figure 10. Lower Rio Mimbres Valley. This area is transitional between the Lower and Upper Chihuahuan life zones.

squirrels, and gophers. Also present are reptiles, insects, breeding and migratory birds. In the mountainous areas are found many of the desert animals plus mule deer, white-tailed deer, bear, wolf, and aquatic mammals such as beaver and muskrat. Few fish remains have been recovered from excavations, suggesting that fish were not an important exploited resource. In other words, there was a great diversity of animal resources available to the pre-historic hunter, assuming no major changes from the prehistoric fauna to that found at present. Those interested in the fauna of the study area should consult Findley et al. (1975) or Bailey (1932).

Climatic Fluctuations

Environmental change through time has been documented for the Southwest. Various data bases are used to infer change, and they are often in marked disagreement. Basically, four approaches have been used: sedimentology, dendroclimatology, palynology, and pack rat midden studies. Each measures slightly different phenomena

Figure 11. Transitional life zone in the Black Range Mountains just east of the Rio Mimbres Valley. The relatively level area in the middle of the photograph is a "mountain park."

with differing degrees of sensitivity. Next, environmental changes, both prehistoric and historic, will be considered. Finally, I will outline a basic reconstruction of the prehistoric environment.

While we can accept the fact of general Holocene environmental stability, there has been variation in climate that was critical to prehistoric groups, particularly agriculturalists. Two methods are commonly used to infer specific archeologically relevant climatic fluctuations--palynology and dendroclimatology. There has not yet been definitive work using either data set for the Mimbres Foundation study area, so more detailed analyses from the Pine Lawn Valley will be used here. Schoenwetter (1962) has analyzed the pollen record, and Dean and Robinson (1978) present a tree-ring record from A.D. 580 to A.D. 1287.

On the basis of work near Vernon, Arizona, and in the Pine Lawn Valley, New Mexico, Schoenwetter sketched an outline of vegetational and environmental change. Contrasting pollen from cheno-am (chenopod and amaranth families), Compositae, and pines he correlated these with changes in rainfall patterns. Dominance of cheno-am pollen, he believes, is indicative of heavy summer rain

Figure 12.   Environment of the high elevations in the Black Range Mountains.   The area in the background is the Rio Grande Valley.

fall, whereas large amounts of Compositae pollen indicate light summer precipitation.   He then divided the pollen sequence into four periods, one of which is undated.   Schoenwetter noted a major shift about A.D. 1000, when all pollen profiles are dominated by cheno-am, indicating more erosion and a basically drier climate. Unfortunately, one of the assumptions necessary for this model is that the prehistoric human population had no effect on the pollen spectrum.   Numerous studies, however (e.g., Martin and Byer 1965; Lytle-Webb 1978; Minnis 1978; Stiger 1977; Wyckoff 1977; Kelso 1980), have documented the often widespread effects that human population has on the local vegetation.   Therefore, one must investigate major factors of soil disturbance including human activity, such as agriculture, as well as natural factors, such as erosion, in order to reconstruct past environments.   Further, the processes of pollen deposition in archeological sites is very poorly known, so that archeological pollen spectra can be difficult to interpret.

A much more reliable approach for inferring climatic change is dendroclimatology.   The use of tree-ring indexes for environmental reconstruction has become more sophisticated because complex analytic techniques. Fortunately, a long term tree-ring sequence is available for the Reserve area (1,860 m elevation), approximately 110 km north of the study area. The other relatively close tree-ring sequence is from Casas Grandes, about 160 km south of Mimbres in northern Chihuahua (Scott 1966).

The Reserve tree-ring index is taken from Dean and Robinson (1978). This index was generated as a part of the major reassessment of southwestern tree-ring data undertaken by the Laboratory of Tree-Ring Research at the University of Arizona. Two problems plague the available preliminary Mimbres sequence. First, the Mimbres sequence does not cover as long a time period as the Reserve sequence. Second, many of the Mimbres yearly values are based upon a very small sample. Given these problems with the Mimbres sequence, it would be useful to determine if the Reserve sequence could be used as an adequate predictor of the tree-ring sequence in the Mimbres area. To do this, various segments of the two sequences were correlated. First, Mimbres tree-ring values that are well documented were correlated with the corresponding Reserve tree-ring values. As can be seen in figure 13, the correlation is adequate. For the years between A.D. 813-37 the correlation coefficient is .80 and for A.D. 970-94 it is .75. In contrast, some poorly documented Mimbres values were correlated with the Reserve values. For A.D. 600-624, the correlation coefficient is only .56. Therefore, it is clear that the relation between well documented Mimbres and Reserve values is better than that for the poorly documented Mimbres years. Because the Reserve sequence is more thoroughly documented than the Mimbres sequence and because the Reserve sequence is an adequate predictor of Mimbres values, the Reserve tree-ring sequence will be used here as an indicator of prehistoric precipitation patterns for the study area.

The Reserve sequence is presented in figure 14. The tree-ring value for each year is graphed on a distribution curve with a mean of 100. The standard deviation for the Reserve sequence is 42.8. The methodology for constructing the tree-ring index is presented in Dean and Robinson (1978); also see Stokes (1968); Fritts, Mosimann, and Bottoroff (1969); Fritts (1976).

Tree-ring indexes have been used to infer periods of low moisture that might have constituted agricultural droughts for prehistoric populations in the Southwest (Douglass 1935). Objections to this method have been raised. Gladwin (1940) asserted that tree-rings primarily measure winter precipitation, whereas summer precipitation is more critical for farming. How-

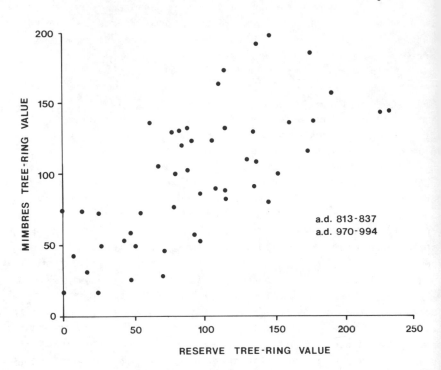

Figure 13. Correlation between the best-documented prehistoric Mimbres tree-ring sequence and contemporary Researve area tree-ring sequence.

ever, Fritts, Mosimann, and Bottoroff (1969) have shown, using multivariate statistics, that tree-ring widths can be used as an adequate measure of summer precipitation.

Stockton (1975) obtained good correlations between yearly streamflow values and tree-ring widths for the corresponding twelve-month period. To test the applicability of using the Reserve tree-ring sequence as a predictor of streamflow in the Mimbres drainage, I correlated the modern Reserve tree-ring sequence (from Dean and Robinson 1978) and values for the yearly Rio Mimbres steamflow (United States Geological Survey 1974). The correlation coefficient between the 1931-59 Reserve tree-ring index and average flow of the Rio Mimbres is .77 (fig. 15), within the range of correlation values between tree-rings and streamflow in the same drainage (Stockton 1975). This further supports the use of the Reserve area tree-ring index for the Rio Mimbres drainage.

A general view of figure 14 indicates several periods of low

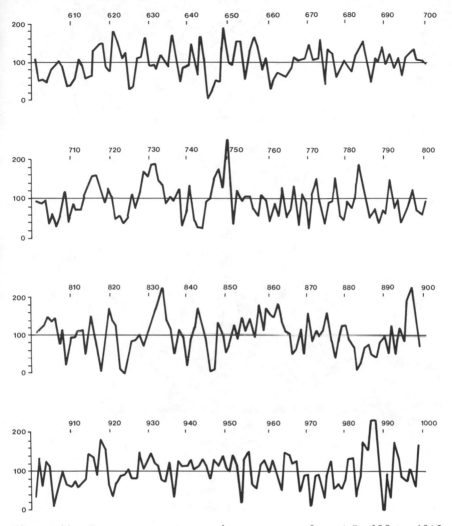

Figure 14.   Reserve area tree-ring sequence from A.D. 600 to 1249 (after Dean and Robinson 1978).

precipitation in the Reserve area and by extension in the Rio Mimbres region. Of particular interest in regard to Late Pithouse and Classic Mimbres periods are the late 700s, 880s, 900s, 970s, 1030-40s, and 1090-40s. The tree-ring index will be discussed later as it relates to agriculture.

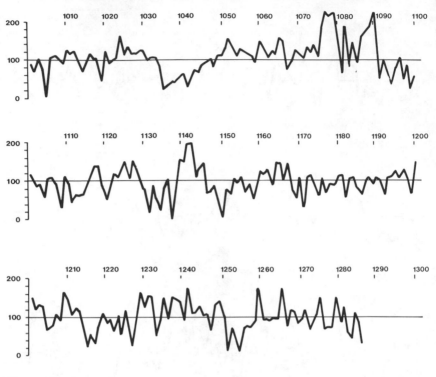

Figure 14 (cont.).

Documented Prehistoric Environmental Change

Several changes in the study area environment created by the prehistoric population have been documented by various Mimbres Foundation analyses. Four broad changes have been noted: (1) reduction of arboreal floodplain vegetation, (2) changes in stream-flow characteristics, (3) increase in disturbed soil habitats, and (4) changes in faunal assemblage.

Evidence for the reduction of the floodplain trees has been inferred from two data bases, fuel woods and construction woods. The macroplant evidence has been presented in greater detail else-where (Minnis 1978). Over two thousand individual pieces of char-coal have been identified from numerous sites ranging from Early Pithouse to Salado. Most of this charcoal is from hearths and represents wood fuel. The species present were divided into two categories, phreatophytes growing only on the floodplain and other woody plants that primarily grow on the hills surrounding the

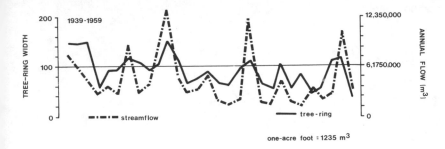

Figure 15.   Relation between modern Reserve tree-ring sequence and Rio Mimbres streamflow.

floodplain.   The first category includes cottonwood/willow, ash, box elder, sycamore, and walnut, whereas the second group is primarily juniper, piñon, oak, and a rosaceous shrub (probably mountain mahogany).   Figure 16 shows the percentage of floodplain charcoal recovered from sites of each of the five archeological periods.   It is assumed that changes in the ratio between flood-plain and nonfloodplain woods reflect changes in their relative use.   Studies of wood fuel collection by modern nonindustrialized societies indicate that the closer suitable fuel resources are to the location of use, the greater their use (Agency for International Development 1980).   That is, availability is a major determinate of fuel wood use; therefore the frequency of woods recovered should be a relative measure of local availability. Figure 16 shows a large reduction in the amount of floodplain wood used during the Early Pithouse and Classic Mimbres periods.   The small amount of floodplain charcoal from Early Pithouse sites is probably the result of the fact that these sites are on high knolls farther away from the floodplain than sites of other periods, and hillside fuel wood was more easily procured.

The same does not apply for the Classic Mimbres period, since these sites are just above the floodplain like sites of all other periods except the Early Pithouse.   It is most probable that this reduction reflects reduction in the phreatophyte community.   The high population density of the agricultural Classic Mimbres period is probably related to this reduction because of increased flood-plain clearance for fields.

This pattern of little fuel wood from floodplain plants during the Classic Mimbres period is mirrored in the percentage of flood plain wood used for construction.   The large pieces of charcoal recovered during excavation, which are generally construction

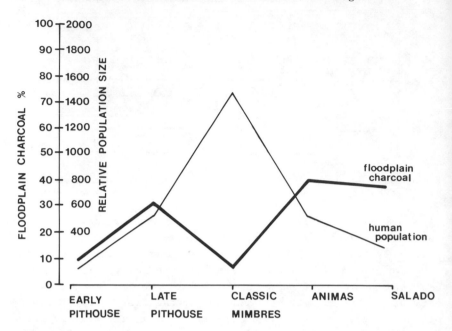

Figure 16.   Correlation between prehistoric human population size
and precentage of wood charcoal from floodplain plants recovered in
Mimbres Foundation flotation samples.

timbers, were identified by the Laboratory of Tree-Ring Research,
University of Arizona. The ratio of floodplain to nonfloodplain
charcoal is similar for this data set, as for the fuel wood remains. Also, there is a noticeable reduction in the amount of
pollen from floodplain trees during the Classic Mimbres period
(Minnis et al. 1982). Two data sets representing fuel wood and
construction wood use, which represent generally independent wood
procurement strategies, confirm the same conclusion that there has
been a significant reduction in the arboreal floodplain vegetation
during the Classic Mimbres period. Until 1979, permission could
not be secured to excavate any Animas site in the Upper Chihuahuan
zone, where most of the excavated Classic sites are situated.   In
1979 a short testing program was undertaken on a dual component
(Classic Mimbres/Animas) site in the Upper Chihuahuan zone. The
charcoal identified from this site, Z:1:6, is presented in figure
17. Although the sample size is small, the general pattern of
floodplain charcoal absence during Classic Mimbres sites or components is confirmed. No floodplain charcoal was recovered from
the Classic Mimbres component, whereas nearly one-quarter of the
Animas wood charcoal was cottonwood/willow.

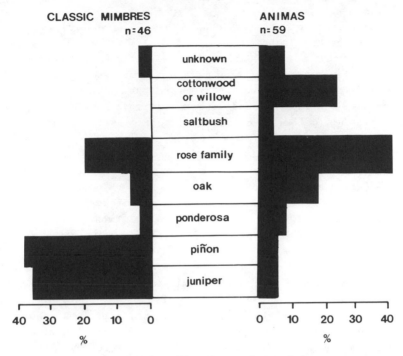

Figure 17. Wood charcoal remains from site Z:1:6.

It is not clear what impact this relative reduction of the phreatophyte community had on subsistence strategies. What is particularly interesting is the relationship between floodplain vegetation, water level, and severity and periodicity of flooding. Loren Potter, professor of biology at the University of New Mexico (personal communication, 1979), doubts that clearance of large floodplain trees would have had much effect on flooding. However, a reduction of this vegetation may have added the small amount of water the trees would have transpired (Bowie and Kam 1968). Long term research on phreatophyte removal along the Gila River at Safford, Arizona, studied these questions. From this research, two conclusions were reached: (1) phreatophyte vegetation increases the lag time from precipitation to runoff; and (2) during floods, large bankside trees increase erosion by taking soils with them if they are uprooted (Burkham 1972, 1976; McQueen and Miller 1972; Turner 1974).

Prehistoric changes from the modern floodplain environment are reflected in several artifact categories. Four indicators of ponded or slow-moving water have been recovered from Mimbres sites;

these indicators are not now found or are found in very small relic stands in the Rio Mimbres Valley today. First, remains of muskrat have been recovered from Classic Mimbres sites (Langenwalter 1979); muskrats are not now present in the Rio Mimbres drainage. Second, remains of the common reed are frequently found in Classic Mimbres period site excavations, and none are at present in the study area. Third, cattail pollen is common from soil sampled in Classic Mimbres period deposits, but only a single very small stand is found along the Mimbres River at present. The fourth indicator of floodplain change is bulrush, whose seeds have been recovered from Animas period site samples but which is not now found in the study area. Although not identified from archeological remains, the Chihuahuan chub was more abundant in the past than today; in fact, a pathetically small population (thirty-five individuals) is all that remains of the chub in the Rio Mimbres. Miller (1961) attributes this population decline to a reduction in the number of pools in the river. The prehistoric fish remains from Mimbres Foundation excavations have not been identified, so we do not have concrete evidence for the prehistoric presence of the chub. All these indicators of change require "ponded water." Common reed, bulrush, and cattail are associated with slow to negligible water flow with little scour (Haslam 1978). Muskrats also prefer slower, mud-bottomed streams with dirt banks. The picture is more complicated however, since cattail, bulrush, common reed (Haslam 1978), and muskrats (Findley et al. 1975) can inhabit irrigation ditches. Therefore, it is unclear whether these four species represent prehistoric irrigation or changes in the river flow. Since these taxa are not found in the numerous modern irrigation ditches, it is reasonable to conclude that their prehistoric presence indicates change in the streamflow from a slower, more meandering flow prehistorically to a faster flow today. This point is supported in part by the fact that periods of low precipitation and runoff create narrow, meandering channels, whereas high runoff creates straighter, more rapidly flowing rivers (Burkham 1976). The later part of the Classic Mimbres period is characterized by lower than normal precipitation and probably lower runoff.

Another prehistoric change noted was an increase in plants that thrive on disturbed soils. Analysis of pollen samples from all five time periods indicates that with increased human population size, there is an increase in pollen from weedy plants (primarily cheno-ams) compared with pollen from nonweedy plants (Minnis et al. 1982). However, this pattern was not noted for charred seeds from weedy plants (primarely goosefoot, pigweed, and purslane). There is little change in the relative frequency of these plants from flotation samples; these seeds are very common from all time periods. This lack of a change, compared with the pollen remains, may be because these seeds are edible and probably were collected in quantity when present. In addition, some of these seeds may be prehistoric "seed rain," seeds naturally dispersed (Minnis 1981b). Therefore, these macroplant remains may represent two processes of deposition, so that this analysis is insensitive to changes in the abundance of disturbance vegetation.

A further change noted in the fauna used (Powell 1977; Powell and Langenwalter 1977). Specifically, during the Classic Mimbres period there is an increase in jackrabbits compared with cottontails. Jackrabbits prefer open habitats (e.g., fields), and cottontails prefer more shrubby covers (Bayham 1976). Extensive floodplain clearance would have increased the jackrabbit habitats.

Thus, during the Classic Mimbres period there seems to have been a significant reduction in the phreatophyte population and an increase in soil disturbance. Both of these are related to increased field clearance, which also affected the faunal distribution, favoring animals adapted to these conditions.

Documented Historic Environmental Change

The present environment has been drastically affected by modern human activity, and it is essential to understand this alteration in order to reconstruct the prehistoric environment.

The ranching, farming, and mining of the past hundred years have in some areas radically altered the hydrology and vegetation of the study area. Using a novel technique that involves comparing modern vegetation with old photographs of the same area, Hastings and Turner (1965; Turner 1974) document surprising vegetation change in the Southwest, particularly in the Sonoran desert of southern Arizona and northern Sonora. However, the causes of these changes are not agreed upon. Generally, livestock grazing, reduction in fires, and slight climatic shifts have been posited as factors in these changes, but each is inadequate as a single factor explaining all vegetation change (Hastings and Turner 1965:275–83). Hastings and Turner conclude that the changes were due to synergistic interaction between slight climatic fluctuations toward a drier/warmer climate and the often devastating effects of overgrazing.

There is some documentation of historic vegetation change within the study area. York and Dick-Peddie (1969), using historical documents from early survey teams, have discussed vegetation change in the desert areas of southern New Mexico, including the region around Deming. They conclude that the dominance of desert shrubs, primarily creosote bush and mesquite, is a recent phenomenon correlating with grassland reduction. They suggest that before large scale ranching the desert areas could properly be considered desert grasslands, with mesquite and creosote bush confined to isolated stands. They believe that one type of mesquite pocket, denoted as "Indian campsites," is where mesquite was introduced as a result of prehistoric human activity. This problem is a classic chicken-and-egg argument. Are the sites near stands of mesquite because of prehistoric exploitation of these stands, or are the stands a result of prehistoric exploitation that created them?

Boles and Dick-Peddie (1983) studied the modern wood riparian vegetation along the Rio Mimbres in the Mimbres Foundation study area. They suggest that modern livestock grazing has altered this vegetation. Specifically, they noted that the absence of immature cottonwoods may be due to trampling and browsing by livestock.

Some of the changes in the desert areas are related to the lowering of the water table owing to extensive irrigation pumping for cotton, sorghum, and maize. White (1934) reported an average 0.6-0.9 m drop in the Deming area water table between 1914 and 1929. A local county commissioner (C. Gaines, personal communication, 1975) estimates that the water table has been lowered at the rate of 0.6 m a year for the past twenty-five years. Other evidence supports his conclusion. Darton (1916, 1917) prepared a geological atlas for the Deming quadrangle and Luna County, and on his hydrology map he illustrated a lake. Today "Florida Lake" has no standing water, though it is the first area to flood when the Rio Mimbres flows as far south as Deming. Similarly, I have identified common reed fragments from a bulldozed site next to Florida Lake. Common reed indicates a high water table, and to the best of my knowledge it is not present in the Rio Mimbres drainage today. There is a chance, however, that the reed was imported from higher elevations along the Mimbres River, where it assuredly grew prehistorically, if not historically.

The dense modern human occupation of the Upper Chihuahuan zone in the Rio Mimbres Valley proper has most likely also affected the water supply. Much of the Rio Mimbres floodplain is cultivated at present. Many of these fields are planted in high water consuming crops such as alfalfa and orchard trees. The fields are irrigated from streamflow supplemented by groundwater pumping. Where stream-flow irrigation alone is used, there are occasional seasonal short-ages of irrigation water (New Mexico State Engineer Office 1975), indicating seasonal water utilization above that available in streamflow. In addition, there is an active program of levee construction and channel straightening.

The reduction of the grass cover by grazing in the whole water-shed has probably increased the speed of runoff, since vegetation slows runoff and stabilizes the soil from erosion (Burkham 1976). Hence the present streamflow characteristics are not necessarily the same as prehistoric ones. In particular, the intensity of rapid runoff and flooding has probably increased during historic times.

Historic vegetational change is not well documented for the Upper Chihuahuan and Transitional zones. However, these areas have been the focus of farming and mining along with ranching, so that anthropogenic vegetation change is quite likely. Using

Figure 18. Rio Mimbres Valley, 1880s.

Figure 19. Rio Mimbres Valley, 1976. This photograph was taken from about the same location as was figure 18. Note the increase in juniper.

Hastings and Turner's technique, I collected several old photographs of the Rio Mimbres around the "town" of Mimbres, taken in the 1880s. I returned to the same locations where the old photos were taken and took similar ones. Unfortunately, my lens angle did not accurately match that used for the old photos, but the two sets are close enough to make comparisons of the vegetation. As can be seen in figures 18 and 19, there have been remarkable changes in the past ninety years or so. Particularly noticeable is the large increase in the amount of juniper on the slopes, illustrated in the foreground of figure 19, as the hills in the background. Numerous factors may account for this increase, including fire suppression and seeds spread in cattle droppings. However, figure 20 indicates that wood use may be an important factor. This photograph shows the Georgetown smelter and illustrated the large amount of fuel wood used (note the two men standing on stacked wood). Hence it is quite likely that a dense modern human occupation using large amounts of fuel wood and construction wood may have contributed to the woodland reduction during the early historic occupations.

There is no evidence of such profound changes in the Transi-

Figure 20. Georgetown Smelter, 1880s. This smelter was situated in the Rio Mimbres Valley near site LA 12077. Note the two men (circled) standing on a large stack of fuel wood.

tional zone vegetation during the historic period, although logging and grazing have probably had an effect.

From historical records, it is reasonable to conclude that modern economic activity has affected the vegetation and water supply. Specifically, grazing has reduced the grass cover, particularly in the desert regions, with a resulting increase in desert shrubs. Also, wood use has reduced the wood vegetation in the mountainous areas, and modification of the Mimbres watershed may have increased the rapidity of runoff, probably increasing the frequency and intensity of floods.

Environmental Reconstruction

What is known about historic and prehistoric changes in the hydrology, vegetation, and fauna of the study area is used here to reconstruct the environment for the time periods under consideration. Obviously, there will be variation in the environment through time, including variation in critical parameters for a successful crop harvest, but I will discuss later when we consider the productivity of agricultural strategies.

Generally, as has been discussed previously, the prehistoric environment was similar to that of today. Undoubtedly the water table was higher, both in the desert and in the mountains. The water flow in the perennial streams was greater, ephemeral streams probably flowed longer, and springs and seeps were more regular. This is particularly true for the desert area, where modern water pumping has had the greatest impact. Some areas in the desert may have prehistorically had surface flow or standing water where today it is dry. The changes in the desert area were probably not as great in the upper river valleys and mountains. The Rio Mimbres was probably less prone to the flooding, caused by the reduction in grass cover over the whole watershed, and during periods of normal flow it was a slower, more meandering channel with ponded water or marshes where hydrophytic plants thrived. It thus was probably better suited for irrigation than the rapidly moving Rio Mimbres of today.

The prehistoric vegetation in the desert was radically different. The Deming plains were more like grasslands, with mesquite restricted to areas of higher water table and with creosote bush on rocky substrates. In the Upper Chihuahuan zone the vegetation change was less pronounced. The woody plants found at present are those found prehistorically. The prehistoric needs for fuel and construction timber undoubtedly had an effect on the woody vegetation, but this is difficult to assess, and I will assume there has been little change. The forb and grass cover in the Upper Chihuahuan zone was greater before modern cattle grazing, thus increasing the availability of some edible resources. Wherever there was a dense prehistoric population, more ground was disturbed, increasing the biomass of edible weeds such as purslane and goosefoot and reducing the floodplain phreatophyte assemblage.

With the exception of the muskrat, the animal remains recovered archeologically are of species still present in the study area. As has been discussed, the Classic Mimbres period population affected the composition of the faunal resources, increasing the proportion of small mammals. This may indicate a reduction of large game near human habitations, a pattern that has occurred in historic times.

5

Estimating Food Stress
in the Study Area

Estimating prehistoric food stress in this chapter is a two-step procedure. I first describe the prehistoric subsistence economy of the Rio Mimbres, then consider the effects of specific potentially limiting factors on the food production system. This second step involves analyzing how these limiting factors affect the periodicity and magnitude of food shortages.

To model the prehistoric subsistence economy I use various data sets including pollen, macroplant, and faunal remains, which provide a record of procurement activities. However, in order to interpret the prehistoric subsistence remains, it is necessary to discuss factors such as differential deposition and preservation, which complicate the inference of prehistoric economy from raw archeological data.

Next, I consider possible limiting factors on the prehistoric economy, discussing in detail two potential constraints, amount and quality of land and quantity of water. Other potential economic and natural environmental constraints on production (e.g., labor scarcity, variation in length of growing season) are not modeled. I show that the lack of water from precipitation and streamflow is the primary constraint on successful crop harvest, a conclusion to be expected considering that the study area is in an arid to semi-arid environment (Kirkby 1978). I use variation in the water supply, as documented by the dendroclimatological data to estimate the potential frequency and magnitude of food production shortages faced by Late Pithouse and Classic Mimbres populations and part of the Animas population. Use of the naturally available foods is also considered.

The evidence presented in this chapter documents increased probability of prehistoric food stress in the study area and sets the stage for the following chapter, which examines expected economic and organizational responses to food stress.

Prehistoric Mimbres Subsistence Economy

Recovered Plant Remains

Table 5 lists forty-one plant taxa recovered from the Mimbres flotation samples. All are charred, indicating that they are prehistoric (Minnis 1981a); uncharred seeds, presumably modern contamination, are not discussed in this work. These are food resources that were present during prehistoric times, not necessarily the food plants actually consumed. Many natural and cultural processes form the prehistoric ethnobotanical record, and only one set of these is resource utilization. Some seeds and fruits might be accidentally charred natural seed rain and thus not direct evidence of resource use.

Also, table 5 is not an exhaustive list of foods available prehistorically. Many potential plant resources have a low probability of archeological survival. Munson, Parmalee, and Yarnell (1971:244) divide food plants into three categories characterized by their probability of preservation:

1. foods that have a rather dense, inedible part (maize cobs).
2. plants that are somewhat dense but are normally ingested in their entirety" (small seeds or maize kernels).
3 nondense foods with a high water content (tubers and greens).

These categories reflect decreasing probabilities of preservation, and usually only plants in the first two categories will be recovered from open sites. In addition to the physical characteristics of food resources, different processing/cooking techniques will affect the probability of survival. Boiling, by increasing water content and destroying cellular structure, is less conducive to preservation than parching, which can easily lead to charring. Therefore it is not surprising that most types listed in table 5 are small hard seeds or nuts. The absence of tuberous or soft fleshy fruits in table 5 should not be taken as evidence of their nonuse by the prehistoric peoples. In fact, we can be as-

Table 5

Potential Food Plants Recovered from Mimbres Foundation Excavations

Taxon	Part Found[a]	Taxon	Part Found[a]
Cotton	Seed, fiber	Acacia	Seed
Maize	Cob, kernel	Canyon grape	Seed
Common bean	Seed	Stickleaf	Seed
Tepary bean	Seed	Hedgehog cactus	Seed
Squash	Fruit rind	Prickly pear	Seed
Goosefoot	Seed	Banana yucca	Seed
Pigweed	Seed	Spanish bayonet	Flower stalk
Purslane	Seed	Grama grass	Seed
Peppergrass	Seed	Bristle grass	Seed
Bugseed	Seed	Ricegrass	Seed
Sunflower	Seed	Dropseed	Seed
Tansy mustard	Seed	Love grass	Seed
Beeweed	Seed	Paspalum sp.	Seed
Knotweed	Seed	Bulrush	Seed
Walnut	Nut	Cactus family	Seed
Alligator-bark		Malva family	Seed
juniper	Seed	Bean family	Seed
One-seed juniper	Seed	Morning glory	
Piñon	Nut	family	Seed
Chokecherry	Seed	Grass family	Seed
Saltbush	Fruit	Sunflower family	Seed
Mesquite	Seed, fruit		

Note: All taxa are represented by charred specimens.
a. Plant parts are common names

sured that greens were a frequent prehistoric dietary item, as they are ethnographically (Ford 1968; Bye 1979).

Table 6 lists plant species now common in the study area that have not been recovered by flotation. An examination of tables 5 and 6 suggests several points of interest. Numerous cultivated plants such as maize, common bean, tepary bean, squash, and cotton have been recovered. Gourd is the only cultivated plant that was probably grown but has not been recovered archeologically. Cotton and tepary beans have been recovered only from sites in the southern segment of the Mimbres Valley and in the desert plains, areas with a long growing season. A substantial number of the taxa (e.g., love grass, peppergrass, goosefoot, pigweed, sunflower, tansy mustard, purslane, beeweed, bugseed, and dropseed) are weedy

Table 6

Potential Food Plants Found in the Study Area
but Not Recovered from Excavations

Taxon	Part Eaten	Taxon	Part Eaten
Gourd	Flower,	Century plant	Stem
	Seed	Sotol	Stem
Oak[a]	Fruit	Cattail[a]	Tuber
Squawbush	Fruit	Unicorn plant	Seed,
Wild currant	Fruit		Immature plant
Desert hackberry	Fruit	Onion	Plant
Buckthorn	Fruit	Cholla	Flower bud,
Red sage	Seed		Fruit
Buffalo gourd	Seed	Nut grass	Tuber
Coyote melon	Fruit	Groundcherry	Fruit
Elderberry	Fruit		

a. Pollen of these plants have been recovered.

annuals that thrive in disturbed habitats such as cultivated and fallow fields. Given the documented soil disturbance, particularly during the Classic Mimbres period, it is not unexpected that these resources would be frequent in flotation samples. Perhaps the prehistoric Mimbreños allowed some of the plants to grow in fields as do the Tewa of San Juan pueblo (Ford 1968). In addition, they simply may have gathered these weeds from other disturbed habitats. All the potential plant resources recovered are readily available within the study area, and thus there is no evidence of long distance importation of plant resources.

Two potential resources that are at present very common in the study area, acorns and century plants, are conspicuously absent from table 5. If used extensively, both resources should have left remains. This is particularly true for the century plant, since the underground pits commonly used for processing the hearts are easily seen. No "agave pit" has been located in four years of survey in the Mimbres region, and the region is conspicuously bare on a map showing the distribution of agave pits in the Southwest (Castetter, Bell, and Grove 1938:37). The lack of century plant remains and processing facilities, I believe, can best be explained as a substantial lack of use. The situation is not clear for acorns, but oak pollen aggregates have been found on the surfaces of grinding stones, suggesting the use of acorns.

A detailed study of pollen deposited on grinding stones as a result of human use has not been completed. However, C. Halbirt (personal communication, 1978) indicates that ten pollen types are found in unusually high quantities on metate surfaces and may represent processed plant foods. These are maize, prickly pear/cholla, juniper, oak, walnut, marsh elder/ragweed, sagebrush, elderberry, grass, and high-spine Compositae such as sunflower. Halbirt believes that these resources were being processed and presumably eaten.

Recovered Animal Remains

Numerous mammalian remains have been recovered from excavations in the study area. Table 7 lists these. Some of these animals, particularly burrowing animals, may be the remains of post-occupation burrowing unassociated with prehistoric exploitation. Similarly, this list does not include birds or lower vertebrates. Like the plant remains, all animals recovered are present in the study area today or would have been present prehistorically.

Quantitative Assessment of Changes in Resource Use

Simply enumerating recovered plant and animal types is of limited utility. Unfortunately, quantitative analysis, particularly of macroplant remains, requires numerous assumptions, many of which are gross simplifications. The quantitative approach that requires the fewest assumptions is to look for relative changes in the same category of remains.

Flotation samples are the least biased record of macroplant remains, because many sizes of remains will be recovered, not just pieces large enough to be caught in a large-mesh screen. Therefore, changes in the presence and quantity of taxa are best examined by using flotation data. A common quantitative approach is simply to tabulate the frequency of remains. For example, 95 percent of the seeds recovered from stratum B are type 1, whereas 25 percent of the seeds from stratum C are type 1. There are numerous problems with this method. As is common with flotation samples, some sample contain hundreds of seeds, whereas most have many fewer. Therefore a single sample with many seeds of a single type, which may represent only a single charring accident,

Table 7

Mammalian Remains Recovered from Mimbres Foundation Excavations

Common Name	Scientific Name
Desert Cottontail	Sylvilagus audubonii
Eastern Cottontail	Sylvilagus floridanus
Jackrabbit	Lepus sp.
Black-tailed jackrabbit	Lepus californicus
Chipmunk	Eutamias sp.
Antelope squirrel	Ammospermophilus sp.
Ground squirrel	Spermophilus sp.
Black-tailed prarire dog	Cynomys ludovicianus
Tree squirrel	Sciurus sp.
Pocket gopher	Thomomys sp.
Botta's pocket gopher	Thomomys bottae
Pocket gopher	Geomys sp.
Pocket mouse	Perognathus sp.
Kangaroo rat	Dipodomys sp.
Beaver	Castor canadensis
White-footed mouse	Peromyscus sp.
Wood rat	Neotoma sp.
Vole	Microtus sp.
Muskrat	Ondatra sp.
Dog, coyote, or wolf	Canis sp.
Dog	Canis familiaris
Gray fox	Urocyon cinereoargenteus
Ringtail	Bassariscus astutus
Badger	Taxidea taxus
Skunk	Mephitis sp.
Cat	Felis sp.
Mountain lion	Felis concolor
Deer	Odocoileus sp.
Mule deer	Odocoileus hemionus
Pronghorn	Antilocapra americana
Mountain sheep	Ovis canadensis

will grossly overrepresent that taxon. If food resources are primarily charred because of accidents, then tabulation measures the magnitude of some accidents.

An alternative approach is presence/absence analysis or "ubiquity." I prefer this approach. Ubiquity is simply the percentage of samples that contain a particular type. For example, maize cob fragments were found in 20 percent of the five Early Pithouse period samples, in 64 percent of the thirty-three Late Pithouse period samples, and so forth. Making the assumption that

Table 8

Ubiquity Index for Plant Remains from Flotation Samples

Taxon	EP	LP	CM	A	S
Maize cob	20.0	63.6	57.1	84.0	76.9
Maize kernel	0.0	9.1	17.1	36.0	32.7
Cultivated bean	0.0	3.0	0.0	4.0	3.8
Squash	0.0	0.0	0.0	0.0	1.9
Cotton	0.0	0.0	0.0	8.0	11.5
Goosefoot	60.0	72.7	60.0	64.0	50.0
Pigweed	0.0	24.2	8.6	28.0	7.7
Purslane	60.0	45.5	51.4	40.0	34.6
Peppergrass	0.0	3.0	2.9	0.0	1.9
Bugseed	0.0	3.0	2.9	0.0	0.0
Sunflower	0.0	6.1	8.6	0.0	1.9
Tansy mustard	0.0	0.0	5.7	0.0	1.9
Beeweed	0.0	0.0	0.0	0.0	1.9
Knotweed	0.0	3.0	2.9	8.0	0.0
Walnut	0.0	0.0	2.9	4.0	3.8
Juniper	20.0	27.2	17.1	24.0	23.1
Pinon	0.0	3.0	0.0	0.0	0.0
Chokecherry	0.0	6.1	0.0	0.0	0.0
Saltbush	0.0	3.0	5.7	4.0	0.0
Mesquite	0.0	0.0	2.9	28.0	0.0
Acacia	0.0	0.0	0.0	0.0	1.9
Canyon grape	0.0	3.0	0.0	0.0	0.0
Stickleaf	0.0	0.0	2.9	0.0	0.0
Hedgehog cactus	0.0	0.0	2.9	8.0	1.9
Prickly pear	0.0	6.1	8.6	12.0	0.0
Banana yucca	0.0	0.0	2.9	8.0	0.0
Grama grass	0.0	0.0	2.9	4.0	3.8
Ricegrass	0.0	0.0	2.9	4.0	0.0
Dropseed	0.0	0.0	0.0	8.0	1.9
Love grass	0.0	3.0	0.0	0.0	0.0
Nightshade	0.0	3.0	0.0	0.0	0.0
Bulrush	0.0	0.0	0.0	8.0	0.0
Paspalum	0.0	3.0	0.0	0.0	0.0
Cactus family	0.0	6.1	5.7	4.0	1.9
Malva family	0.0	3.0	0.0	0.0	0.0
Bean family	0.0	3.0	0.0	0.0	1.9
Morning glory family	0.0	0.0	2.9	0.0	1.9
Sunflower family	0.0	12.1	14.3	20.0	5.8
number of taxa	5	23	23	21	22
number of samples	5	33	35	25	52

Note: EP = Early Pithouse; LP = Late Pithouse; CM = Classic Mimbres; A = Animas; S = Salado.

charred remains are primarily the result of accidents, then ubiquity tends to measure the number of accidents, which is more closely related to the degree of utilization than is tabulation. Thus, I will assume that a change in the number of samples in which a taxon is present is an imprecise but useful measure of the relative change in the use of that resource. Obviously, this type of analysis can easily be taken too far, given our present ignorance of depositional and preservation factors. This approach also tends to overestimate the importance of uncommon remains, and it does not take into account nutritional differences in various resources. Nevertheless, the ubiquity indexes generated from the data are a useful base to judge general resource use changes. Table 8 lists the plant remains and their ubiquity by time period, and figure 21 graphically presents the changes in ubiquity for the nine categories of plant remains found in all time periods from Late Pithouse through Salado. Because of the small number of samples from Early Pithouse period contexts, this period has been deleted from further analysis.

As can be seen in table 8, there is no evidence for a diversification in plant resource use with increasing population density, disregarding the inadequately sampled Early Pithouse period. Also, there are no startling changes in the ubiquity of these potential resources. This similarity can be shown by statistical tests that compare the relative rank of each taxon by time period with the corresponding rank from the other time periods. This was done for the Late Pithouse period and Classic Mimbres period types (which have ubiquity values of over 5 percent in either assemblage). Using a Spearman's coefficient of rank-order correlation, it was found that the ranking of these thirteen taxa in these two assemblages was very similar (r_s=.90). Consequently, the evidence suggests that the proportional use of these resources was similar in the Late Pithouse and the Classic Mimbres periods. There is no evidence that with increased food stress during the Classic Mimbres period the Classic Mimbreños increased their use of naturally available resources. However, it is unlikely that short term increases in foraging would be detected in such a small flotation sample with broad time period boundaries. What can be stated is that the plant resources (which are represented by charred remains) seem to have been used in very similar proportions during the Late Pithouse and Classic Mimbres periods.

Maize cob fragments, goosefoot seeds, and purslane seeds are uniformly ubiquitous. Elsewhere (Minnis 1978, 1981a) I have argued

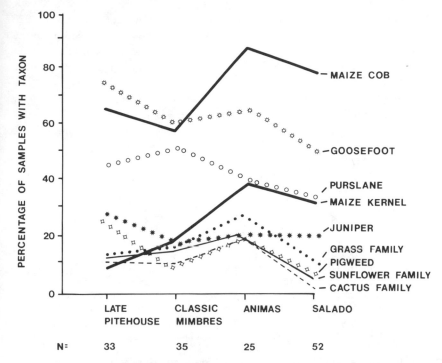

Figure 21.   The most common plant remains from Mimbres Foundation flotation samples.

that the presence of small weed seeds such as goosefoot and purslane overrepresents their dietary importance, since some of these charred seeds may well represent prehistoric seed rain, not their utilization.   Maize cob fragments are probably the result of the use of the cobs for fuel, which would inflate the ubiquity of maize.   However, I agree with Bohrer (1976) that maize kernels are underrepresented in the paleoethnobotanical record, because maize is prepared in numerous ways, many of which are not conducive to preservation.   Therefore the true "importance" of maize is probably somewhere between the ubiquity of maize cobs and that of kernels. Clearly then, maize is one of the most important resources, perhaps more important than any other plant resource.   Potential resources other than weed seeds and maize are present in smaller quantities in these samples.

Other flotation macroplant assemblages from the puebloan Southwest document the common occurrence of maize (Struever 1977; Minnis 1978; Cowan et al. 1977; Gasser 1978).   Further, maize remains are quite common in areas where they would be expected not to occur. For example, in areas of high elevation such as Chimney Rock, southwestern Colorado (Minnis and Ford 1977), and the Upper Mimbres drainage (Minnis 1979), where the frost-free period is very short, maize is commonly recovered.

Changes in faunal use have been recorded by Powell (1977) and Powell and Langenwalter (1977). They note that during the period of highest population density there are three changes in the faunal assemblage:

1. jackrabbit quantities and proportions apparently increased greatly from the Late Pithouse period to the Classic period, so that by the Classic period jackrabbits were used more than any other single species and so that the ratio of cottontails to jackrabbits decreases during the Classic period;
2. during the Classic period it appears that hill rodents were hunted much less and in much lower proportions than during the Late Pithouse period;
3. the artiodactyls, deer and antelope, compared with small mammals were used in low proportions during both the Late Pithouse and the Classic periods. (Powell and Langenwalter 1977:3-4)

They further argue that these changes are a result of vegetation changes due to increased agricultural activity. Thus, during the Late Pithouse and Classic periods smaller mammals were being used more frequently than during later periods. These results are consistent with the conclusions derived from analysis of macroplant and pollen data.

From the macroplant, pollen, and faunal remains we find that all populations from the Late Pithouse to the Salado period were practicing similar general patterns of food procurement, although some changes in magnitude of the resources have been noted. It is clear that agricultural products, particularly maize, were critical resources for all these time periods. To develop a more precise model of the prehistoric economy, we must estimate of dietary contribution of maize.

Dietary Contribution of Maize

The macroplant and pollen evidence cannot be used directly to estimate the percentage of the diet contributed by cultigens, but such an estimate is critical to this study. What has been docu-

mented is that maize constitutes a substantial percentage of macroplant remains. Further, several data sets--faunal remains, wood
charcoal, charred seeds, and pollen--suggest extensive floodplain
clearance for fields, indirectly indicating substantial use of
cultigens. To estimate the contribution of cultigens to the
prehistoric diet, I will use two sources of information, ethnographic examples and prehistoric southwestern coprolite analysis.

Ethnographic Analogies

   The subsistence economies of the indigenous puebloan populations of the Southwest have been substantially altered since the
first Spanish occupation. The change has been so great that for
even supposedly conservative Hopi Kuhnlein and Calloway (1977:161)
report that "in fact, today the dietary mix is much like that found
elsewhere in America." These changes from the original dietary
patterns include: (1) introduction of new cultigens, primarily
wheat, chiles, cultivated fruit, and garden vegetables; (2) increased purchasing power and access to market commodities; (3)
altered agricultural techniques; (4) increased livestock raising;
(5) increased wage labor with decreased time for traditional subsistence activities; (6) decrease in available sustaining area; (7)
environmental changes such as changes in agriculturally relevant
hydrology and depletion of potential resources; and (8) increased
government programs affecting food production and consumption patterns. Despite these changes, ethnographic description and
analysis of relatively early pueblos exist, and from these sources
it is useful to look at the importance of cultigens, primarily
maize.
   Ford (1968) estimates that about 1890, the Tewa of San Juan
Pueblo were very dependent on cultigens. Of the food consumed, 84
percent was grown by the Tewa, and 46.5 percent of total human
energy needs came from maize. If we combine wheat and maize, their
contribution to the diet was about 75 percent. In addition, maize
was also grown to feed livestock, but this maize is not included in
the percentage of human energy met by maize as cited above.
   Stephens (1936) estimates that the per capita Hopi maize use in
the latter half of the nineteenth century was 314 kg. Hack (1942)
points out that 71 percent of the average Hopi acreage was planted
in maize. An indirect but nevertheless impressive indication of
the role of maize is that at least seventy different Hopi dishes

used maize (Hough 1898).

We can roughly estimate the percentage of energy contribution by knowing the amount of food consumed and its caloric value. One kilogram of maize contains approximately 3,600 calories (National Institute for Arthritis and Metabolic Diseases 1961). Therefore 314 kg would yield approximately 1,130,400 calories. Assuming an average daily per capita requirement of 2,100 calories, the 314 kilos will supply 147 percent of one person's annual caloric requirement. Obviously, some maize was sold, fed to animals, lost, indirectly fed to pests, or stored, so that maize contributed much less than this amount to the diet. If, as Stephens suggests, only 40 percent of the 314 kilos was consumed during that year, then this would equal 59 percent of the human energy needs met by maize alone. This is in the same range as Ford's estimate of maize used by the Tewa.

Farther afield, Tepehuan informants of northern Chihuahua consider 318 kg of cereal in the form of maize (245 kg) and wheat (73 kg) necessary per capita (Pennington 1969). Using the same calculations as for the Hopi, this amount of maize and wheat would account for 149 percent of the Tepehuan diet. As with the Hopi, assuming disposal of half of the maize by other than human consumption, over half of the caloric energy was still from maize. In the case of the Tepehuan, large amounts of maize were indirectly consumed as tesquiño, a potent alcoholic drink. For example, Merrill (1978) estimates that a single large fiesta for one hundred Tarahumara, neighbors of the Tepehuan, would require 70 kg of maize to produce the necessary amount of tesquiño.

From this short ethnographic survey, it is reasonable to conclude that maize was a dietary staple for the historic agricultural groups in the Southwest, often accounting for over 50 percent of the total human consumption needs. This large figure is despite the fact that numerous introduced plants have been added to the indigenous inventory of cultivated plants.

Prehistoric Coprolite Analysis

The best evidence for documenting the prehistoric dietary importance of various resources is the analysis of prehistoric feces. However, the relationship between the materials in feces and their dietary importance is not a completely direct inference. Some remains are difficult to identify, and an individual coprolite is often a mixture of several meals. Nevertheless, what is in feces is a closer approximation of diet than any other archeological data set.

Conveniently, Stiger (1977) has compared numerous analytic sets of Anasazi coprolites. Most coprolites were recovered from the Mesa Verde region (Hoy House, Lion House, Step House, Mug House, Long House), but sites in other areas were also discussed (Inscription House, Glen Canyon, and Antelope House). Thirty-six types of macroplant remains were identified from the feces, and figure 22 illustrates the ubiquity of the eight most common plant remains. Even though there is great variability in the presence of resource types, the constant high ubiquity of maize is clear. For the Pueblo II through Pueblo III samples, for example, slightly over 80 percent of the samples of the coprolites contained maize, and of these "meals," if only 60 percent was maize, then 48 percent of the food consumed was maize. Making the same assumptions and calculations, maize would have constituted one-third of the food

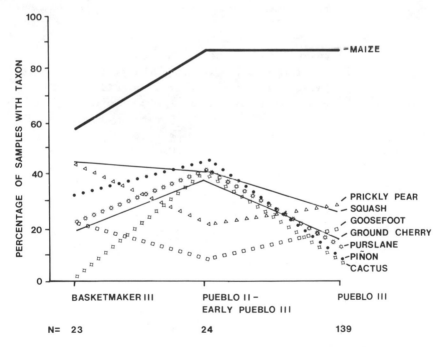

Figure 22. Plant remains from Anasazi coprolites (data from Stiger 1977).

consumed (fifty-six samples with maize x 60 percent) by the BM III
population. After more detailed analysis, Stiger reaches these
conclusions:

> 1) Anasazi diet relied heavily on corn but made use of a
> wide variety of "wild plants," 2) these "wild plants" are
> mainly plants which grow in disturbed areas or are found
> where farmlands are not practical, and 3) the Anasazi inten-
> sified their use of high production crops through time and
> decreased their use of pinyon nuts and other low yield
> resources. (1977:55)

Piñon and other "low yield" plants are not so much low yield as
erratic, unpredictable resources. Further, Stiger concludes that
the Mesa Verde inhabitants were exhausting the soil, leading to the
final abandonment of the area. Scott (1979:278), on the basis of
the pollen analysis of coprolites and archeological pollen samples,
takes exception to Stiger's interpretations and concludes that
"Stiger's hypothesis that corn contributed in ever increasing
amounts to the Anasazi diet cannot be substantiated by the pollen
analysis of these coprolites" and that "pollen analysis of these
coprolites does not indicate that Zea was the dominant element in
the diet of the people at Hoy House." Unfortunately, Scott's data
do not have sufficient time depth to judge the possible long term
trends observed by Stiger. Scott did provide evidence of significant field clearance and the ubiquity of weedy plants that is
further evidence of large scale field clearance. Generally,
Scott's data do not contradict Stiger's conclusions, as she
indicates.

Although there is some disagreement concerning the dietary
importance of cultigens, the evidence, direct or indirect, still
supports the contention that maize was a, if not the, major plant
staple consumed. The ubiquity of field weeds indicates the extent
of field clearance in many areas of the Southwest and indirectly is
an index of the significant extent to which agriculture was
practiced. It is clear from both the prehistoric coprolite
evidence and the ethnographic cases that maize was a very important
resource, contributing 50 percent or more of the human energy
requirement. Therefore I will assume that 50 percent of the prehistoric food need was met by maize. I will not account for other
crops but will consider maize the only crop.

The Early Pithouse period population most likely was not as
dependent on agricultural products. There are few or no data to

decide the dietary contribution of maize for this period, so using the analogy that the Anasazi BM III period is similar to the Early Pithouse period, I will somewhat arbitrarily estimate this figure as 35 percent.

Modeling Subsistence Failure

As we have seen, the archeological evidence supports the contention that the post-Archaic populations in the study area, particularly during the Late Pithouse through Salado periods, were heavily dependent on agriculture. I will assume that for groups where food production contributes a majority of the diet, agricultural strategies take priority over other activities in subsistence decision making. That is, many food gathering strategies are generally considered in relation to the perceived and actual success of food production strategies. Therefore, these models of subsistence failure will concentrate first on factors influencing successful crop harvest.

Modeling subsistence failure for this study involves two steps. First, I examine potential limiting factors. Second, I consider the most important limiting factor through time in order to estimate the frequency and magnitude of crop production failure. These two steps constitute a catchment analysis. Unlike most catchment analyses, this work will not be concerned with the range of potential activities that could be used to extract food energy from the environment. Rather, it will emphasize the most reliable agricultural strategy in the study area, floodplain farming. With the exception of flooding, factors which decrease crop productivity have a greater impact on nonfloodplain farming than on floodplain farming. Both edaphic and moisture conditions are most favorable for agriculture on the floodplain, and nearly all agriculture in the study area today is confined to the floodplain. Further, a small farming study was conducted in the area during 1977. Several small maize plots were planted, one on the floodplain and one on the first bench above it. The Pima maize was watered weekly in both plots. The estimated productivity of the floodplain plot was two to four times greater than that of the first bench.

I am mainly concerned with the most reliable agricultural strategy, because nonstratified groups do not adjust their subsistence activities to the maximal energy capture. For example, Sahlins (1972:44) summarizes the population density of groups of swidden agriculturalists, and all are well below the theoretical maximum. Because of the yearly variation in swidden crop productivity, given the absence of significant storage, it makes no sense for a swidden food producer to maximize output (Dalton 1971; Sahlins 1972).

Limiting Factors in Prehistoric Mimbres Agriculture

Two physical factors limiting the agricultural potential of the study area will be considered: the amount and quality of floodplain soils and the amount and distribution of water, both as streamflow and as precipitation. Only the floodplain from the Mitchell site south to Old Town will be used in this analysis (see figure 5). This area includes the vast majority of floodplain that could have been prehistorically farmed, and it had the densest concentration of prehistoric occupation in the study area. Other areas could have been farmed, but they were much smaller or were less reliable locations.

Land as a Limiting Factor

To assess the possibility of land as a limiting factor, we must know how much land was available and how much land was necessary. To calculate the floodplain available for fields, I assembled a composite of aerial photographs, traced an overlay following the floodplain, and then measured it using an electronic digital planimeter lent by the Remote Sensing Laboratory at the University of New Mexico. Several distances on the air photo composite were checked against those distances on the United States Geological Survey maps to make sure that the scale used for the air photos was correct. The error was less than 10 percent, and the air photos were used.

From the air photos, I estimated that the floodplain within the restricted study area consists of 1,890 ha. However, not all of this is arable, since this figure includes the stream channel. Maker, Neher, and Anderson (1971) estimate that 92 percent of the floodplain in Grant County is arable. I will subtract 20 percent for the stream area because the prehistoric stream was undoubtedly more meandering and took up a larger area, there probably were swampy areas of drainage in the past that were not arable, and the floodplain was not as level, thus decreasing the area available for fields. Therefore, I calculated that the arable floodplain is 1,512 ha.

Determining the land necessary for agriculture is much more difficult. The approach used here will be to determine the land considered necessary per capita by modern southwestern agriculturalists and to compare this with the land available. Modern Eastern and Western Pueblos are agriculturalists. Because the Western Pueblos, particularly the Hopi, have not been as influenced as other groups by Spanish, Mexican, and Anglo occupations, archeologists use them as an ethnographic base for determining arable land requirements. For example, Woodbury (1961:37) concludes:

> None of the New Mexican pueblos now has an economy that is sufficiently like the aboriginal situation to make their acreage under cultivation a safe basis for inferences about the past. More suggestive data can be obtained from the Hopi, since their remoteness and their conservatism have slowed the process of acculturation.

Despite Woodbury's admonition, I will use data from the Eastern Pueblos, since they cultivate floodplain fields, whereas the Hopi for the most part use dry farming or floodwater farming. The agricultural situation of the Eastern Pueblos is more similar to that at Rio Mimbres than are Hopi agricultural strategies.

The inhabitants of Cochiti Pueblo plant an average of 0.31 ha per capita in maize (Lange 1959), and at San Juan Pueblo the average is 0.29 ha (Ford 1968). As Wetterstrom (1976:191) points out, "since wheat has been an important food during the historic period, combined maize and wheat acreage figures would provide a more valid basis for extrapolation. The combined figure for San Juan is .456 hectares per person (Ford 1968) and for Cochiti, .447 hectares." Wetterstrom then concludes that for the prehistoric pueblos around Santa Fe a reasonable approximation of per capita acreage is 0.3 to 0.4 ha.

It is doubtful that 0.4 ha would have been considered an adequate landholding, since a farmer would want enough land to plant during poorer-than-average agricultural years. In addition, crops besides maize were planted, and no explicit compensation for fallow has been considered. Therefore, I will add 50 percent to the land required as a safety margin, so that I will assume per capita land need as 0.6 ha, in all probability a conservative estimate. For the Early Pithouse period this estimate is reduced to 0.4 ha per person because of the lower contribution of cultigens to the diet.

Using this figure of 0.6 ha, the floodplain could itself support 2,525 people with 50 percent of the diet from cultigens. Assuming the 0.6 ha as a constant through time (0.4 ha for the Early Pithouse period) and no change in maize productivity, we can then figure what percentage of the floodplain would have to have been cultivated to supply the prehistoric populations. Figure 23 presents this information. Note that two estimates were made for the Classic Mimbres and Animas periods.

The population estimates used in figure 23 are for the entire study area excluding the desert regions. During the Classic Mimbres period and perhaps the Animas period (if the higher population estimate is used), there would have been insufficient floodplain to support these populations. If we consider only population sizes derived from sites immediately adjacent to the Rio Mimbres floodplain, 70 percent to 90 percent of the floodplain would have to have been cultivated during the Classic Mimbres period. It appears that the Classic Mimbreños were impinging on the upper limit of floodplain cultivation. This supports the wood charcoal analysis documenting the reduction in floodplain phreatophytes. An impingement is not evidence of shortages but rather suggests an increasing vulnerability if the most dependable agricultural strategy was unable to provide adequate energy. The Classic Mimbreños would have had to seek alternative farming strategies to supplement their inadequate floodplain holdings.

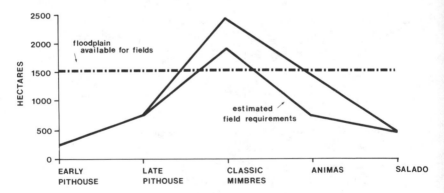

Figure 23.   Availability of floodplain for prehistoric fields.

Soil fertility should be considered as another potential factor limiting prehistoric agriculture. How long could prehistoric fields have been cultivated without depletion of soil nutrients necessary for cultigen growth? Unfortunately, this is a very difficult question. This difficulty arises because the relation between soil fertility and the nutrient needs of a plant population grown under aboriginal conditions is very complex and not well understood.

A great deal of experimental work using modern agricultural conditions has established what nutrients are necessary for maize growth. Thirteen minerals must be supplied to maize from the soil or through irrigation water (Larson and Hanway 1977; Arnon 1975). Three of these, nitrogen (N), phosphorus (P), and potassium (K), are used in large quantities, and the other ten are used in much smaller amounts. For example, Mohr and Dickinson (1979), in their studies of South African maize, indicate that every metric ton of grain removes 15-18 kg of N, 2.5-3 kg of P, and 3-4 kg of K from the soil.

Southwestern soils tend to be low in nitrogen, phosphorus, zinc, and iron (Fuller 1975a,b; Glover et al. 1980; Dregne 1959). Consequently, we would expect that if continuous cropping of maize in the study area affected the nutrient reserves in the fields, it would be these four elements that would present the mineral limiting factors for maize growth. We have no data that might be used to infer mineral deficiencies in prehistoric maize in the study area. The one exception is a study of human skeletal remains from the Classic Mimbres period component of the Galaz site. Provinzano (1968) finds evidence of dietary calcium deficiency that he believes developed from consumption of maize grown on fields deficient in calcium.

Even if the soils were subject to depletion of minerals necessary for maize growth, prehistoric cropping practices could have reduced this depletion. We do not know if the prehistoric Mimbreños fertilized their fields as do the modern Moenkopi Hopi, who leave maize stalks in the fields (Nagata 1970). This practice returns many nutrients, particularly potassium, to the soil. They also may have spread wood ash on fields, as do the modern occupants of Zia (Euler 1954). Growing nitrogen-fixing crops, such as beans, along with maize would have supplemented the nitrogen in the soil. A novel palynological study from Hovenweep National Monument suggests that some prehistoric southwesterners did intercrop these cultigens, but we do not know in what proportions (Winter 1977).

If flooding was frequent, nutrient-rich sediments would have been added to floodplain fields. This situation has been described by Castetter and Bell (1942:172) for the Pima:

> The fact that many of the Piman fields have been under cultivation for hundreds of years, producing sustained crop yields without additions of manures or other fertilizers, is evidence that considerable plant nutrients were carried by the waters used for irrigation in the Gila Basin. Allowing fields to lie fallow in order to build them up was unknown, although it was recognized that new ground produced larger yields than the old.

Castetter and Bell (1952) report a similar situation for the Yuma. We do not know how frequent the Rio Mimbres flooded prehistorically.

Southwestern ethnographic analogies are not sufficiently well documented to provide a solution to the question posed above. Some sources indicate that loss of soil fertility was a problem for some southwestern agriculturalists (e.g., Euler 1954; Bradfield 1971; Page 1940). In other cases, such as for the Pima and Papago, there is no evidence of serious soil depletion. Franke and Watson (1936) found that after sixteen years of continual dry farming of a maize field in Mesa Verde National Park, there was no noticeable reduction in yields due to soil depletion. They also cite a study of dry farming in Colorado that reported no yield reductions after thirty years of continual planting in the same field.

Sandor (1983) conducted investigations of prehistoric terrace systems just north of the Mimbres Foundation study area, as well as within the study area. On the basis of soil profiling, chemical studies of soils, and plant growing tests, he found evidence of soil degradation due to farming. Bulk density increased, and there was a reduction in organic carbon, nitrogen, and certain phosphorus fractions among the terrace soils compared with soils from nonterraced locations. However, we do not know if this reduction of fertility was of sufficient magnitude to severely affect crop yields.

This discussion of soil fertility has not come to any clear solution. I cannot answer the question of how long a field in the study area could have been under crop production without substantial loss of fertility. It is certain that continuous cropping would not have increased fertility, but it is not certain that under the prehistoric Mimbres condition yields would have decreased on floodplain fields. Consequently, I will assume there was no decrease. This is consistent with the methodological bias of making liberal estimates of the prehistoric productive capacity in the study area.

Water as a Limiting Factor

In regard to crop maturation, water can be a limiting factor in two ways. First, assuming that the floodplain was irrigated, it is possible to calculate the maximum acreage that could be irrigated given the available streamflow. The second limiting aspect is the amount and distribution of precipitation, primarily during the growing season.

The first factor involves assessing whether there was adequate streamflow to irrigate the whole floodplain. This is not as easy as it seems, since we must estimate streamflow and then the water necessary for irrigation. There are six gauging stations along the Rio Mimbres that monitor streamflow, but only two of these have records of thirty years or more. Unfortunately, the annual flow recorded for any or all the gauging stations does not equal the streamflow, since there is upstream diversion for irrigation that is not recorded as streamflow. Two methods were used to estimate the average annual streamflow. The first method uses recorded streamflow from gauging stations not affected by large scale diversion. This is then compared with the drainage area of these stations. A water flow per square kilometer can then be derived, and this factor is multiplied by the drainage of the affected gauging stations.

Table 9 lists the six gauging stations, their drainage catchment, annual average flow, and a derived streamflow per area of watershed. The first three stations, McKnight, Bear Canyon, and Mimbres, will be used to compute the flow per land unit, because they are basically unaffected by upstream diversion. The last three, Faywood, Spalding, and Wamel, are biased by heavy diversion or unfavorable geological conditions that cause the water not to rise to the surface. The estimated flow factor is 2,03 14.2 m^3/km^2 from the first three stations.

The station at Faywood is the best location for calculating the streamflow available for the study area, because its catchment includes nearly all of the study area that could be irrigated from surface flow. If we multiply the flow factor times the Faywood drainage area (1,139.6 km^2), we estimate an annual average flow at

Table 9

Water Gauging Stations along the Rio Mimbres

Station and Years of Operation	Drainage Catchment[a]	Average Annual Streamflow[b]	Volume Flow per Square Kilometer of Catchment[b]
McKnight (6)	252.0	4,625,625	18,355.7
Bear Canyon (?)	37.6	714,196	18,994.6
Mimbres (40)	393.7	9,288,255	23,592.2
Faywood (30)	1,139.6	12,865,405	11,289.2
Spalding (5)	1,222,5	11,520,890	9,424.0
Wamel (5)	2,851.6	2,022,940	709.4

Source: United States Geological Survey (1974).
a. Square kilometers.
b. Cubic meters (1,235 m^3 = 1 acre-foot);
   average for the first three stations is 20,314.2 m^3/km^2.

Faywood station of 23,150,062 m^3.

The second method for estimating annual streamflow at Faywood adds the recorded average streamflow, 12,865,405 m^3, to an estimate of the water diverted upstream. Upstream from the Faywood station, 708 ha are irrigated. If we assume that all of this is planted in alfalfa (New Mexico State Engineer Office 1975), which is the most common crop, then we can calculate the water necessary for 708 ha. Blaney and Hanson (1965) and Henderson and Sorenson (1968) provide methods for estimating irrigation needs for various crops. Alfalfa in the Deming area requires 83.1 cm irrigation water. In the Hillsboro region, which is more like the upper Mimbres Valley, alfalfa requires 77.9 cm of irrigation water. These figures do not account for irrigation efficiency, which will run about 65 percent. If we average the alfalfa irrigation requirements for Hillsboro and Deming and then multiply this by 1.54 (the reciprocal of .65) to account for irrigation efficiency, then alfalfa requires 1.25 m of irrigation water. This figure, multiplied by the upstream irrigated acreage, results in an estimate of upstream diversion of 8,850,362 m^3. This, added to the recorded Faywood flow, yields an annual streamflow of 21,678,763 m^3.

The first method estimates an average flow of 23,120,724 m^3 and the second estimates 21,678,763 m^3. The similarity of these figures is striking given the assumptions necessary to make these calculations. For example, one factor involved in calculating irrigation efficiency is the water that percolates through fields and rejoins the stream. This would tend to lower annual flow calculated by the second method. Similarly, the first method does not take into account increased evaporation in the warmer southern part of the valley. Despite these problems, the similarity of the two estimates adds confidence that the annual average flow at Faywood is about 22,220,300 m^3, and this is the figure I will use.

Of this average annual flow at Faywood, only a fraction flows during the growing season. From 1961 through 1969, flow during the growing season (May through August) was 53.5 percent (New Mexico State Engineer Office 1975). This figure is a little high, because in 1967 an unusually high proportion of flow was during the growing season. September is not included here, because rainfall is high in this month and the water requirements of mature maize are low. Therefore flow during the growing season is about half of the 22,220,300 m^3 and so is 11,101,500 m^3. This estimate is probably a little low for prehistoric conditions because of a suspected higher water table in the past and the fact that vegetation was not overgrazed. Thus, there would have been a greater lag time in runoff, which would somewhat even out the seasonal flow. To account for this, I will add 1,233,500 m^3 flow available for irrigation for the average growing season.

The next step is to estimate irrigation requirements of the 1,512 ha of irrigable land. Irrigated maize requires 48 cm of water in Deming and 21.6 cm in Hillsboro (Henderson and Sorensen 1968), which averages to 39.8 cm. This average must be multiplied by 1.54 to account for a 65 percent irrigation efficiency. Therefore, a hectare of maize requires 6,129.2 m^3 of water during the growing season. The 1,512 arable hectares would then require 9,267,350 m^3 during the growing season. Therefore, during an average year, 75 percent of the streamflow would have to be diverted to irrigate all the arable land.

While theoretically there is enough surface water to irrigate the maximal acreage, practically there is not enough water for four reasons. First, the 65 percent irrigation efficiency is probably a little high. The soils at the southern end of the valley have low permeability, which would increase surface evaporation. Furthermore, if fields are not level, and it is doubtful that prehistoric agriculturalists leveled their fields, then the efficiency of irrigation is reduced. A second and greater problem is that streamflow is not constant but rises and falls in relation to precipitation. Many summer storms drop large amounts of water in a short time, so that there were periods of rapid flow that could not be diverted efficiently. The third reason is perhaps the most important. The archeological evidence suggests that each village was basically autonomous, and to utilize 75 percent of the growing season flow along this 50 km section of the Rio Mimbres probably would have necessitated organizational coordination, of which there is no indication. In addition, at present there are periods during the growing season when fields irrigated from streamflow go dry, and as a result only approximately 2000 ha are planted today. Because there is barely enough water to irrigate the entire flood-plain under normal conditions, during periods of below-average flow it is certain that there would not be enough. Given these points, it is doubtful that more floodplain land could have been managed effectively or efficiently prehistorically than is irrigated today. This is certainly true during periods of low streamflow.

The second aspect of water as a limiting factor is precipitation patterns in relation to the possibility of dry farming. Dry farming in a semiarid area is an uncertain enterprise. For example, no dry farming is practiced today in the study area, though during periods of heavier-than-average precipitation beans and oats have been dry farmed on the first bench along the Rio Mimbres around LA 635. Similarly, I was not able to mature a crop of Pima maize without artificial watering in 1977, and even with equal watering, the plot on the first bench produced only one-quarter to one-half the yield of the plot on the floodplain. Last, agricultural experiment stations in eastern New Mexico reported an average of 27 percent total crop failure with dry farming of non-hybrid maize in the early part of this century (Stanten, Burnham, and Carter 1939). The precipitation pattern in the eastern part of New Mexico is more conducive to dry farming than that in the western part of the state because of early spring rain in the eastern areas.

Several factors contribute to the difficulty of dry farming. First, maize requires more moisture for successful crop harvest than falls during the growing season in the study area. Maize needs approximately 45 to 60 cm of water during its growing season (Pendleton 1979; Shaw 1977), and an average of only 43 cm of precipitation falls during the entire year in the central Mimbres Valley. Second, May and June are very dry months in southern New Mexico, and the rainy season usually does not begin until July.

Assuming that maize requires 120 days to mature, then crops should
be planted at least 120 days before the first annual average frost,
which is the first week in October in the Upper Chihuahuan zone.
Thus, maize should be planted by early June. At present, maize is
planted in the Rio Mimbres about the beginning of June and harvested about the first of October (Henderson and Sorensen 1968).
This means that the first month the maize seeds are in the field
will be quite dry, and after the dry month of May there probably is
little residual moisture in the soil. However, as Demead and Shaw
(1960:273) conclude, "it is probable that the reduction in plant
size occasioned by stress during the first 30 days after planting
would not retard plant size sufficiently to produce a noticeable
effect on grain yield." This, of course, assumes that the stress
is not severe enough to kill small maize seedlings.

The distribution of precipitation during the life cycle of
maize is also important. Water stress during different periods of
plant growth has substantially different effects on the ultimate
grain yield. Jensen (1968:18) points out that "the yield of the
marketable product of a farm crop may not be linearly related to
total water use when plants are stressed." For example, he reports
that with a 20 percent reduction in water, grain sorghum yield was
reduced 35 percent, and with a 40 percent water reduction yields
fell 70 percent. Using both field experiments (Demead and Shaw
1960) and laboratory studies (Robins and Domingo 1953), the effects
of water stress on maize yields were investigated and found to be
similar. Robins and Domingo found that water stress when grains
were mature made little difference in yields and that the biggest
difference in yields occurred when there was water stress on the
plant during the tasseling period. They found a 22 percent
reduction in yields with a one to two day period of water stress
before tasseling, and this reduction was increased to 50 percent
from a six to eight day water stress period before tasseling.
Demead and Shaw's study found moisture stress before tasseling
reduced yields 75 percent, stress during tasseling reduced yields
50 percent, and stress after tasseling reduced yields 21 percent.
These findings have been replicated (Classen and Shaw 1970).

From the agronomy studies, it seems that maize would be able to
recover from an early mild water stress, but a water shortage
during tasseling/silking has devastating effects on yields. Like
early growth stress, water stress to mature plants has a small
effect on grain yields. What this seems to mean for dry farming in
the Rio Mimbres region is that young maize plants may be able to

survive the dry month of June with the use of conservation techniques such as planting in clusters and with no excessive winds.
With the rains coming in July and an average rainy season, maize
can be matured to successful harvest. However, a particularly dry
winter and hot and windy June might kill the young plants, and a
dry rainy season would surely reduce yields. Dry farming on the
floodplain might alleviate the effects of a dry rainy season if the
roots grew deep enough to tap groundwater. Assuming that the
seedlings did not survive the dry month of June, replanting the
fields as early as the beginning of July would mean that the maize
might not have matured until the end of October, and the crop would
have been vulnerable to frost, further reducing the yield. In
short, dry farming would be a delicate balance, a balance often
tipped against the farmer.

Variation in Agricultural Productivity

So far I have shown that two basic variables, land and water,
pose constraints on the limits of agricultural productivity and
that it is unlikely that the Classic Mimbres period population
could have supported itself on floodplain farming alone. Average
values have been used, but variation in these values is the
critical consideration for subsistence failure. Next I will
examine how variation in precipitation patterns affects agricultural strategies. I have previously established indications of
population size, dietary patterns, and farming strategies. The
link that needs to be considered in detail here is how dendroclimatological data relate to precipitation and crop production.
To clarify this relationship, I will review and simplify the correlation between tree-ring indexes and climate and will detail
assumptions about the effect of precipitation and runoff on crop
production. Finally, I will discuss prehistoric variation in crop
production success.

As stated previously, the correlation coefficient (.77) between
tree-ring width in the Reserve area and streamflow in the Rio
Mimbres drainage permits the use of the former to predict the
latter. In fact, the relation between streamflow during the agriculturally important season of April through September in the Rio
Mimbres area and the Reserve tree-ring data index is .73. Therefore tree-rings are a reasonable predictor of growing season
streamflow and indirectly of growing season precipitation. There

is one potential problem with using modern tree-ring data to extrapolate to the prehistoric sequence. The modern sequence was derived from Douglas fir, whose growth is a good predictor of summer precipitation. The prehistoric sequence is based on several species, including juniper, piñon, ponderosa pine, and Douglas fir. The growth of most of these trees is not as good a predictor of summer precipitation as that of Douglas fir. Obviously this causes some problems with using prehistoric tree-ring growth as a predictor of prehistoric growing season precipitation. However, with the available data, it is impossible to correct for this distortion. Analytically, this problem will be ignored, although it must be mentioned. Unfortunately, there is no way to detect variation in precipitation within the growing season. As has been discussed, this is important for crop yield. Because I have no analytic tool to understand intraseason moisture variation, I will assume that the lower the moisture throughout the growing season, the lower the crop yield. The yearly tree-ring indexes from A.D 600 through 1249 were scored into four arbitrary categories: more than one standard deviation above the mean, within one standard deviation above the mean, within one standard deviation below the mean, and more than one standard deviation below the mean. These values can be related to actual precipitation. A regression formula was derived for relating tree-ring width to growing season precipitation. The data used were modern (1931-60) tree-ring widths from the Reserve area and growing season precipitation (April through September) data collected at the Fort Bayard station, approximately 30 km west of the Mimbres Valley and with environmental conditions similar to the Mimbres region. The mean tree-ring width (93.6) for this period yields an estimated mean growing season precipitation of 25 cm. One standard deviation below the mean tree-ring width estimates approximately 11 cm precipitation. Figure 24 illustrates the scattergram and the regression line used for these calculations.

There are few data on the effect of precipitation variation on aboriginal agriculture. Page (1940:51) states that for the Hopi region "a drop of two or three inches in the total yearly precipitation will lower production in agricultural products 15-30 percent." He found that for one drought year (1939) a 35 percent reduction in yearly precipitation correlated with a 60 percent reduction in crop yield. While this information is not adequate for projecting a trend, it does illustrate the effect of deficient moisture on agricultural productivity.

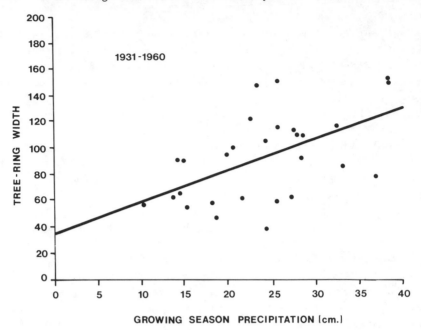

Figure 24. Correlation between modern Reserve area tree-ring values and Fort Bayard growing season precipitation.

Adding to the conservative nature of the estimates of crop failure made here is the fact that many factors that decrease yields and cause total crop failure are not considered. Minimally, these factors include insect and animal predation, decreased soil fertility, floods, disease, frost, low temperatures, high winds, hail, fire, and excessive moisture during harvest. For example, with dense continual cropping, insect predation increases, and with the extensive field maintenance during the Classic Mimbres period, it is quite likely that insect damage was a problem.   Interestingly, one Classic Black-on-White bowl shows people picking insects off what appear to be crops. Similarly, floods not only destroy a year's harvest but also temporarily decrease soil fertility, erode fields, and destroy field facilities, thus affecting subsequent crops. Not considering these factors makes the estimates of the frequency and magnitude of reduced yields quite conservative.

Table 10 illustrates the guidelines for relating precipitation to crop success. Four classes of crop success are presented. It is assumed that precipitation more than one standard deviation above the mean allowed excellent floodplain and dry farming yields

Table 10

Guidelines for Relating Growing Season
Precipitation to Crop Success

Tree-Ring Value	Agricultural Strategy	
	Floodplain Farming	Dry Farming
Above average (width more that one standard deviation above the mean)	++	++
Average (width within one standard deviation above the mean)	++	+
Below average (width within one standard deviation below the mean)	+	--
Failure (width more that one standard deviation below the mean)	--	--

++ Successful harvest with surplus for storage.
 + Successful harvest but with no surplus.
 -- Poor harvest to complete failure.

with a storable surplus beyond the yearly needs of the production group. Precipitation within one standard deviation above the mean indicates that a surplus floodplain crop could be harvested and dry farming is possible. Within one standard deviation below the mean, it is assumed that dry farming is not possible but an adequate floodplain crop could be harvested. A growing season more than one standard deviation below the mean would result in no dry farming crop and a severely reduced floodplain yield that would not be adequate for the year's food needs. These rules are based on the conclusion previously drawn that dry farming is possible only with above-average precipitation. A reduction in precipitation would have different effects on irrigated crops than on floodplain dry farming. Low precipitation would reduce streamflow, so that under extensive irrigation there would not be enough water; and, as we

Estimating Food Stress in the Study Area

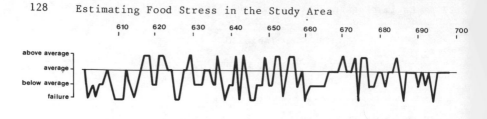

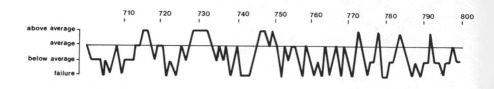

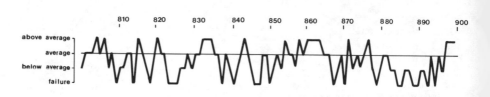

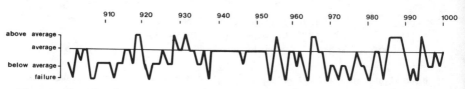

Figure 25.   Estimates of crop success from A.D. 600 to 1249.

have seen, in an average year there is not enough water to irrigate the whole floodplain. Low growing season precipitation would affect floodplain dry farming as well. Unless the plants were large enough for the roots to reach groundwater, they would not produce an adequate crop. Without enough precipitation, the roots would not reach a sufficient depth. Using the guidelines from table 10, the periodicity and magnitude of food production failures for each year are shown in figure 25.

Three levels of stress are outlined in figure 26:   mild, moderate, and severe. A mild stress would occur in a year with precipitation more than one standard deviation below the mean. A

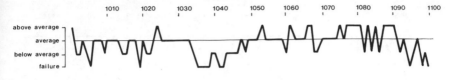

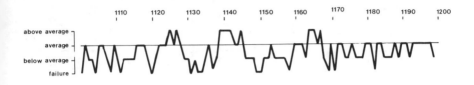

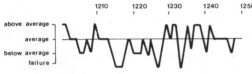

Figure 25. (cont.).

single failure year is considered a mild stress because of the
potential for using resources stored in earlier years. Many modern
puebloan groups try to keep at least a one year supply stored in
the event of crop failure (Ford 1968; Stephens 1936). A moderate
stress is defined as occurring in a year more than one standard
deviation below the mean that was preceded by two consecutive years
of below average precipitation. This situation is a greater stress
because it is assumed that the earlier years would not have allowed
an adequate buildup of stored surplus. A severe stress is when at
least two failure years occur together. I assume that in this
situation all stored resources would have been exhausted long
before an adequate crop could be harvested.

Another crop failure category is presented in table 11. This
is the frequency of upland dry farming success. I assume that all
years with below average precipitation would not have allowed an
upland dry farmed crop, except in a few restricted areas. Table 11
illustrates the frequency of these stress categories in fifty-year
intervals. The prehistoric Mimbreños would have been mildly stressed 10.2 percent of the years, or once every 9.8 years; 3 percent
of the time, or once every thirty-three years, they would have been
moderately stressed; and 4 percent of the years, or once every

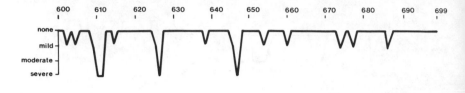

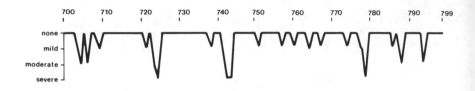

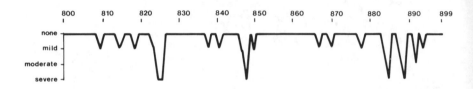

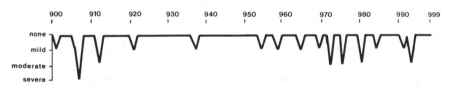

Figure 26.   Estimates of food stress from A.D. 600 to 1249.

twenty-five years, they would have been severely stressed.   On an
average, nearly half of the years would have had insufficient
precipitation for successful dry farming.

It seems a poor economic strategy to rely on dry farming unless
necessary, as seems to have been the case with the Classic Mimbreños.   As I have shown, the Classic Mimbres period farmers
probably could not have supported their population on floodplain
farming alone.   Interestingly, much of the Classic Mimbres period
was the best time for farming.   The half-century from A.D. 1050 to
1099 had the lowest failure rate for upland dry farming, only once

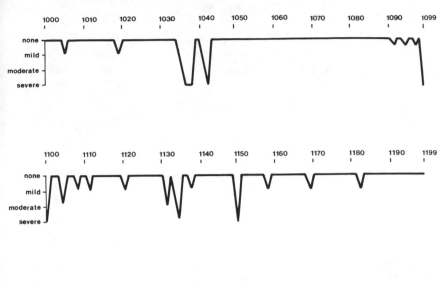

Figure 26 (cont.).

every four years. This is similar to the percentage of crop
failure years reported for eastern New Mexico dry farming at the
turn of the century. For this period, maize crops failed an
average of once every 3.5 years (Stanten, Burnham, and Carter
1939).

The distribution of crop failures during the Classic Mimbres
period is particularly interesting. The earliest part of the
Classic Mimbres period was quite favorable for agriculture. Except
for a drought in the late 1030s, the precipitation regime was
unusually favorable for crop success. However, starting in the
1090s precipitation levels returned to a more normal condition and,
in fact, were even worse than normal. The half-century from 1090
to 1139 was a very unfavorable period for agriculture in the study
area. During this time period there would have been 1.4 times the
average number of mildly stressed years, 2.0 times the average of
moderately stressed years, 1.5 times the average of severely stressed years, and 1.5 times the average of dry farming failures.

Table 11

Periodicity of Farming Failure Based on Precipitation Estimates

Time Period	Mild[a]	Moderate[b]	Severe[c]	Only Dry Farming[d]
610–649	14	0	8	56
650–699	10	0	0	38
700–749	8	6	6	50
750–799	16	4	2	68
800–849	14	0	6	44
850–899	10	6	4	50
900–949	6	2	2	48
950–999	12	8	0	54
1000–1049	6	2	8	48
1050–1099	6	0	2	26
1100–1149	8	8	4	56
1150–1199	6	0	2	48
1200–1250	6	0	4	36
Average	10	3	4	42

a. Percentage of years more than one standard deviation below the mean.
b. Percentage of years more than one standard deviation below the mean that were preceded by two below-average or failure years.
c. Number of times two or more years more than one standard deviation below the mean occurred together.
d. Percentage of years below the mean.

Precipitation Predictability

I will discuss one further characteristic of the moisture regime important for considering prehistoric farming. The predictability of precipitation refers to the degree of variation between years. Rainfall is one of the least predictable climatic factors important to agriculture in warm, semiarid regions. Although the coefficient of variation for solar radiation and annual temperature averages 5 percent in these regions, the coefficient of variation of rainfall averages 20–30 percent (Swinedale, Virmani, and Sivakumar 1981). Kirkby's study (1973, 1978) of Oaxacan peasant farmers clearly demonstrates how agricultural decision making relates to the farmer's perception of the amount and distribution of precipitation: "the ultimate success of the harvest is, to a large extent, the result of correctly matching planting conditions with rainfall conditions" (1973:55). Although we cannot model the specific decisions made by prehistoric Mimbres farmers, consideration of the effects of precipitation constancy is based on the assumption that <u>the more variable the rainfall, the greater the risk of crop failure or reduced yields</u>. That is, the more variable the moisture patterns, the less likely it is that prehistoric farmers could match their planting strategies to the precipitation patterns. No data are available on intrayear variation, so discussion will focus on variation between years.

As with other precipitation variables, predictability will be based on the analysis of the Reserve tree-ring record from A.D 650 to 1259 (see Dean and Robinson 1978 for the basic data). A coefficient of variation (CV) is used here as the measure of predictability. CV values were calculated by ten-year intervals (e.g., A.D. 1200-1209), and these values are plotted in figure 27. The lower the CV, the more predictable the precipitation amount. The mean CV for these sixty-six intervals is 40.6 percent with a standard deviation of 16 percent. The mean and one standard deviation are plotted on figure 27 as a guide for comparing CV values.

As can be seen in figure 27, there are several periods of relatively high predictability. These include A.D. 650-99, 850-69, 920-49, 1040-1129, and 1150-1209. Following the basic assumption used here, these periods represent relatively stable precipitation regimes for farming. In contrast are periods of unusually high variability, and these are A.D. 720-79, 870-909, 970-99, and 1130-49. These periods represent unusually unstable precipitation conditions and therefore increased risk of crop failure or low yields.

Not knowing the exact farming strategies employed by prehistoric Mimbres farmers, it is difficult to discuss how precipitation variation interacted with amounts of precipitation. However, we can derive a general understanding of the effects of precipitation on prehistoric farming by combining the measure of amount of precipitation with the measure of precipitation predictability. By emphasizing the extremes, we can identify periods unusually favorable for agriculture (high predictability and high moisture) and periods unusually unfavorable (low predictability and low precipitation). The middle values are harder to interpret, since they can result from low predictability/high precipitation, high predictability/low precipitation, or average values for both

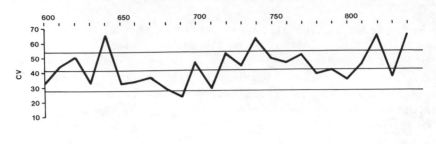

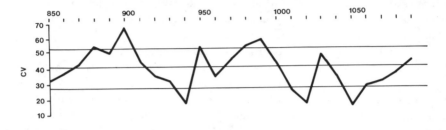

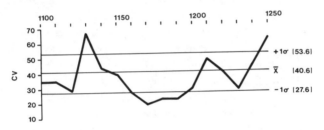

Figure 27. Coefficient of variation in tree-ring widths by ten-year intervals.

variables.

Figure 28 presents this composite measure, which is the mean for each ten-year interval multiplied by the reciprocal of the CV for the same time period. The mean for this "precipitation efficacy" measure for all sixty-six intervals is 2.89, with a standard deviation of 1.42. The higher the figure, the more predictable and wetter; the lower the figure, the less predictable and drier. Again, the middle range values are less clear, but since we do not know the specific farming strategies employed by prehistoric Mimbreños, emphasis on the extremes is warranted. The period A.D. 600-900 lacked extremes and tended to have slightly lower values. The Classic Mimbres period is particularly interesting. The first part (A.D. 1000-1089) was unusually favorable

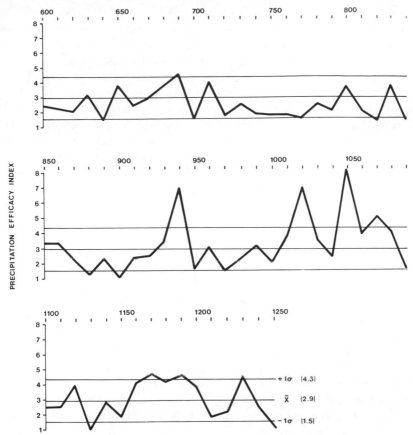

Figure 28.   Precipitation efficacy from A.D. 600 to 1249.
This measure combines precipitation variation with amount of precipitation.

for agriculture, particularly dry farming, which was very dependent
on precipitation. However, from A.D. 1090 until 1149 the precipitation effectiveness is more typical--that is, less predictable
with lower amounts of moisture.

Reliability of Food Acquisition from Naturally Available Resources

Estimates of the magnitude and periodicity of farming failures
in the Rio Mimbres Valley from A.D. 600 to 1250 have already been
made. Estimates of farming failure are not necessarily estimates
of food acquisition failure, since many strategies ("buffers") can
be used to supply adequate food during times of farming failure.

One such buffer, storage of foods, was built into the estimation of farming failure. The next strategy to consider is the intensive harvesting of naturally available resources in the vicinity of the sites to make up for a deficit caused by an unsuccessful crop harvest. Was it possible for the prehistoric populations in the study area to obtain sufficient energy from wild foods without a widespread population dislocation? The attempt to answer this question falls under the rubric of carrying capacity--"the maximum number of organisms which can maintain themselves indefinitely in an area" (Zubrow 1971:128). Rather than attempting to estimate a maximum homeostatic population size, I will be estimating whether the prehistoric populations in the study area could have been supported through the use of naturally available resources.

Equation for Estimating Naturally Available Foods

Table 12 presents the equation I will use to estimate the maximum energy available from wild foods. The logic of this equation is to derive estimates of the natural environment productivity of animals and plants and then to estimate what percentage of this productivity could have been realistically available to prehistoric groups in the study area.

Tables 13 and 14 give the values assigned to each variable and the total estimated energy available from the biotic environment of the study area. Because the values assigned to each variable are derived primarily from indirect sources, I present detailed justification of these values and then give estimates of the human population caloric need at different periods. The availability of energy from wild foods can then be compared with estimates of the nutritional needs of the population under different conditions of crop harvest success, providing an estimate of the reliability of using wild foods to make up a caloric deficit from farming failures.

Value Justification

Value **a** (net primary productivity, NPP). Net primary productivity represents the production of organic matter by autotrophs after respiration and is an indication of the organic matter potentially available to organisms in the food chain. While there

Table 12

Equation for Estimating the Energy Available from
Naturally Occurring Food Resources in the Study Area

$A = E_p + E_s$

where:

    A = energy available from naturally occurring food resources
    E_p = energy available from autotrophs
    E_s = energy available from heterotrophs

$E_p = abcdes_p$

where:

    a = net primary productivity (NPP)
    b = fraction of edible NPP
    c = collectible fraction of edible NPP
    d = nutritional value of NPP
    e = digestible NPP
    s_p = area of exploitation

$E_s = ghijks_s$

where:

    g = net secondary productivity (NSP)
    h = fraction of edible NSP
    i = collectible fraction of NSP
    j = nutritional value of NSP
    k = digestible NSP
    s_s = area of exploitation

---

have been numerous studies of NPP over the past twenty years, there
often has been marked disagreement concerning the rates of NPP
under various conditions. Many of the early estimates of NPP were
inadequate, primarily because they tended to underestimate below-
ground productivity (Bray 1963) and the productivity of nonperen-
nial organs (e.g., leaves). More recent work has become
increasingly sophisticated, resulting in more accurate methods for
estimating NPP.

There are only two estimates of NPP for southwestern environments similar to the study area. Zubrow (1975b) investigated NPP
in the Hay Hollow Valley of Arizona, approximately 160 km northwest

Table 13

Calculation of E_p in the Study Area

Variable	Value
a Net primary productivity (NPP)	5,000 kg/ha/year
b Edible NPP (2%)	100 kg/ha/year
c Collectible NPP (10%)	10 kg/ha/year
d Energy value (4,000 Kcal/kg)	40,000 Kcal/ha/year
e Digestible NPP (90%)	36,000 Kcal/ha/year
s_p Area of exploitation (90,000 ha)	3.24×10^9 kcal/year

Table 14

Calculation of E_s in the Study Area

Variable	Value
g Net seconday productivity (NSP)	35.3 kg/ha/year
h Edible NSP (60%)	21.2 kg/ha/year
i Collectible NSP (10%)	2.1 kg/ha/year
j Energy value (5,000 Kcal/kg)	10,590 Kcal/ha/year
k Digestible NSP (90%)	9,531 Kcal/ha/year
s_s Area of exploitation (90,000 ha)	8.58×10^8 kcal/year
TOTAL ENERGY AVAILABLE IN THE STUDY AREA	4.10×10^9 Kcal/year

of the Rio Mimbres area. Zubrow estimates NPP as 1,589 kg of dry
organic matter per hectare per year. Compared with the NPP estimates made by a variety of researchers for environments somewhat
analogous to the study area, it is clear that his estimate is very
low; this is probably due to inadequate sampling procedures. The
second southwestern estimate of NPP is reported by Whittaker and
Niering (1975) for a number of plant associations in the Santa
Catalina Mountains near Tucson, Arizona. For their "pigmy conifer-
oak shrub association," they estimate NPP at 3,500 kg per hectare
per year. This association is similar to the plant assemblages in
most of the Mimbres study area. Their "Pinus ponderosa-Quercus
hypoleucoides association" (which had an estimated NPP of 6,200 kg
per hectare per year) is roughly analogous to the more mesic parts
of the Rio Mimbres study area. From Whittaker and Niering's study
it is reasonable to conclude that the NPP in the study area is
somewhere between 3,500 and 6,200 kg per hectare per year.

This range can be compared with other estimates of NPP in
environments similar to the study area. Table 15 provides NPP
estimates calculated by various researchers. These estimates are
not specific to the Southwest but generally include arid to semiarid regions. Eliminating Zubrow's low estimate, the estimate from
Whittaker and Niering is within the range proposed by others.
Rodin, Bazilevich, and Rozov (1975; Bazilevich, Drozdov, and Rodin
1971) estimated NPP on a global scale. Their NPP estimate for
class 12 zones (which include semiarid woodland), 6,100-8,000 kg
per hectare per year, compares favorably with Whittaker and
Niering's estimate of NPP. Annual precipitation is an excellent
predictor of NPP up to about 800 mm annual precipitation (Whittaker
1970; Rosenweig 1968; Walter 1954). Therefore the study area NPP
of 5,000 kg per hectare per year will be used in this equation.
This value is halfway between Rodin, Bazilevich, and Rozov's
minimum estimate of 6,100 kg per hectare per year and Whittaker and
Niering's estimate of 3,500 kg per hectare per year.

Value **b** (edible fraction of NPP). Clearly, not all NPP goes
into organic matter that is directly edible by humans, and in fact
most does not. What NPP is indirectly available to humans by
consumption of heterotrophs will be considered later. The vast
majority of NPP goes into production of roots, wood, leaves, and
other vegetative structures that humans generally cannot use
directly (Whittaker 1975). With a few exceptions, such as some
edible underground parts, leaves, and cambium, the edible fraction
of NPP is in the form of reproductive structures--seeds and fruits,

Table 15

Estimates of NPP for Environments Similar to the Study Area

Reference	NPP (kg/ha/year)
Zubrow (1975b)[a]	1,589
Walter (1954)[b]	2,900
Whittaker and Woodwell (1971)[c]	2,000-12,000
Odum (1959)[d]	750-6,250
Rodin, Bazilevich, and Rozov (1975)[e]	6,100-8,00
Whittaker and Niering (1975)[f]	3,500-6,200

a. Zubrow's estimates are based on work in eastern Arizona. His study considers only aboveground NPP and underestimates the productivity of green assimilating organs.
b. Walter's estimate is from work in East Africa and is an estimate of only aboveground NPP.
c. Estimates for "woodlands and shrublands."
d. Odum's estimates are for "grasslands, deep lakes, mountain forests, and some agriculture" (1959:75). His calculations are for gross primary productivity of 1,825 to 10,950 kg/ha/year. This was then corrected for net productivity using Odum's suggestion that NPP is 40 percent to 60 percent of gross productivity.
e. Rodin and colleagues estimate NPP based on a worldwide survey. The Mimbres study area falls within their NPP category 12 (xerophytic woodlands and shrub communities in mountains). Also see Bazilovich, Drozdov, and Rodin (1971).
f. Estimates are for woodlands in the Santa Catalina Mountains, Arizona.

and to a lesser extent flowers. There is a wide range in the percentage of NPP that goes into reproductive structures. Whittaker, Cohen, and Olsen (1963) found that the fruits of white oak (Quercus alba) and short leaf pine (Pinus echinata) in Tennessee constitute only 0.3 percent and 0.2 percent of NPP respectively. Ovington, Heitkamp, and Lawrence (1963) and Rodin and Bazilevich (1965) report similarly low estimates of the percentage of NPP that results in reproductive structures. Only one study, Whittaker and Niering (1975), provides estimates of the percentage of NPP that goes into producing seeds and fruits. They do not directly estimate the percentage of seeds and fruits for all plants in their study area, in that they do not differentiate the percentage of herbaceous NPP that constitutes reproductive structures. One can derive a fairly reliable estimate of edible NPP from their work. For their "pigmy conifer-oak shrub" association, which is most analogous to the study area, they provide estimates of the percentage of NPP that is composed of "fruits, flowers, etc." For trees 6.2 percent of the NPP goes into reproductive structures, and for shrubs the percentage is 4.3. The percentage of NPP in the form of herbaceous plants is not broken down into plant parts. However, the portion of NPP that goes into herbaceous plants was estimated to be only 1 percent. The herbaceous NPP added to the NPP percentages of reproductive structures from trees and shrubs accounts for only 3.6 percent of NPP. A significant percentage of reproductive NPP is inedible by humans, including most flowers and fruit integuments. The percentage of edible NPP should be less than 3.6. Therefore, an estimate of 2 percent of the NPP as directly edible by humans is reasonable.

Value c (fraction of edible NPP that could be collected). Obviously, not all of the potentially edible NPP could have been collected by the human population at any given time. Much of the edible NPP is available in a short period of time, and it is unlikely that the human population could mobilize sufficient labor to exploit all resources completely. This is the basis of Flannery's (1968) concept of scheduling conflicts. Not only would potential resources become available within a short time, primarely summer and early fall, but they would be spread over wide distances, further complicating harvest efficiency. Also, humans would be competing with other predators for these resources. This competition would be greatest during times of resource scarcity such as droughts.

Unfortunately, there is no anthropological information on which to base an estimate of the harvest efficiency for this case study. E. Odum roughly estimates that only 0.02 percent of net primary productivity would be consistently available for human exploitation (letter to L. Binford, 1966). This was an estimate and was not based on empirical studies. Interestingly, this estimate is approximately one-tenth the estimate used here. I believe that a harvest efficiency value of 10 percent is reasonable. Unfortunately, there is no empirical justification for this value.

Obviously, then, this variable constitutes the weakest link in the equation for estimating the usable biomass in the study area.

Value **d** (nutritional value of edible NPP). The average caloric value for each kilogram of plant tissue is about 4,000 Kcal (Whittaker 1970). It is a little higher for seeds but is still under 5,000 Kcal per kilogram (Reichman 1976; Kendigh and West 1965). Since seeds and fruits include inedible integuments, an assigned value of 4,000 Kcal per kilograms will be used here.

Value **e** (digestible fraction of edible, collectible NPP). Not all of the energy available from food plants can be assimilated by the human body. Herbivores tend to be very inefficient in this regard, and often 90 percent of the energy value of plants is excreted (Phillipson 1966). While the digestive efficiency of carnivores is higher, it is still not completely efficient; "In carnivores as much as 75 percent of the food eaten may be as-similated..., although 30-50 percent is more normal".(Phillipson 1966:6). However, these energy efficiencies are not applicable to humans, for food processing, particularly cooking, can increase the energetic efficiency. Most studies of human energetic efficiencies have been performed using a modern highly processed and cooked diet. Experimental studies have shown that about 97 percent of the ingested carbohydrates in these studies were normally absorbed by the human body (Davidson and Passmore 1969). I doubt that the efficiency of foods processed with the technology available to the prehistoric Mimbreños would have been as high. This is parti-cularly true for the wide range of naturally available foods in the study area. Therefore, it is reasonable to consider the digestible fraction of the energy available as 90 percent, but I suspect that this is high, given the milling and cooking technology used.

Value s_p (size of catchment region). It is very difficult to determine the regional catchment area for prehistoric peoples. This is particularly true for times of food provisioning problems, when a much wider area probably had to be exploited. The size of the Mimbres Foundation study area in the mountainous river valleys, including the Rio Mimbres Valley, will be used for this areal estimate. This region, which covers about 90,000 ha, is used for several reasons. First, it is in this area that the vast majority of the prehistoric sites occurred, with the exception of the Animas period. Second, this area is a good average of the environment of southwestern New Mexico, because it is so large and includes most of the environmental variation found in this part of the state.

Value **g** (net secondary productivity, NSP). Net secondary productivity is a very difficult estimate to make because of the complexity of heterotrophic interaction and the methodological difficulty in the census of mobile organisms. Consequently, there is little information on NSP. Whittaker (1975) provides the only estimate of NSP for regions similar to the study area. He estimates NSP for "woodlands and savannas" at 35.5 kg per hectare per year. In the absence of other estimates and considering that Whittaker's estimates of NPP are in line with estimates made by other researchers (see table 15) this approximation will be used for this variable.

Value **h** (edible fraction of NSP). Not all NSP can be consumed by humans, although the fraction is higher than for the edible percentage of NPP. White's work (1953a,b) has been used by zoo-archeologists as the basis for estimating the percentage of live-weight that can be consumed by humans. He suggests that 50 to 70 percent of the liveweight is potentially usable for human food. There has been recent criticism of these figures (e.g., Stewart and Stahl 1977; Lyman 1979). Stewart and Stahl, for example, find that White's estimates are almost consistently too high, and their average of the edible portion of liveweight is about 50 percent. As a result of these corrections, a value of 60 percent of NSP assigned here to this value is very generous in adding to the overestimate of potential energy available to the prehistoric inhabitants of the study area.

Value **i** (collectible fraction of edible NSP). Like the collectible fraction of NPP, not all the potentially available NSP could be harvested. Under normal conditions and on a sustained basis, the yield of any trophic level cannot exceed its ecological efficiency. "If harvest is in the form of the meat of herbivorous animals, the harvest efficiency must be lower than the trophic level efficiency, hence less than 10 percent" (Whittaker 1970). This does not necessarily apply to the situation under consideration here, because it is doubtful that when faced with severe food provisioning problems, the prehistoric population would have been concerned with overexploiting the resource base. Conversely, however, many of the conditions that would create conditions of crop loss would also lower the potentially edible NSP.

The value assigned to this variable (10 percent) has little empirical justification in anthropological and biological literature other than the theoretical consideration expressed above by Whittaker. However, I believe this estimate is quite reasonable when one considers that much of the NSP is in the form of small,

difficult-to-acquire resources such as insects and small herbivores. Hassan (1981) has selected a rather arbitrary estimation
of 10 percent sustainable yield of ungulates while noting that
studies have shown that deer populations, under specific circumstances, can withstand a 10 percent cropping. Obviously, this
variable, along with variable c, has the least empirical justification and consequently is the most open to criticism.

Value j (energy value of NSP). In general, the energy
available in animal tissue is higher than that in plant tissue, and
it provides a more complete nutritional complement. Whittaker
(1970) estimated that animal tissue averages about 5,000 Kcal per
kilogram, and this figure will be used here for the average energy
value. However, there is a good deal of variation around this
average. For example, lean meat has a much lower caloric value
than fatty tissue, so that this value probably adds to the overestimation of edible NSP.

Value k (digestible fraction of collectible, edible NSP). As
discussed for value e, energetic efficiency is not complete.
Therefore, a value of 90 percent will be used for this variable.

Value s_s (size of regional catchment). The same size, 90,000
ha, used for variable s_p will be used here. However, it is quite
likely that the hunting territory used by the prehistoric Mimbreños
was larger than their plant collecting area, because animal resources can be more efficiently transported over long distances
than can plants, with some important exceptions such as piñon nuts
(Lightfoot 1979). Still, the size of the study area is very large.
It is unlikely that much potential hunting grounds outside the
study area would have been available for peoples living within the
study area, since Mimbreños had to compete with people living in
these areas, thus infringing upon established hunting territories.
While this value may be low, I doubt that it is small enough to
alter significantly the estimates of foods available from naturally
occurring resources.

Several of the values assigned to variables used to calculate
the study area carrying capacity have been without adequate
empirical or theoretical justification. While these specific
values (particularly for variables c and i) cannot be evaluated
independently, the overall estimate of the number of people who
could have been supported from naturally available resources in the
study area can be compared with the population densities of modern
hunter/gatherer groups. The density of these groups is not
completely comparable to the carrying capacity estimate made for

the study area, which calculates how many people could have been supported using naturally available foods. The density of hunter/gatherers should be lower than the estimate for the study area because these modern populations do not utilize all the resources they could consume (Lee and Devore 1968). Nevertheless, this comparison provides insights into how high the carrying capacity estimate is in relation to modern foraging population densities.

The total energy available to humans in the study area is 4.1 x 10^9 Kcal. Within this 900 km^2 area, this energy would support 5,349 people (at 766,500 Kcal per capita), a potential population density of one person per 0.17 km^2. Under drought conditions, this figure drops to one person per 0.27 km^2. For comparison, Hassan (1981:table 2.1) lists population density estimates for thirty-five hunting/gathering societies from throughout the world. Densities for these groups ranged from one person per 0.11 km^2 (Haida) to one person per 97.1 km^2 (Asiagmuit). The Owens Valley Paiute, whose environmental setting is very similar to that of the study area, have a population density of one person per 5.4 km^2 (Steward 1938). For the !Kung San, a desert hunter/gatherer group, the density is one person per 6.3 km^2 (Lee 1968). Therefore the estimated potential population density in the study area supportable from natural resources is higher than all of the groups listed by Hassan with the exception of the Haida, is twenty times the Owens Valley Paiute density, and is twenty-three times the !Kung San density. Generally, only hunter/gatherer groups that have access to and use marine and/or fish resources have higher population densities than the Rio Mimbres region estimate. These groups include the Haida, California hunting/gathering/fishing groups (Hassan 1981), and the Kaiadilt of Australia (Tindale 1962).

This is not a completely fair comparison, since the natural productivity of these regions is not the same. Great Basin NPP averages 50 percent that of the Mimbres region, and the NPP of the !Kung San environment is only 20 percent that of the study area (see Bazilevich, Drozdov, and Rodin 1971). Consequently, for a more realistic comparison, the densities of these modern groups should be reduced according to the differential productivity of their environments. Making the density estimates comparable to that of the study area by multiplying the population density by the NPP differential, the potential supportable population in the study area is ten times that of the Owens Valley Paiute and five times that of the !Kung San. These comparisons indirectly suggest that, in fact, the estimates of the carrying capacity of the study area are quite generous, although I cannot directly estimate how generous.

Energy Needs of the Prehistoric Groups in the Study Area

Now that estimates of the potential energy available from natural resources in the study area have been calculated, it is necessary to approximate the caloric needs of the prehistoric populations. This value can then be compared with the energy available from the natural environment. There are many important factors such as sex, age, work expenditure, and health that are important in determining the caloric requirements of humans. Since these factors cannot be measured for the prehistoric populations under consideration, a more general level of abstraction must be used. Wetterstrom (1976) estimates that the average caloric requirement for the prehistoric Arroyo Hondo Pueblo population was approximately 2,100 Kcal per day or 766,500 Kcal per year per person. This is in general agreement with older data cited by Davidson and Passmore (1969) for a "temporary maintenance level" and for modern hunter/gatherer caloric intake (e.g., Lee 1979; Wilmsen 1978). Therefore, it will be assumed here that an average per capita daily caloric need is 2,100 Kcal.

Table 16 shows the caloric requirement that would have to be derived from naturally available foods at three levels of crop harvest success for the five prehistoric periods under investigation. Population size estimates used were presented in chapter 3. The three levels of crop harvest are (1) for an average year, when only half of the caloric need had to be obtained from wilds; (2) partial crop failure, when 75 percent of the energy would have to be taken from naturally available resources; and (3) total crop failure, when all the energy would have to be supplied by wild foods.

Figures 29 and 30 illustrate the estimates of actual prehistoric population size during the five time periods under consideration as compared with the maximum population size that could be supported by the energy available from noncultivated resources. Figure 29 is predicated on the assumption that the factor(s) causing crop failure did not have an impact on the wild productivity. Figure 30 takes into account situations where the factor(s) creating crop losses will also affect the availability of

Table 16

Estimated Caloric Requirements for the Prehistoric Populations in the Study Area

Percentage of Diet from Naturally Available Foods	Time Period				
	EP	LP	CM	A	S
50% (385,500 Kcal/person/year)	1.8×10^8	4.6×10^8	1.2×10^9(a) 1.5×10^9(b)	4.7×10^8(a) 9.2×10^8(b)	2.6×10^8
75% (575,250 Kcal/person/year)	2.7×10^8	6.9×10^8	1.8×10^9(a) 2.3×10^9(b)	7.0×10^8(a) 1.4×10^9(b)	3.9×10^8
100% (767,000 Kcal/person/year)	3.7×10^8	9.2×10^8	2.4×10^9(a) 3.1×10^9(b)	9.4×10^8(a) 1.8×10^9(b)	5.2×10^8
Estimated population size	478	1,205	3,187(a) 4,021(b)	1,221(a) 2,404(b)	680

Note: EP = Early Pithouse; LP = Late Pithouse; CM = Classic Mimbres; A = Animas; S = Salado

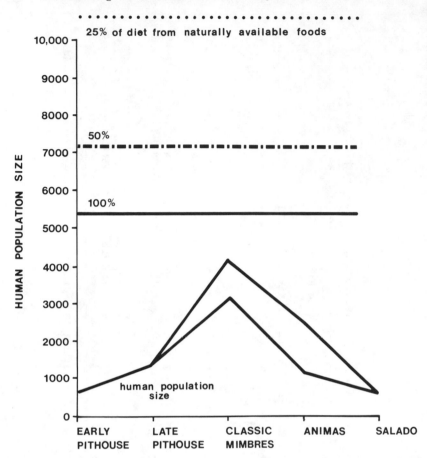

Figure 29.   Human population supportable from naturally available resources in the study area (normal precipitation).

noncultivated resources.   In some circumstances such as localized flooding, the situation represented in figure 29 would be the one faced by the prehistoric Mimbreños.   However, this whole discussion of crop failure is based upon regionwide precipitation values; therefore figure 30 is of more interest in this discussion.

The estimates of the maximum supportable human population presented in figure 30 were calculated by making the assumption that the decrease in potentially edible biomass was linearly related to the decrease in moisture.   Thus, as we have seen earlier, one standard deviation below the mean in growing season precipitation is a reduction of 56 percent in potentially edible biomass (see figure 24).   Therefore, with one standard deviation

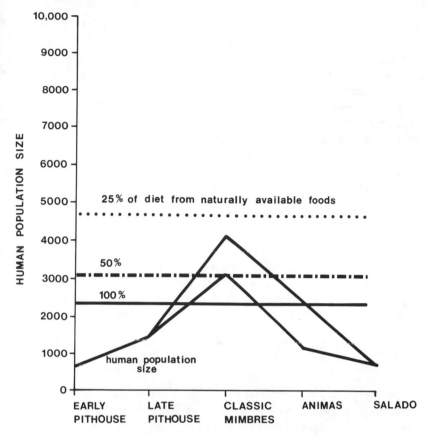

Figure 30. Human population supportable from naturally available resources in the study area (drought conditions).

reduction in precipitation, the caloric energy would be reduced by over half. There is good reason to suspect that this approach again tends to overestimate the food supply available from non-cultivated resources. It could be argued that the reduction in the edible biomass, which would be primarily in the form of seeds and fruits, would be curvilinear rather than linear. Consequently, there would be a greater reduction in edible biomass than the assumption used here indicates. During times of inadequate precipitation many annuals, including edible ones, would simply not germinate. Similarly, with water stress, less energy could be invested in reproductive structure by perennials and most would have to be used just to maintain the plant. Therefore, the human population limits shown in figure 30 are probably very conservative, and the actual situation would have been a graver problem for the prehistoric occupants of the valley.

Even using these conservative estimates of the energy available from noncultivated resources, figure 30 indicates that during the Classic Mimbres period the human population would have had a very difficult time sustaining itself using the naturally available foods in the event of crop failure without having to resort to the importation of food or massive population movement to other areas. In addition, the Late Pithouse period and perhaps the Animas period populations also would have found it difficult to sustain themselves under the conditions modeled here. Figure 30 further suggests that the Early Pithouse period and Salado period populations probably had little difficulty obtaining enough food when faced with an inadequate crop harvest. Figure 29 does not conflict with the assumption made earlier that half of the food supply came from wild resources during "normal" times, but figure 30 indicates that during periods of low precipitation even half of the food supply from wild resources may have been difficult to gather, notably for the Classic Mimbres period population.

Summary

Too often southwestern archeologists explain patterns in the archeological record as the result of subsistence problems without attempting to estimate the severity of these problems. Consequently, the detailed calculations in this chapter are a necessary prerequisite for studying the consequences of food provisioning problems in the Mimbres region. In order to estimate the magnitude of the problems the prehistoric Mimbreños faced in securing a stable food supply, three subsidiary goals were established: to describe the subsistence economy, to explore how particular potentially limiting factors affected the capacity of the prehistoric economy to support the population present, and to estimate variation in the potential subsistence strategies using prehistoric climatic data.

Before summarizing the results presented in this chapter, I must reinterate one methodological point. Describing any archeological system is a very difficult task because of the incomplete data available for understanding critical variables in that system. Consequently, there is a potential for great error in the calculations used in this chapter. To minimize some of this error, these calculations were biased toward an overestimation of the production capacity of the prehistoric subsistence economy. By analytically considering maize the only crop grown prehistorically, estimates of agricultural productivity were made generous. Maize is a very efficient energy "factory" compared with other crops that were grown prehistorically. For example, Pennington (1969) estimates that Tepehuan maize yields approximately 1,000,800 Kcal per hectare and that beans will produce 516,520 Kcal per hectare. If these estimates are accurate, maize produces 1.9 times the energy of beans. Maize would be even more efficient in relation to cucurbits and other high water content crops. Therefore, the analytic assumption that maize was the only prehistoric crop increases the estimates of energy available from prehistoric fields, since we have evidence that other crops were being grown.

The greatest overestimation in this chapter results because low precipitation was used to estimate frequencies of prehistoric crop failure. Numerous other natural environmental factors will decrease cultigen yields. These include fire, hail, early or late frost, flooding, insect and animal predation, high winds, too much moisture, and various crop diseases. By not considering these, the estimates of crop failure are certainly made quite conservative.

It is difficult to assess the accuracy of the estimate of energy available from naturally occurring resources in the study area. The discussion of modern hunter/gatherer population densities, compared with the potential human population that could have been supported from naturally occurring resources in the study area, suggests that the carrying capacity estimate made in this chapter was quite generous. Since even these conservative estimates of food acquisition problems show that the Classic Mimbres period population had serious difficulty in acquiring enough foods, we can be fairly certain that these problems were worse than portrayed here.

After reviewing ethnographic information and data from southwestern coprolite studies, I suggested that, for the prehistoric periods in the study area except the Early Pithouse period, cultivated plants constituted approximately 50 percent of the diet on the average. Based on weaker inferences, I assigned a figure of 35 percent to the domesticated plant contribution to the Early Pithouse period diet.

The most reliable prehistoric farming strategy in the study area was floodplain agriculture. Approximately 1,500 ha of floodplain fields were available along the Rio Mimbres. Assuming 0.6 ha per capita, the floodplain would support 2,525 people. This amount of land would have been insufficient for the Classic Mimbres and perhaps the Animas period populations. For the other periods there appears to have been sufficient floodplain to support their field requirements. It is clear from these calculations that the Classic Mimbres population became dependent upon less reliable agricultural strategies such as using farming locations more vulnerable to periods of low precipitation.

I calculated that approximately 12,335,000 m^3 of water was available for irrigation during the growing season. If all possible floodplain fields were planted, 75 percent of this water flow would have had to be used for irrigation. For reasons stated previously, it is very unlikely that this would have been possible. Therefore, water for irrigation limited the possible extent of floodplain cultivation. This further suggests that the Classic Mimbres population was dependent upon less reliable agricultural strategies.

Although we cannot estimate how growing season precipitation specifically affected variation in crop yields, it is safe to conclude that low precipitation would seriously affect yields of nonfloodplain agriculture. Using tree-ring data and four guide-lines for relating tree-ring width to farming success, I calculated year-by-year estimates of farming success. Because stored foods could be used to supplement poor yields, three levels of food stress were considered, depending upon the farming success of previous years. A "mild" stress is defined as occurring in a single year with precipitation more than one standard deviation below the mean. A "moderate" stress is defined as a year with precipitation more than one standard deviation below the mean preceded by two consecutive years with below average precipitation. A "severe" stress would have occurred with at least two consecutive years of precipitation more than one standard deviation below the mean. On an average from A.D 600 to 1249, there was a mild stress every 9.8 years, a moderate stress every thirty-three years, and a severe stress about once every twenty-five years. Generally, about every other year would have had inadequate precipitation for dry farming.

These estimates, grouped by fifty-year periods, show that the best time for crop harvest was during the Classic Mimbres period, from A.D 1050 to 1099. The rest of the early Classic Mimbres period was usually good for agriculture, with the exception of a single thirteen-year drought in the 1030s and 1040s. However, toward the latter part of the Classic Mimbres period, starting about A.D. 1090, the precipitation pattern was closer to the average of the whole prehistoric period.

The predictability of precipitation measured by ten-year intervals was considered. Based on the assumption that the less predictable the precipitation, the greater the risk of crop failure or reduced yields, this analysis suggests that certain time periods had unusually high predictability and others unusually low predictability. Of particular interest was the Classic Mimbres period. From A.D. 1000 to 1089, precipitation was very predictable, whereas the later part of the Classic Mimbres period (A.D. 1090-1149) was much less predictable. Not only was the first part of the period quite moist, it was also quite predictable, indicating a generally favorable agricultural climate. The last part of the Classic Mimbres period was not only relatively unpredictable, but also less moist, indicative of a poorer agricultural climate.

Finally, it was estimated that within the study area considered in this chapter approximately 4.1×10^9 Kcal per year were available to the prehistoric occupants from naturally available resources. During a year of average precipitation this amount of foods would easily supply the population's needs during any of the five time periods considered here. It was assumed that under drought conditions yields of naturally available foods would be linearly related to precipitation, and under these conditions it appears that there would not have been sufficient food from wild sources to supply the Classic Mimbres and perhaps the Animas period populations in the event of farming failure. In fact, it appears that there would have been barely enough "wilds" to supply half of the calories necessary for the Classic Mimbres population during drought years. Note that it was assumed that half of the energy ration came from naturally available foods. This indicates that under drought conditions the Classic Mimbreños may have had a hard time provisioning themselves even if crop yields were not reduced.

The various calculations in this chapter indicate that the largest prehistoric population, during the Classic Mimbres period, had become reliant upon nonfloodplain agriculture, which is vulnerable to variation in precipitation. During the early part of the Classic Mimbres period precipitation patterning was unusually favorable for expansion of nonfloodplain agriculture. Toward the end of this period, however, precipitation returned to a more normal pattern, which was detrimental to nonfloodplain farming, but this population had already become dependent upon these strategies.

Given that during droughts the Classic Mimbres population could not have gathered enough food from naturally available resources to make up for harvest failure, we can see that this population zenith was in a very vulnerable position. While we cannot say that the Classic Mimbres population had exceeded the "carrying capacity" of its economy, these estimates strongly indicate that this group was in very poor condition with respect to its ability to sustain itself, given the agricultural and foraging possibilities in the study area. If the calculations are correct, then the explosive population growth during the Classic Mimbres period probably occurred during the first two-thirds of this period when conditions for agriculture were favorable.

Unfortunately, we do not have documentation of the physical effects of food stress episodes on the prehistoric occupants of the Rio Mimbres region. Part of this is due to the poor condition of skeletal remains. Most Classic Mimbres period burials were placed in pits dug into sterile soil, and the accumulation of water in these pits over the centuries degraded the bones. For example, out of 1,009 burials recovered from the Swarts Ruin, a Classic Mimbres period village excavated by Cosgrove and Cosgrove (1932), only eight complete skeletons and 20 craniums were in good enough condition to analyze (Howell 1932). Similarly, Bradfield (1929) reportes that most of his 606 burials were badly disintegrated. However, Provinzano (1968) did analyze the burial remains from the Galaz site. He concludes that "the apparent carbohydrate diet, the tooth decay, the long bone demineralization, the pathology involved with calcium metabolism all point to a calcium deficiency at Galaz" (1968:81). He further suggests that this calcium deficiency was due to dietary dependence on maize grown on calcium-deficient soils, a conclusion similar to that reached by Hooton (1930) in his classic study of human remains from Pecos. Other studies documenting nutritional inadequacies suffered by prehistoric southwestern populations dependent on maize-based agriculture have shown evidence of various chronic deficiencies (e.g., Palkovich 1980; El Najjar et al. 1976; Sabels n.d.).

Few have studied human remains from the prehistoric Southwest to assess the frequency of acute food shortages. Woodall's (1968) preliminary study of growth arrest lines on Casas Grandes skeletal remains suggests increased food provisioning problems during the Medio period, the time of highest population density. No such studies have been undertaken with Mimbres region human remains. If my calculations of food stress frequency are correct, then we would expect that late Classic Mimbres period human remains should show greater evidence of episodic food shortages than remains from the earlier Classic Mimbres period.

This chapter has not "proved" that the Classic Mimbres period population did not sustain itself because of the conditions outlined here. However, these cautious estimates suggest that this was the case.

6

Responses to Food Stress
in the Study Area

In this chapter, I will examine responses to periods of food stress by the prehistoric occupants of the study area. The previous chapters set the stage for this analysis. Chapter 2 outlined a model for predicting the sequence of responses to food stress by some human groups. In chapter 5, I estimated the severity and frequency of periods of food acquisition problems in the study area. The conservative calculations indicate that the late Classic Mimbres period population had a very difficult time sustaining itself given precipitation fluctuations, the absolute size of this human population, and the resource base available in the local region. Therefore, we have good reason to believe that the late Classic Mimbreños would have had to use more inclusive responses than the earlier populations. Given that the Classic Mimbres cultural system collapsed (from an archeological perspective), we might expect that with increased risk of food stress there would be no increase in more inclusive responses.

Inclusiveness can be measured in many forms, but two will be considered here--sociopolitical integration (vertical inclusiveness) and noncentralized economic exchange (horizontal inclusiveness). Sociopolitical integration is expressed through the interaction in "power," "the ability to channel the behavior of others" (Fried 1970:13). Economic exchange refers to the movement of goods and services between groups. These two forms of interaction are often interrelated, since exchange in nonstratified societies is usually embedded in the sociopolitical organization. In this chapter these two types of integration will be considered separately. First I will examine the archeological evidence for increasing sociopolitical integration, and then discuss in detail the dynamics of exchange.

As mentioned in chapter 2, the analysis of changes in one

response category is one of two approaches that could be used. The other involves analyzing a wide number of responses and comparing their timing and inclusiveness. The first approach is used here because of problems with archeological visibility of some types of human activity.

There are two potential problems with the analyses in this chapter. First, the logical item to be exchanged during times of food stress is food. However, foods tend to be more perishable than other material culture goods. Also, it is difficult to demonstrate that various foods were exchanged between groups. Consequently, evidence for exchange involving groups in the study area will concentrate on nonfood items. During times of food stress in traditional populations, the affected group tends to interact with others with whom they have established contacts. This was the case with the Gwembe Tonga and the Fringe Enga, as discussed in chapter 2. The logic of this chapter is that the prehistoric relationships between social groups, which act as mechanisms for food distribution, may be mirrored in the exchange of durable goods or in the sociopolitical integration of prehistoric populations. The economic and social relationships are often maintained through the ongoing exchange of goods (such as hxaro) even though changes in the nature of this exchange can occur, as Laughlin (1974) documents. In other words, I will be discussing indirect indexes of potential food distribution or measures of relationships that could act as sources of food for prehistoric Mimbreños.

The second problem concerns the Late Pithouse period and Classic Mimbres period samples. Most Late Pithouse contexts excavated by the Mimbres Foundation are from the later part of this time period. The Classic Mimbres period assemblage from Mimbres Foundation excavations covers the whole period, and at this point it cannot be assigned to a more detailed division within the Classic Mimbres period. Therefore, any differences between the Late Pithouse and Classic Mimbres period assemblages should underrepresent the differences that actually occurred. The lack of internal analytic division in the Classic Mimbres period is a particularly troublesome problem. As discussed in the previous chapter, the earlier part of the Classic Mimbres period was unusually favorable for agriculture, whereas the last part was unusually poor. That the Classic Mimbres period artifact assemblages are a mixture of these two parts means that changes in exchange patterns will be less clear in the analyses in this chapter.

Sociopolitical Integration

Increasing sociopolitical integration can take two forms. On one hand are hierarchical changes such as increased centralization of decision making. This is the case with some modern puebloan groups in the Southwest. For example, in numerous Eastern Pueblos, some ceremonial, land use, and water control decisions are vested in a small group of individuals (Ortiz 1969; Ford 1968). On the other hand, increased sociopolitical integration can be horizontal, in that the increased integration does not involve hierarchical differentiation. In the Southwest this pattern involves a complex, interwoven system of sodalities, all of which are ideally required in order to form a complete social and ritual system. An example of this process is also found among the Pueblos (Dozier 1970; Eggan 1950; Ortiz 1979).

A major interest of Southwestern archeologists within the past fifteen years has been patterns and transformations of prehistoric social organization. Some of the initial studies (Longacre 1970; Hill 1970) have been criticized, and it has proved difficult to define patterns of social organization from the archeological record.

Few studies concerned with increased Mogollon social integration have been undertaken compared with studies of the Anasazi. Lightfoot and Feinman (1980) analyzed data from sites to the northwest of the Mimbres region. They tested expectations about increasing social differentiation and simple hierarchical leadership development during the Early Pithouse and Late Pithouse periods. Their analysis supports the observation that the largest sites show the greatest storage volume, most exotic goods, and most frequent presence of cultivated plants and are closest to great kivas. These characteristics, they believe, are consistent with the conclusion that simple extrahousehold leadership had developed between Mogollon villages. Because of a lack of adequate published data, their analysis did not include Rio Mimbres sites.

Kennedy (1982a) investigated the patterns of thirty-six burials from the NAN Ranch Ruin, a moderate sized Late Pithouse and Classic Mimbres site. She found that NAN Ranch burials were segregated by sex; females were buried only with ceramics, whereas males had ceramics and jewelry. Furthermore, she notes that some children were interred with large amounts of grave goods, and she suggests that this may be characteristic of ascribed status for children.

However, as Saxe (1970) and Braun (1979) point out, simple abundance of grave goods with children cannot distinguish between ascribed status and achieved status of the child's family.

These studies hint that Mogollon social structure may have involved simple hierarchical differentiation. Yet both Lightfoot and Feinman's and Kennedy's results are also consistent with a society in which there was little hereditary differentiation between social individuals or groups.

One index southwestern archaeologists use to indicate changing patterns of social interaction is the distribution of presumed ceremonial structures (kivas). Steward (1937) was one of the first to use the number and distribution of kivas to argue for changes in levels of social integration. More recent examples include Plog (1974) and Lightfoot and Feinman (1980). There are obvious problems with this, such as assuming that prehistoric kiva use was functionally and culturally equivalent to modern kiva use. Nevertheless, looking at these special purpose structures as indicators of social interaction may be useful.

Anyon and LeBlanc (1980) have summarized the distribution of communal structures in the Mimbres region. They prefer not to call these structures "kivas" because of the lack of similarities between Mogollon communal structures and Anasazi kivas. Unlike Anasazi kivas, Mogollon communal structures exhibit a lack of internal features until the later part of the Late Pithouse period. The major criterion that distinguishes communal structures from other presumably domestic structures is size. For example, during the Georgetown phase, communal structure floor area averaged 37 m^2 with a range of 34-44 m^2. In contrast, domestic pithouses averaged 17.3 m^2 with a range of 11.8-20.4 m^2. Another more subtle criterion for distinguishing domestic from communal structures is lobing of the pithouse walls on each side of the entrance. While these two indicators are less than overwhelming, they are enough, in my mind, to show that Anyon and LeBlanc's characterization of these structures as something more than simple domestic pithouses is correct.

During the Early and Late Pithouse periods these communal structures have a distinctive distribution. There appears to be only one communal structure per site. Further, there seems to be a relation between the size of the site and the size of the structure. In general, the largest, those with from 90 to 175 m^2 of floor area, are found only on large sites with more than fifty pithouses. This trend is in addition to a general increase in

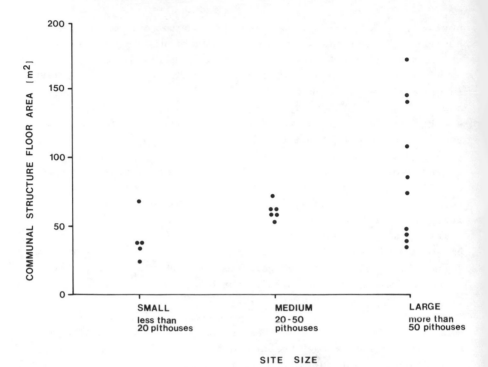

Figure 31. Relation between size of site and size of communal structures (data from Anyon and LeBlanc 1980).

floor area of these structures through time. Figure 31 shows the size distribution of communal structures from Early and Late Pit-house period sites in relation to three classes of site size.

There is a radical shift in the size and composition of communal structures during the Classic Mimbres period compared with the earlier periods. Large villagewide communal structures were no longer used during this period, although some Three Circle phase structures were used during the early part of the Classic Mimbres period. Anyon and LeBlanc isolate four possible architectural loci of ceremonial interaction: kivas, large surface rooms, walled plazas, and unwalled plazas. Classic Mimbres period kivas are subterranean structures, often remodeled pithouses, that have some features similar to those of contemporary Anasazi kivas. The kivas have about the same floor area as Classic Mimbres period surface rooms. Large surface rooms are exceedingly large. Their average floor area is 37.2 m^2, over three times as large as the average Classic Mimbres period room size of 12.2 m^2. Walled plazas are small, often with a prepared surface. Unwalled plazas are large open spaces between room blocks. The kivas and large surface rooms are so distinctive in their architecture that they are assumed to have been the loci of rituals. While Anyon and LeBlanc assume that the plazas were also used for ceremonial activity, there is no direct archeological evidence for this.

Kivas, large surface rooms, and walled plaza surfaces exhibit nonrandom distributions. Kivas appear to be associated with room blocks, either near or incorporated within the room block. Only one kiva per room block is present. The only exception is two kivas at Rock House Ruin, but these do not appear to be contemporary. Similarly, only one large surface room is present in room blocks having large surface rooms. No room blocks with kivas have large surface rooms and vice versa. Anyon and LeBlanc note that generally the larger the room block, the larger the large surface room. Few walled plazas have been excavated. Where they have been reported, they are associated with or enclosed within a room block. There is no way at present to determine the relationship between an unwalled plaza and a particular room block.

Anyon and LeBlanc suggest that Early Pithouse and Late Pithouse period communal structures in the Mimbres area involved community-wide interaction. The larger the community, the larger the structure necessary. With the advent of the Classic Mimbres period, there are substantial changes. Kivas, large surface rooms, and perhaps walled plazas were the loci of rituals in the room block, not the whole community. Communitywide ritual activity, assuming it occurred during the Classic Mimbres period, was conducted in the unwalled plazas between room blocks. Obviously, this analysis refrained from assigning specific functions to these communal structures and has avoided making comparisons with specific ethnographic practices. While we do not have an understanding of the specific symbolic/ritual system involved, Anyon and LeBlanc have documented a change in the location of the ritual system during the Classic Mimbres period.

It appears that there was a change during the Classic Mimbres period involving a hierarchical use of ritual space. Given the absence of archeological information on the use of plazas as loci of communitywide interaction, one could make the case that there was less communitywide ritual integration during the Classic Mimbres period. If Anyon and LeBlanc are correct about the use of plazas, there appears to have been a shift in the patterns of ritual integration. The apparent change to several types of ritual loci during the Classic Mimbres period may indicate an increased complexity of the ceremonial system. However, the data are too weak to make a definitive statement that there is an increased level of sociopolitical integration during the Mogollon sequence in the study area.

Exchange

There are many reasons for prehistoric exchange; one of these is to cement relationships with people who, during times of food provisioning problems, can be used as points of refuge, sources of foods, or sources of information about regional food availability. As discussed in chapter 2, intensification of exchange is a common ethnographically documented response to food shortages. The Fringe Enga and Gwembe Tonga are but two examples of this pattern. Therefore, it is expected that an increase in the exchange of goods might correlate with an increased vulnerability to subsistence failure. While it would be ideal to have an understanding of the particular mechanisms of exchange, the documentation of transfer of goods from one group to another illustrates that interaction has occurred. In nonmarket economies, where a primary function of exchange is to strengthen alliance (Mauss 1967), the documentation of the transfer of goods can be used to infer the creation and maintenance of some form of relationship between social units.

Exchange can be viewed in two ways. First, one can consider the organization of material culture production, particularly any evidence of economic specialization that is a priori evidence of exchange. Second, one can analyze artifact categories that seem to have been exchanged. Evidence of the latter appears in the form of goods that are not locally available and which had to have been imported through some mechanism or in the distribution of artifact types that may indicate patterns of local exchange in goods locally available. Both of these approaches will be discussed in this chapter.

Little can be said about economic specialization in the study area, simply because there is little evidence of specialization now available for the Mimbres region. LeBlanc (1977) suggests that the most sophisticated Classic Mimbres Black-on-White ceramics (about 20 percent of the total) were of such artistic sophistication that they probably were produced by at least part time specialists who traded their wares for other goods or services. Unfortunately, pattern recognition studies have not been done that can independently confirm this suggestion. The presence of pottery workshops, for example, might suggest craft specialization in ceramic manufacture, but none have been located in the study area. The lack of evidence of economic specialization in ceramics is mirrored for other goods. For example, there are no workshops or craft manufacturing tool kits that might indicate specialization. A possible exception is an assemblage of grave goods from a burial on the Swarts Ruin. With a male burial Cosgrove and Cosgrove (1932:63) recovered a cache of stone beads in various stages of manufacture. About thirty pieces of raw material and several hundred partially completed or finished beads were in this burial. Another possible exception to the lack of evidence for specialization was from the Mattocks site. Nesbitt (1931) reported finding several caches of "hoes," long tapered stone artifacts, but it is not clear that these are indeed "hoes" or that the caches indicate specialization.

These examples are hardly convincing evidence of anything more than a possibility of minimal economic specialization in the study area, and they pale in comparison with clear examples of specialization from the Southwest such as at Casas Grandes (DiPeso 1974), Snaketown (Haury 1976), and Pueblo Bonito (Pepper 1920; Judd 1954). Therefore, we have to look at the broad distribution of goods for evidence of exchange in the study area.

Many types of artifacts will be considered for evidence of exchange involving the prehistoric inhabitants of the study area. Artifacts recovered by the Mimbres Foundation will be emphasized, since these data are from the largest number of sites in the study area. Earlier artifact assemblages, such as those from Harris Village, Cameron Creek, Swarts Ruin, and Nesbitt's excavation on the Mattocks site were collected without benefit of screening, so that fragile items, small materials, or low density artifacts are underrepresented. Preliminary analysis of artifacts for the NAN Ranch Ruin excavated by Texas A&M University are considered here.

Artifacts of exchange will be considered under three categories: extraregional, interregional, and intraregional exchange. Extraregional exchange concerns goods that may have originated outside of the American Southwest. Interregional exchange concerns goods originating within the American Southwest, and intraregional exchange involves artifacts originating and being traded within the Rio Mimbres region. The boundaries between these three categories are rather imprecise but will be made more specific in regard to the specific kinds of artifacts considered.

Another level of exchange, intrasite exchange, will not be discussed here because we lack detailed intrasite analyses for the Mogollon remains in the study area, for two reasons. First, heavy vandalism at most sites excavated has distorted much intrasite patterning. Second, the overall research design of the Mimbres Foundation stresses a regional perspective, so less effort has been directed toward understanding intrasite patterning.

Extraregional Exchange

For many decades southwestern archeologists have recognized that many goods circulated within the Southwest originated outside the area. Some archeologists (e.g., C. C. DiPeso and J. C. Kelly) have gone so far as to suggest that the culture history of the Southwest is a direct reflection of changes in trading patterns originating in Mesoamerica, an interpretation with which I do not agree. While it is clear that some Mexican goods are present in the Southwest, the mechanisms involved in the acquisition of these goods and the effect of this interaction on the cultural processes of the Southwest are not clear (McGuire 1980) Three classes of artifacts, macaws, copper bells, and shell remains, will be considered here as evidence of extraregional exchange.

Macaws

Macaws are one of the most interesting items of extraregional exchange recovered from southwestern sites. Hargrave (1970) inventoried all known remains of macaws from southwestern sites. Of the 145 examples, only one was a military macaw, and 100 were scarlet macaws. The remaining 44 could not be identified as to species. Military macaws extend as far north as southern Arizona. On the basis of age distribution analysis of southwestern macaw remains, Hargrave suggested that southwestern macaws were not a breeding population but rather were young birds transported into the Southwest from somewhere in Mexico. DiPeso (1974) reports the presence of nesting cages, over three hundred macaw skeleton, and macaw eggs at Casas Grandes, indicating that macaws were bred as far north as this site.

The few macaws from the Mimbres region cannot be taken as evidence of an extensive trade in macaws. Those macaws present, however, are restricted to Classic Mimbres period sites; no macaws from earlier contexts have been reported from the study area. Table 17 lists the occurrence of macaws from sites in southwestern New Mexico.

Table 17

Macaw Remains from Sites in the Mimbres Region

Site	Number of Macaws	Time Period
Cameron Creek[a]	2	Classic Mimbres
Galaz	4	Classic Mimbres

Source: Data from Hargrave (1970).
a. Cameron Creek is outside the immediate Mimbres Foundation study area.

Copper Bells

Another item of extraregional exchange found in southwestern sites is copper bells (Jernigan 1978). Sprague and Signori (1963) cataloged 450 copper bells from sixty-two sites in the Southwest. There is currently no evidence for the manufacture of these bells in the American Southwest. Copper goods were manufactured at Casas Grandes, but this probably postdated the Classic Mimbres period (LeBlanc 1980c). On grounds of artifact morphology, they appear to be of Mexican origin (Pendergast 1962). These bells represent only a small fraction of the types of prehistoric Mexican copper artifacts. The small size of these bells undoubtedly contributed to ease of distribution into the Southwest. The lack of evidence of indigenous southwestern coppersmithing is ironic given that veins of native copper are found in the Southwest, including the area just west of the Rio Mimbres drainage around Santa Rita, New Mexico.

The greatest concentration of southwestern copper bells is from Hohokam sites and Casas Grandes. DiPeso (1974) documented the

Table 18

Copper Bells from the Mimbres Region

Site	Number of Bells	Time Period
Cameron Creek	7	Classic Mimbres
Galaz	5	Classic Mimbres
Mattocks	1	Classic Mimbres
Old Town	1	Probably Classic Mimbres
Osborn	11	Probably Classic Mimbres
NAN Ranch	1	Classic Mimbres

fabrication of copper items at Casas Grandes. In light of the great number of Anasazi and northern Mogollon sites excavated, it is clear that a comparatively small number of copper bells were circulated in these areas.

No copper bells have been recorded by the Mimbres Foundation, but twenty-six have been found at sites in the Mimbres region (listed in Sprague and Signori 1963). In addition, Kennedy (1982b) reports that one copper bell was recovered from the NAN Ranch Ruin. These are listed in table 18. All are from Classic Mimbres period contexts. No copper bells have been reported from Late Pithouse period sites in the study area, although a large number of Late Pithouse period sites have been excavated. Similarly, none have been recovered from Early Pithouse period sites. However, few Early Pithouse period sites have been excavated in the area. The lack of Animas period copper bells is interesting in light of the copper artifacts recovered from the contemporary site of Casas Grandes (DiPeso 1974). No copper bells were found in Salado sites in the study area.

The distribution of copper bells in the study area is clear; they are restricted to Classic Mimbres period sites. Except for the Early Pithouse period, this distribution cannot be a result of sampling bias, since many sites of other time periods have been excavated.

Shell Remains

Shell artifacts are the last item of extraregional exchange to be considered. Numerous pieces of marine and freshwater mollusks

Table 19

Taxa of Shell Artifacts Recovered by the Mimbres Foundation

Taxon	Origin[a]	Number of Identifications[b]	Percentage of Total
Aeguipecten circularis	G	2	0.7
Andonta californiensis	F	8	2.7
Columbella major	G	23	7.8
Conus sp.	G	3	1.0
Conus perplexus	G	1	0.3
Glycymeris sp.	G	113	38.3
Haliotis sp.	P	1	0.3
Haliotis fulgens	P	1	0.3
Laevicardium elatum	G/P	2	0.7
Oliva sp.	G	1	0.3
Olivella sp.	G	38	12.9
Oreohelix sp.	T	4	1.4
Pecten sp.	G	2	0.7
Spondylus califer	G	93	31.5
Spondylus princeps	G	2	0.7
Vermitidae	G	1	0.3

a. G = Gulf of California; P = Pacific coast; F = freshwater; T = terrestrial.
b. Only 42 percent of shell artifacts have been identified.

were used in the Southwest for beads, pendants, and other ornamental items. Unlike the other two items of extraregional exchange considered here, large amounts of shell have been recovered by the Mimbres Foundation. Sharon Urban (University of Arizona) has identified 708 individual shell artifacts from Mimbres Foundation excavations. Seventeen shell taxa were identified, and these are listed in table 19. All but three taxa are marine shells. Anodontia californiensis is a freshwater mollusk found in the Rio Mimbres drainage. The genus Oreohelix is composed of land snails found in the Southwest, including the Rio Mimbres area. Except for Haliotis and Laevicardium elatum shells, all come from the Gulf of California. Haliotis is from the Pacific coast, and Laevicardium elatum is found on both the Pacific coast and the Gulf of California.

Evidence suggests that finished goods, primarily beads and pendants, were imported into the Mimbres area. It does not appear that a significant amount of shell manufacture was carried out by

prehistoric Mimbreños. Of the 708 shells identified, fewer that
1 percent (7 pieces) were raw material. The rest were finished
goods. Also, only 4 percent of the identified shells were from
locally available resources. This also suggests that local shell
manufacture was not a significant source of shell goods used by
prehistoric occupants of the Mimbres area.

Where these finished goods were manufactured is not known.
They may have been obtained from their points of origin along the
coast. Another option is they were obtained from other groups away
from the coasts that manufactured the beads and bracelets. Haury
(1976) convincingly argues that shell fabrication was practiced at
the Hohokam site of Snaketown. Whether the inhabitants of the Rio
Mimbres region obtained their shell from the Hohokam is uncertain.

Unlike copper bells and macaws, shell artifacts have been
recovered from all prehistoric time periods under consideration.
Table 20 summarizes the shell remains recovered from the Mimbres
Foundation. Only shell from excavated sites is included in this
tabulation, and shell from excavation units of uncertain temporal
placement is excluded. Unfortunately, the shell from the Disert
(Salado) and Montoya (Animas) sites has yet to be identified.

As can be seen in table 20 and figure 32, few shell pieces were
recovered from Classic Mimbres and Salado period sites. Single
proveniences with a great number of shell goods bias the Animas
period and Late Pithouse period samples. Nevertheless, all Late
Pithouse period sites have a slightly greater number of shell goods
than the Classic Mimbres period sites.

Interregional Exchange

In all likelihood, numerous goods were exchanged between prehistoric groups within the Southwest. In fact, the most recent
models of Anasazi prehistory, particularly those concerned with the
Chacoan phenomenon, focus on the development of complex interregional exchange (e.g., Marshall et al. 1979; Judge et al. 1981).
It is difficult to detect patterns of interregional exchange,
primarily because sufficiently sophisticated methods have not been
used to determine the source of exchanged goods or manufacture
points.

For this reason only one artifact category, ceramics, will be
discussed under the topic of interregional exchange. Other arti-

Table 20

Shell Remains from Mimbres Foundation Excavations

Site by Time Period	Number of Shell Artifacts	Number of Excavated Rooms	Shell Pieces per Room
Early Pithouse			
Z:5:35	3	0.75	4.0
Late Pithouse			
LA 636	202	11.0	18.5
Z:1:27	4	0.75	5.3
Z:14:6	781	1.0 (?)	781.0
Classic Mimbres			
LA 676	46	17.0	2.7
Y:4:35	7	4.0	1.8
LA 12076	9	6.0	1.5
Z:14:3	1	0.5 (?)	2.0
Animas			
Z:5:80	341	4.0	85.3
Salado			
LA 12077	6	6.0	1.0
Z:1:78	3	2.0	1.5

facts (cotton, turquoise, obsidian) that are often considered by southwestern archeologists as artifacts of interregional exchange will be discussed as intraregional exchange, since we cannot be certain that they did not originate within the Rio Mimbres region.

Ceramics

Southwestern archeologists once simply characterized pottery as either indigenous, locally made wares, or tradewares, exotic pottery whose presumed center of manufacture was far enough removed from an excavated site or region to suggest that these wares were somehow traded. It is beginning to be recognized that this simple distinction glosses over a great deal of variation in the exchange of ceramics (Plog 1980).

The pottery of the Late Pithouse and Classic Mimbres periods in the study area is an excellent data base for investigating exchange

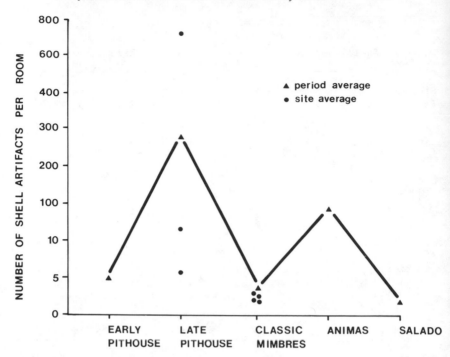

Figure 32. Distribution of shell artifacts from Mimbres Foundation excavations (data from Stailey, n.d.).

in ceramics.   The painted wares of these two time periods are very distinctive.   The painted ware tradition is characterized during the later part of the Late Pithouse period by Boldface Black-on-White.   There is a recently described intermediate type, Transitional Black-on-White.

Mimbres Black-on-White pottery has an interesting distribution. Very few Mimbres Black-on-White sherds have been found outside the Rio Mimbres region (Gilman 1980). For example, only eight Classic Mimbres Black-on-White sherds were recovered from Snaketown (Haury 1976;figure 16.3).   In contrast fifty-six Boldface Black-on-White sherds, eleven Mogollon Red-on-Brown sherds, and three Three Circle Red-on-White sherds were found at this site.   Given the distinctive style of Classic Mimbres Black-on-White pottery, it is unlikely that this distribution is a result of misidentification or sampling problems.   In addition, Classic Mimbres Black-on-White pottery has been recovered from San Cayetano del Tumacacori in southeastern Arizona (DiPeso 1956) and the Forked Lightning site near Pecos, New Mexico (Breternitz 1966).

Two areas adjacent to the Mimbres region regularly obtained Mimbres wares. While not abundant, Mimbres Black-on-White pottery is found in sites to the north and northwest of the Mimbres region. Martin and Rinaldo (1950) found sixty-five Mimbres Black-on-White sherds from three Reserve phase pueblos in the Pine Lawn Valley. These amount to only 0.5 percent of the total sherds from these sites. Farther to the northwest, in the Point of Pines region 180 km from the Rio Mimbres Valley, Breternitz (1959) recovered 701 Mimbres Black-on-White sherds. These represent only 1 percent of the total sherd assemblage. However, they are 20.5 percent of the painted wares present on the site. Of this number, Classic Mimbres Black-on-White are only 25 percent and Boldface Black-on-White are 74 percent of the Mimbres pottery. The prevalence of Boldface sherds and the small number of Classic Mimbres Black-on-White sherds on sites outside the Rio Mimbres region is a common pattern (P. Gilman, personal communication, 1980).

The second area outside of the Mimbres region where Mimbres sherds are fairly common is the Jornada region east of the Rio Grande (Lehmer 1948). Whalen (1980:381) concludes that, "Mimbres Black-on-White ceramics are the only nonlocal wares commonly found on late Jornada pithouse sites, although absolute frequencies of Mimbres pottery are never very great." Whalen also notes a lack of Mimbres wares during the Puebloan period in the Jornada region. This may be because exchange networks changed or because much of this period is later that the Classic Mimbres period.

Very few nonindigenous wares have been found on Classic Mimbres period sites. One potential exception is pottery that has Classic Mimbres designs but appears to have a construction similar to that of the Reserve area pottery (Gilman 1980). These may be simply a variation of Classic Mimbres wares. Some obvious tradewares that have been found on Classic Mimbres period sites now appear to be from very late or post-Classic contexts (Gilman 1980; R. Anyon, personal communication, 1979). Animas period ceramics, such as El Paso Polychrome, St. Johns Polychrome, Chupadero Black-on-White, Gila Polychrome, Playas Red, and a variety of Chihuahua Polychromes, are the most common types recovered from post-Classic components of primarily Classic Mimbres period sites. Taylor (1982) indicates that fewer than 1 percent of the NAN Ranch Ruin sherds were "tradewares." As with the lack of Classic Mimbres period tradewares on non-Mimbres sites, there are very few nonlocal ceramics on Classic Mimbres sites. Therefore, it appears that there was very minimal exchange of painted wares between Classic

Mimbres period groups and other contemporary groups in the Southwest.

The situation is not clear for plain and corrugated pottery. These ceramics are rarely analyzed in as great detail as painted wares. Later in this chapter I will discuss the circulation of corrugated wares as intraregional exchange.

Nonindigenous ceramics are rare on Late Pithouse period sites. Haury (1936) noted that fewer than 1 percent of the sherds from Harris Village were nonlocal. Lino Black-on-Gray, Red Mesa Black-on-White, and Kiatuthlanna Black-on-White are the tradeware types found at Harris Village. They originated to the north of the Mimbres region. About the same percentage of nonlocal wares as reported by Haury has been recovered from Late Pithouse period sites excavated by the Mimbres Foundation (R. Anyon, personal communication, 1980).

No other artifact categories indicative of interregional exchange have been analyzed. Some possible interregional exchange artifacts are more appropriately discussed under the category of intraregional exchange. Although this has not been a rigorous quantitative study of interregional exchange in ceramics, it leads to the conclusion that few Classic Mimbres period ceramics were circulating outside the Rio Mimbres region. Although not many, a greater number of Late Pithouse period wares were exchanged outside the study area. Very few nonlocal sherds have been recovered from either Late Pithouse or Classic Mimbres period sites, and no difference is noted between these two periods in regard to the amount of nonlocal ceramics present. Therefore, there seems to be a decrease in the exchange of ceramics from the Late Pithouse period to the Classic Mimbres period. Because Early Pithouse period pottery cannot be differentiated by location of manufacture, little can be said about the movement of Early Pithouse period ceramics.

Intraregional Exchange

Five artifact categories (turquoise, copper minerals, ceramics, obsidian, and plant materials) will be considered with regard to their exchange within the Rio Mimbres region itself or in areas immediately adjacent to the study area. There are sources for these goods within the study area. In some cases, particularly with turquoise and obsidian, we cannot be certain that these remains did not originate outside the study area. Because of this ambiguity, it is best to be conservative and to assume that they originated within the region.

Turquoise

Turquoise artifacts are common in southwestern sites and generally are considered trade items. Recent evidence suggests that southwestern turquoise was circulating widely within the Southwest and perhaps outside the Southwest into Mesoamerica (Weigand, Harbottle, and Sayre 1977; Sigleo 1975). Turquoise sources are found just west of the Mimbres region around Santa Rita, New Mexico, and the Burro Mountains. No analysis has been completed on the sources of the turquoise recovered by the Mimbres Foundation; it will be assumed that most was derived from the region and not through longer distance exchange.

Turquoise artifacts, usually beads or pendants, are common in the Mimbres region. Few pieces of raw material or partially worked turquoise items have been recovered. Of the 311 turquoise pieces from sites excavated by the Mimbres Foundation, only 7 percent (22 pieces) are raw material. Kennedy (1982b) enumerates the few turquoise artifacts recovered during the excavation of the NAN Ranch Ruin. These include 9 beads (out of 6,979 beads recovered), 10 pendants (out of 26 total pendants), and 116.7 g of turquoise "raw material" (most of which was unworkable for jewelry manufacture). Near the study area is a small Classic Mimbres period "shrine" at the West Baker site in Hidalgo County, New Mexico (McCluney 1968). Here 3,329 pieces of turquoise were recovered, of which 86 percent were blanks or "waste turquoise." This site is close to the Burro Mountain turquoise sites, but we do not have direct evidence for the source of the West Baker site turquoise. With this one exception, the general lack of residue of turquoise working suggests that the Mimbres area was not a center of turquoise crafting, as Chaco Canyon may have been (Snow 1973).

Stailey (n.d.) tabulates the turquoise recovered from sites excavated by the Mimbres Foundation. Table 21 presents a site-by-site summary of this turquoise, and table 22 gives the average number of turquoise pieces per room for the five time periods. The greatest number of turquoise pieces comes from the Late Pithouse period. An average of a little over 12 pieces of turquoise was found for each Late Pithouse period pithouse excavated. This compares with only 1.6 pieces per room from the Classic Mimbres

Table 21

Turquoise from Mimbres Foundation Excavations

Site by Time Period	Number of Pieces	Number of Excavated Rooms	Number of Pieces per Room
Early Pithouse			
Z:5:35	0	0.75	0.0
LA 12110	0	1.75	0.0
Late Pithouse			
LA 635	201	11.0	18.3
LA 676	0	3.0	0.0
Z:1:30	0	2.0	0.0
Z:1:27	1	0.75	1.3
Classic Mimbres			
Y:4:35	2	4.0	0.5
LA 12076	3	6.0	0.5
LA 676	31	17.0	1.8
Z:1:46	17	6.5	2.6
LA 12109	0	3.0	0.0
Z:1:126	0	1.0	0.0
Animas			
Z:5:112	15	2.0	7.5
Z:5:80	35	4.0	8.8
Salado			
Z:1:78	1	2.0	0.5
LA 12077	3	6.0	0.5
Z:5:10	2	5.5	0.5

Source: Data from Stailey (n.d.).

period. However, these data are skewed by the fact that of the 202 pieces of Late Pithouse period turquoise 117 (57 percent) were recovered from a single burial on the Galaz site (R. Anyon, personal communication, 1980).

If we look at the distribution of turquoise by site, a difference between the Late Pithouse period and Classic Mimbres period is apparent. Almost all of the Late Pithouse period turquoise is from a single site, the Galaz site. In contrast, turquoise is found in most Classic Mimbres period sites. One of the two Classic Mimbres period sites lacking turquoise is LA 12109, a very small,

Table 22

Average Number of Turquoise Pieces per Room

Time Period	Average Number of Pieces per Room
Early Pithouse	0.0
Late Pithouse	12.1
Classic Mimbres	1.6
Animas	8.3
Salado	0.4

Source: Data from Stailey (n.d.).

special activity site (Nelson, Rugge, and LeBlanc 1978). Superficially, it appears from the Mimbres Foundation data that more turquoise was present during the Late Pithouse period than during the Classic Mimbres period. However, the distribution of turquoise is more even during the Classic Mimbres period, suggesting that the exchange in turquoise was more widespread than during the Late Pithouse period. Turquoise is lacking from Early Pithouse period sites. The proportionally large amount of turquoise found and its even distribution during the Animas period may be indicative of a greater degree of exchange in turquoise during this time. This analysis contrasts with Snow's (1973) conclusion that in the Mimbres region there is an increase during the Classic Mimbres period.

Unfortunately, evidence from other excavated sites in the study area does not help us understand the pattern of turquoise exchange. This is because primary data by provenience are not given in the early reports. Bradfield (1929) mentions that turquoise goods were present throughout the occupation of Cameron Creek but does not give a tabulation of the turquoise by provenience. Haury (1936) reports recovering only four pieces of turquoise from Harris Village, and two of these were surface finds. Cosgrove and Cosgrove (1932) do not tabulate their turquoise artifacts from the Swarts Ruin, but they state that turquoise beads were not particularly common, and only forty-three turquoise pendants were found. While these early data cannot be used quantitatively, they do not conflict in a general sense with the pattern of turquoise recovered by the Mimbres Foundation.

Copper Minerals

Copper minerals are another category of artifacts recovered from sites in the Mimbres region that occur in the study area. This category includes mostly chrysocolla, with some azurite and malachite. As for turquoise, the closest sources of these three minerals are in the Santa Rita area and to a lesser extent in the Burro Mountains and the Pinos Altos region, northwest of the study area. Stailey (n.d.) compiles a list by weight of copper minerals recovered from sites excavated by the Mimbres Foundation, and this information is presented in table 23. These weights are corrected for the differential degree of site excavation. The standard of comparison used is the average weight of copper minerals per "room." The unusually high average for Z:1:30 is due to the recovery of a burial vessel filled with chrysocolla. Like so many other categories used here, there is no clear-cut pattern in amount of copper minerals recovered per time period. Generally, Late Pithouse period sites tend to have a greater average abundance of copper minerals than Classic Mimbres period sites. However, there is a great deal of overlap in the averages for these two periods.

Obsidian

Obsidian is found in southwestern New Mexico. The closest sources of consequence to the study area are to the southwest at Antelope Wells, in the Mule Creek and U Canyon sources northwest of the study area, and in the Hueco area near El Paso. All four sources were used by prehistoric occupants of the Rio Mimbres area, but we do not have a sufficient sample of sourced-identified obsidian artifacts to determine more specific patterns of source use. Therefore, obsidian is considered an object of intraregional exchange. Stailey (n.d.) has compiled data on the percentage of chipped stone that is obsidian. Table 24 presents these data for the sites excavated by the Mimbres Foundation. With the exception of Z:1:30 and LA 676 (Late Pithouse period), it is clear that for all periods obsidian represents a small percentage of the material used for chipped stone artifacts. The chipped stone samples from

Table 23

Copper Minerals from Mimbres Foundation Excavations

Site by Time Period	Weight of Copper (g)	Number of Excavated Rooms	Average Weight per Room (g)
Early Pithouse			
Z:5:35	0.0	0.75	0.0
LA 12110	23.1	1.75	13.2
Late Pithouse			
Y:4:35	161.7	2.0	80.9
LA 635	146.9	11.0	15.4
LA 676	12.1	2.0	6.1
Z:1:46	30.3	3.5	8.7
Z:1:30	860.0	2.0	430.4
Z:1:27	17.7	0.75	23.6
Classic Mimbres			
Y:4:35	381.4	4.0	95.4
LA 635	12.1	2.0	6.1
LA 676	271.9	17.0	12.8
LA 12076	37.5	6.0	6.3
Z:1:46	67.3	6.5	10.4
Z:1:30	40.0	9.0	4.4
Z:1:126	1.5	1.0	1.5
Animas			
Z:5:112	74.1	2.0	37.1
Z:5:80	8.7	4.0	2.2
Salado			
Z:1:78	11.1	2.0	5.9
LA 12077	21.2	6.0	3.5
Z:5:10	180.2	5.5	32.8

Source: Data from Stailey (n.d.), excluding turquoise.

these two sites are very small (about thirty artifacts), and they will be disregarded in this analysis. There is an increase in the use of obsidian through the Mogollon sequence in the study area. The average percentage of obsidian chipped stone for the Early Pithouse is 0.06, for the Late Pithouse period it is 1.2, and for the Classic Mimbres period it is 2.0. The percentage of Late Pithouse period obsidian is twenty times that of the Early Pithouse period, and the average for the Classic Mimbres period is 1.7 times times that of the Late Pithouse period.

Table 24

Obsidian as a Percentage of Lithics
from Mimbres Foundation Excavations

Site by Time Period	Percentage of Lithics That are Obsidian	Average for Time Period
Early Pithouse		
Z:5:35	0.1	0.06
LA 12110	0.01	
Late Pithouse		
LA 635	1.1	1.2[a]
LA 676	19.4	
Z:1:27	1.0	
Z:1:30	56.3	
Z:1:46	1.4	
Classic Mimbres		
LA 635	1.5	2.0
LA 676	1.2	
Z:1:30	4.8	
Z:1:46	1.4	
LA 12076	2.0	
LA 12109	0.03	
Y:4:35	2.4	
Z:1:126	2.3	
Animas		
Z:5:42	1.8	1.5
Z:5:80	1.4	
Z:5:112	1.3	
Salado		
Z:1:78	3.7	2.3
Z:5:10	1.8	
LA 12077	1.3	

a. This average excludes LA 676 and Z:1:30.

Ceramics

As Plog (1980) suggests, there was probably a great deal of intraregional ceramic exchange in the Southwest. However, the smaller the region, the more difficult it is to detect patterns of pottery exchange. The Rio Mimbres area is probably a better location than most to detect intraregional exchange in ceramics

because of the large, well known sample of Classic Black-on-White
ware. The Maxwell Museum and the Mimbres Foundation have begun an
archive of all known Mimbres Black-on-White pottery. This project
is not yet complete, so that only preliminary studies of Mimbres
pottery have been undertaken. Two such studies shed some tentative
light on the possible exchange of Mimbres ceramics. The first, by
Dale Rugge (1975), was a petrographic examination of corrugated
wares. The second, by Catherine LeBlanc (1977), dealt with a
subset of Classic Mimbres Black-on-White pottery, the naturalistic
bowls.

Using petrographic techniques, Rugge analyzed the temper of
Classic Mimbres period pottery. An initial sample of 108 thin
sections from corrugated and painted pottery revealed that two
types of temper were used. All painted ware temper was from
volcanic sources. Two types of temper were used in corrugated
vessels, volcanic rock and plutonic material. These categories
were mutually exclusive in that they were never mixed in a single
sherd. On the basis of geological knowledge of the Rio Mimbres
region and mineralogical analysis of the plutonic temper, Rugge
determined that the sources of plutonic temper were outcrops of
Precambrian granites and granite gneiss in the Cook's Range, the
southeastern section of the Rio Mimbres Valley. After examining
the mineral composition of stream samples taken nearest the temper
sources and the morphology of the temper, it was found that the
granitic temper was being procured at the outcrop and was then
crushed.

To gain understanding of the distribution of pottery with
granitic temper, Rugge analyzed 170 rim sherds from large corrugated ollas. Samples from eight sites at various distances from
the sources were analyzed by viewing polished cross sections and/or
thin sections of sherds. Rugge found a decrease in the percentage
of sherds from sites farther from the sources. The correlation
between distance from the site to the source and the percentage of
site sherds with granitic temper was .69. Modifying the distance
to make it the easiest walk from the site to the granite source,
the correlation increased to .81. Several explanations could account for this pattern. On one hand, potters from all of the sites
could have been traveling to the outcrop and procuring the raw
material for the temper. Alternatively, occupants of sites farther
from the source may have been obtaining the temper as part of an
exchange system. The temper, the pots, or the contents of the pots
may have been the object of exchange. Rugge suggests that if the

first explanation is correct, then there should be a very rapid decrease in the percentage of granitic temper once the cost of procuring it outweighted the benefit.   Rugge does not see the dropoff as sharp but rather envisions a steady decline in the percentage of granitic temper the further the site is from the source (figure 33).   He rejects the first explanation and posits that the presence of ollas with granitic temper is a function of some type of exchange pattern.   The exchange mechanisms involved are not known.   Rugge's petrographic study presents a reasonable case for the exchange of a temper type, pottery, or the contents of the pottery within the study area.

Catherine LeBlanc (1977) conducted a pilot study of Mimbres Black-on-White naturalistic bowls, vessels with either a human or

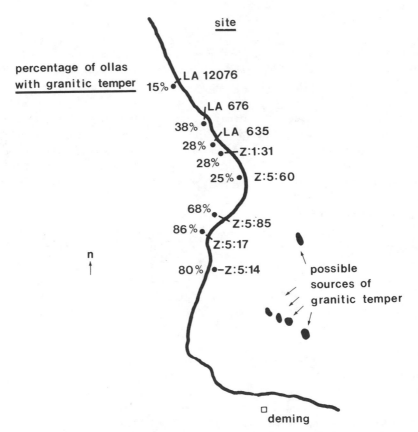

Figure 33.   Percentage of ollas with granitic temper for sites in the Mimbres Foundation study area (after Rugge 1975).

an animal figure.   She estimates that during the Classic Mimbres period about one-third of the painted bowls were naturalistic. This is an increased percentage from earlier Boldface Black-on-White and Transitional Black-on-White.   Using the archive of Mimbres pottery, she selected six sites that had a large sample of naturalistic bowls, a total of 422 pots.   Of fifteen motif types, nine clustered significantly; for example, the bighorn sheep bowls clustered at the Swarts Ruin, and the horny toad motif predominated at the Baca site.   Computing Robinson-Brainerd coefficients of similarity for all site combinations and comparing these with the distances between sites, LeBlanc found that in four of the six sites distance and similarity were inversely related.   This may be an indication of the movement of pots with specific motifs through an exchange network.   Obviously, other factors could account for this patterning, and more detailed studies of Mimbres painted wares are under way.

These two studies of Classic Mimbres period ceramics suggest that there was a pronounced exchange in pottery in the Rio Mimbres area during the Classic Mimbres period.   We do not have as good comparisons for the Late Pithouse, Animas, and Salado periods. Rugge did examine Late Pithouse period neck-banded ollas and found that they were all made with sand temper.

Plant Materials

Given the economic patterns discussed in the previous chapter, it is expected that there would have been a substantial exchange in plant foods in the valley during the Classic Mimbres period.   Unfortunately, it is very difficult to detect patterns of food exchange, for most plant food resources would have been available within the catchment territory of each community.   One possible exception is mesquite, which is most abundant at the lower end of the valley and is quite rare in the upper part of the Rio Mimbres drainage.   A single mesquite seed was recovered from the Mitchell site (LA 12076), which is at the northern end of the valley.   However, at present and perhaps prehistorically, little mesquite grows on south-facing slopes in the upper valley.   Therefore, one cannot eliminate the possibility that mesquite was present within the immediate vicinity of the Mitchell site.

Another potential plant resource that may have been traded within the valley is cotton.   Cotton requires a long and hot

growing season.   Charred cotton cloth has been recovered from the
Mattocks site, but in contrast, cotton seeds, which may be an
indicator of cotton cultivation, have not been recovered from
Classic Mimbres period sites further north than the Swarts Ruin,
from which V. Bohrer identified thirty-three charred cotton seeds
(Peabody Museum of Harvard, catalog number 95752).   These are
probably from the Classic Mimbres period occupation, although they
could be from the Late Pithouse or post-Classic occupations of the
site.   I have identified cotton seeds recovered from a bulldozed
Classic Mimbres period site near Deming.   Therefore, it is
conceivable that cotton was being grown in the more southerly
segment of the valley and traded to the more northerly sites.
However, the cultivation requirements of native cottons in the
Southwest are not well understood, and cotton was grown in areas
previously thought to have been outside their potential range of
cultivation.   Therefore, it is not certain that the area around the
Mattocks site was unsuitable for cotton cultivation.

Summary

Two possible sets of responses--degree of social integration
and exchange--were examined in this chapter.   In line with the
model presented in chapter 2, we would expect to see the increased
use of more inclusive responses during the Classic Mimbres period.
    In terms of social integration, it appears from Anyon and
LeBlanc's (1980) work that there was a definite change in the
spatial organization of the Classic Mimbres period ritual system.
We cannot say if this change involved increasingly inclusive levels
of ritual integration.   Research with non-Mimbres Mogollon data may
indicate that simple hierarchical differentiation may have occurred
during the Early and Late Pithouse periods, a research topic not
rigorously considered with Mimbres Foundation data.
    The patterns are not obvious in regard to exchange from the
Late Pithouse period to the Classic Mimbres period.   Of nine artifact categories examined in this chapter, five indicated increased
exchange, three noted a decrease, and one could not be used to
detect any pattern changes.   Whatever changes in exchange occurred
from the Late Pithouse period to the Classic Mimbres period, they
are not obvious.   Considering the artifacts as evidence of exchange
either within the Rio Mimbres region or involving peoples outside
the study area, there did seem to be a change in the pattern of

Table 25

Evidence of Changes in Exchange during the Mogollon Sequence

Artifact Category	Early Pithouse to Late Pithouse	Late Pithouse to Classic Mimbres
Macaws[a]	0	X
Copper bells[a]	0	X
Shell[a]	X	−
Ceramics[a]	0	−
Turquoise	X	X[b]
Copper minerals	X	−[b]
Ceramics	0	X
Obsidian	X	X
Plant resources	0	0

Note: 0 = no change; X = increased exchange; − = decreased change.
a. Boldface indicates extraregional exchange.
b. Very weak data base.

exchange from the Late Pithouse period to the Classic Mimbres period (see table 25). As weak as the evidence is, it suggested that during the Classic Mimbres period there was an increase in intraregional exchange and perhaps a decrease in the intensity of exchange with peoples outside the Rio Mimbres area. Turquoise, obsidian, and particularly ceramics were evidence of this. Contrasted with this interpretation is the fact that two items of extraregional exchange, macaws and copper bells, are found only during the Classic Mimbres period. However, even combined, these two artifact categories amount to only a few items, and as such they may not indicate an extensive trade in these goods. Furthermore, it is not know if these goods were available as exchange objects before A.D. 1000. LeBlanc (1983) suggests that these changes indicate a shift in Mimbres exchange from the Hohokam region to northern Mexico.

Partitioning exchange on the basis of only the origin of the traded goods is too simple.   Different goods may have been exchanged via different sociological mechanisms.   If incipient rank differences between individuals existed during the Classic Mimbres period, some goods (quite likely items such as macaws and copper) may have flowed along lines of inequality, whereas other goods were exchanged among a wider range of Classic Mimbreño society.   Similar processes may have occurred even if Mimbres society was egalitarian; ritually significant items probably had a much different mode of exchange than largely utilitarian goods.   Unfortunately, we do not have an adequate understanding of the sociopolitical context of exchange for the study area.

These changes in the patterns of exchange from the Late Pithouse period to the Classic Mimbres period are consistent with expectations of the model.   The Classic Mimbres period system did not survive, although some of the Classic Mimbreños undoubtedly did.   Viewed in this light, it appears that under conditions of significantly greater risk of food stress with a possible contraction of response inclusivity, Classic Mimbres society was unable to cope with these problems.

Although bordering on being a circular argument, this chapter suggests that the adaptive behaviors of the Classic Mimbres period population did not let them cope successfully with the food provisioning problems they faced.   Unfortunately there is no way, and it is not likely that a way will be found, to estimate the resilience (the ability of a system to restore itself after a perturbation) of any cultural system.   In other words, we do not have an independent method for understanding what problem threshold it takes to cause systemic change.   Even in more easily modeled biological systems there are no widely accepted measures of ecosystem resilience or inertia (Westman 1978).   Without such a measure, it is impossible to predict what perturbation magnitudes will trigger various response levels.

Another explanation is possible for the apparent lack of more inclusive responses during the Classic Mimbres period.   As I mentioned at the beginning of this chapter, the Classic Mimbres period excavations by the Mimbres Foundation covered the entire period.   The analyses in chapter 5 indicated that the first part of the Classic Mimbres period was an unusually favorable time for agriculture.   It is quite probable that the substantial population increase during the Classic Mimbres period occurred during this time.   If this is correct, then the collection of Classic Mimbres artifacts discussed in this chapter may well overrepresent the favorable early Classic Mimbres period when we would not necessarily expect more inclusive responses to have occurred.   However, that very few Classic Mimbres period ceramics have been recovered from outside the Mimbres region (assuming that both early and late Classic Mimbres period ceramics have equal probabilities of being found in sites outside the Mimbres region) might indicate that there was no increase in more inclusive responses over the Late Pithouse period.   That is, the trajectory of increased local interaction established during the early part of the Classic Mimbres period continued throughout the entire Classic Mimbres period. Until a well dated intra-Classic Mimbres period sequence can be established, the description of changes in exchange and social organizational patterns remains uncertain.

7

Conclusions

This research has been directed toward understanding organizational and economic responses to food stress by nonstratified societies. An archeological case study in the prehistoric American Southwest was used to evaluate a model of the ordering of these responses. In order to properly address this topic, several secondary goals were established:

1. define and discuss food stress;
2. develop a predictive model of responses to periods of food stress by human groups, and evaluate the model with ethnographic examples;
3. estimate the magnitude and frequency of food stress faced by the prehistoric occupants of the Rio Mimbres drainage, New Mexico;
4. examine several potential responses by these peoples in light of the model.

In this concluding chapter, these goals will be discussed and the results of this study summarized. Then I will very briefly consider the implications of this study for the archeological study of food stress, southwestern prehistory, and culture change.

Summary of Research

Food stress was defined here as any shortage of food or perception of vulnerability to food acquisition problems that requires some action on the part of human groups. Food stresses can vary from minor nuisances to devastating catastrophes. Two broad types of food stress were outlined, short term and long term. The three ethnographic examples discussed were short term stresses, and the archeological case study from southwestern New Mexico involved long term food provisioning problems. Ideally, this research was limited to nonstratified societies and not those tied to a colonial- or market-dominated economy. In actuality, few such groups remain in the world, and the ethnographic examples had to be drawn from colonial-dominated groups. However, their involvement in market economies was minimal and, I hope, did not obscure the responses that we would expect in noncolonial situations.

The model developed here predicts a sequence of responses to food stress by nonstratified human groups. The basic perspective from which this model was developed was first outlined in evolutionary biology. Adaptation is posited as a multifaceted and hierarchical set of responses to immediate environmental problems, arranged such that low level responses, those that are quickly activated and easily reversed, are used first. Less reversible and less quickly activated responses occur only after the more superficial responses are found to be inadequate to meet the problem. The model of economic and organizational responses by human groups to periods of food stress is an outgrowth of this perspective, but it requires transformations for its use with sociopolitical phenomena. Specifically, the model suggests that with greater food stress there will be a sequence of responses ordered by their degree of social inclusiveness, such that responses that involve greater numbers of social groups will occur after less inclusive responses are attempted. This model is generally based on the assumption that, in the absence of unrestricted mobility, social groups faced with food provisioning problems will have to enlarge their economic network so as to have access to a more reliable food supply. Three ethnographic examples of groups faced with food stress were discussed in light of this model. Although the time span of these stresses was quite short and the ethnographic descriptions were not as detailed as one would wish, the sequence of responses that occurred seems to be reasonably consistent with the expectations of the model. Finally, a number of response types were briefly discussed in order to provide an understanding of the kinds of responses to food stress that human groups employ.

Background information was presented on the natural environment and archeology of the Rio Mimbres drainage in southwestern New Mexico as a necessary prelude to the detailed study of the responses to food stress by the prehistoric occupants of this region. Of particular importance were population estimates that showed a substantial increase during the Classic Mimbres period over the size of the initial Early Pithouse period population in the Rio Mimbres Valley. Environmental reconstruction presented of the study area was necessary, since archeologists too often do not consider the effects of prehistoric and historic environmental changes but simply use the modern environment as a direct analogue to the prehistoric environment.

The periodicity of food stress in the Rio Mimbres area was then estimated. After documenting the empirical evidence for reconstructing the human subsistence base in the study area and considering other data sources, I suggested that during much of the prehistory in this area an average of half the diet was derived from cultivated plants. The next step in the analysis of the food provisioning problems was to examine the effects of various factors limiting the production capacity of the prehistoric subsistence economy. Two factors, amount of land and availability of water, were considered. I argued that during the population zenith of the Classic Mimbres period there was not enough floodplain land to support the population. Similarly during this period, there was insufficient water to sustain the complete cultivation of the floodplain. Both of these sets of calculations strongly suggest that the Classic Mimbres period population had to have become dependent upon fairly unreliable farming strategies. The Classic Mimbres period settlement pattern supports this interpretation, since a large number of Classic Mimbres period sites are in areas of secondary agricultural potential.

Precipitation is the most critical factor limiting the agricultural potential in the study area. By using dendroclimatological data combined with what is known about the effects of low precipitation on crop harvest success, estimates were made of the frequency of crop failure. These calculations also included the factor of food storage. Finally, estimates were made of the amount of naturally available food resources in the study area. It was found that under drought conditions there probably was not enough food available there to support the Classic Mimbres period population. The analyses suggested that the human population of the Classic Mimbres period had expanded to the point that the people would have had difficulty maintaining themselves given the agricultural potential and the naturally available resources in the study area. It appears that the population had expanded during an unusually favorable climatic regime during the first part of the Classic Mimbres period. Unfortunately, no studies have been conducted that can be compared with the modeling of prehistoric Mimbres economy (e.g., paleopathological attributes of food inadequacy).

If the model of responses to food stress is correct, we should see more inclusive responses culminating during some part of the Classic Mimbres period or that a lack of hierachical sequences should be correlated with system extinction or radical change. Therefore, to evaluate the model from this archeological test case, we need to emphasize the Mogollon sequence (Early Pithouse through Classic Mimbres). Unlike the ethnographic examples, the analytic approach used here was to examine the changes in the inclusiveness in the same response category. Specifically, changes in the level of socioeconomic integration and in the exchange of goods were investigated. From a study of communal structures, a viable case can be made that there was a change in the organization of the ritual system during the Classic Mimbres period. It cannot, however, be asserted that this change resulted in a more inclusive level of integration.

There does seem to be a distinct change in the pattern of exchange from the Early Pithouse period to the Late Pithouse period, which indicates more inclusive levels of exchange. The change from the Late Pithouse period to the Classic Mimbres period is more ambiguous. Of nine artifact categories examined for evidence of exchange, some showed increased levels of exchange while others did not. Breaking these categories into those that indicated exchange within the study area and outside it, the pattern becomes clearer. There appears to be an intensification of exchange within the study area and perhaps a decrease in exchange with groups outside from the Late Pithouse period to the Classic Mimbres period.

The Classic Mimbreños do not appear to have increased their economic network outside the study area. The Classic Mimbres period system did become extinct, and as such, the archeological example fits the model. However, this conclusion is not as well documented as necessary because of the inability to analyze intra-Classic Mimbres period processes. In summary then, this research has presented a reasonable case that some of the prehistoric cultural dynamics in the Rio Mimbres region can be understood as a result of behavior for coping with greater food stresses.

Archeological Study of Food Stress

Given how often "population pressure" or other stress-related models/scenarios have been offered as explanations for prehistoric

change, one would think that the basic problems (such as archeological identification of nutritional stress) would have been
resolved. However, this is not the case.

Some current problems with food stress explanations include
those that affect all archeological research. For example, the
need for middle range studies, which allow us to document what
humans behaviors, cultural system states, and other factors are
represented in the archeological record, is apparent.

Better temporal control of the archeological record is also
necessary. Without intra-Classic Mimbres period divisions, we
cannot fully evaluate responses to food stress by the prehistoric
Mimbrenos. Yet in most areas of the world, the fine chronological
divisions used in much of the Southwest are not available. The
immediate solution for this need is to match theoretical and interpretive sensitivity with chronological sensitivity.

Beyond these general problems with archeological research,
three deficiences inhibit our understanding of the role of food
stress in prehistory: the problem with the definition of food
stress, lack of necessary theoretical constructs, and insufficient
estimation and documentation of the type, intensity, and frequency
of prehistoric food stress episodes. Each of these general problems will be discussed briefly.

There is no explicit agreement on the definition of phenomena
that here have been termed food stress. A broad definition is used
in the research, a research tactic with its own pitfalls. Nevertheless, I believe that a broad definition is preferable to a
narrow one, such as that used by Gerald (1976) in his study of
prehistoric southwestern responses to famines, which includes only
periods of acute starvation. As has been mentioned previously, the
anticipation of food provisioning problems (in the absence of
immediate shortages) is a critical part of the relation between
food stress and culture change. Such was the case with the temwa
fields among the Gwembe Tonga, and it may well have been the factor
responsible for the greater use of less secure farming strategies
by the Classic Mimbreños. Similarly, various types of nutritional
inadequacies (acute/chronic, caloric/protein/mineral) are interactive; famine has a greater effect on chronically malnourished
populations or cohorts than on otherwise well fed populations.
Finally, even in nonstratified societies, the effects of starvation
will be differentially felt by various population segments.
Therefore, a broad definition of food stress, as used here, allows
us to more easily investigate variability in the effects of food

stresses.

The second problem limiting our understanding of socioeconomic responses to prehistoric food stress is a lack of theory. Too often explanations of prehistoric food stress as a cause of culture change are ad hoc commonsense interpretations that are difficult to evaluate and that cannot easily be used to formulate generalizations. The generation of explicit hypotheses (e.g., Hanson 1975) is an improvement, but hypotheses by themselves do not build theory.

Both Dirks (1980) and Hill (n.d.) have adapted Selyes' general stress model for use with human societies. This model proposes a three-stage sequence of responses by organisms to stress. Although it is a step in the right direction, ecological models are preferable to organismic ones, because human societies do not share the same level of coherence as organisms. Various ecologically derived expectations about human responses to stresses have been published. For example, Reid (1978) used the concept of diversity in his study of food stress at Grasshopper Pueblo in Arizona. My work follows in Reid's ecological/evolutionary perspective by emphasizing the sequential nature of human adaptation.

The third major problem with the archeological study of food stress has been the lack of estimates and documentation of the type, severity, and periodicity of the stresses. However, Reid argues that estimating a stress and its parameters is not necessary, because "identification of a subsistence strain is methodologically prior to and should assist in locating the source of the environmental stress" (1978:189) and "in many cases it may be sufficient to know only that a strain was present regardless of the specific stress factor producing the strain" (1978:201). An understanding of the cause of a stress is critical to understanding food stress/culture change relations. Different stresses (not just natural environmental stresses) may produce different assemblages and sequences of responses, although some of the same responses may be used for different problems. Hence our understanding of the source of a food acquisition problem will help us isolate potential responses and build generalizations about common responses and response sequences to similar problems.

Estimating the severity and periodicity of food stress faced by prehistoric peoples requires a description of the prehistoric economy and modeling of factors that may have affected food supply stability. A simple example was presented in chapter 5.

Human remains offer the best data sets to document the types of stresses present and their frequency. Two types of observations can be used as indexes of prehistoric food stress--actual paleo-pathological "markers" of stress and demographic profiles resulting from differential mortality due to food shortages. Many paleo-pathological conditions can be used to understand the type of stress endured prehistorically, be they specific nutrient defi-ciencies or protein/caloric malnutrition (Steinbock 1976; Buikstra 1977; Wing and Brown 1979; and especially see Huss-Ashmore, Goodman, and Armelagos 1982, table 9.14). While specific path-ologies can result from several nutritional and other health conditions, and while there are other interpretive problems with paleopathological analysis, judicious use of multiple indexes can identify prehistoric food stress. Provinzano's (1968) study of a Classic Mimbres period skeletal population, as well as other studies of prehistoric southwestern human remains (Hooton 1930; Palkovich 1980; Sabels, n.d.; Von Endt and Ortner 1982; El-Najjar et al. 1976), have yielded evidence of various chronic deficiencies of specific elements such as iron and calcium. Other paleopatho-logical measures can document the presence, severity, and frequency of acute stress periods. In addition to paleopathological evidence, comparison of prehistoric demographic profiles can help document the nature of prehistoric food stress. High juvenile mortality can be caused by malnutrition. Combining paleopatho-logical and demographic analyses can provide indications of prehistoric food stress.

One important caveat, however, must be maintained, especially when comparing the "hard" data from skeletal analyses with the "soft" data from catchment simulations. Using a broad definition of food stress, allows us to recognize that food stress related culture change can occur in the absence of actual periods of depri-vation. Therefore, estimations of food provisioning problems by modeling prehistoric economies should not be judged soley against evidence paleopathological and demographic evidence of food stress. Rather, these two approach as complementary but do not necessarily investigate the same aspects of food stress.

For archeologists to adequately investigate socioeconomic responses to food stress, a minimal research protocol requires (1) a theoretical perspective with testible deductions that show the specific link between some stress and the resulting culture change, and (2) estimation and documentation of the types, severity, and periodicity of the stresses. Without further developments in both these areas, food stress will remain a convenient but superficial, all-purpose explanation for prehistoric change.

Food Stress and Southwestern Prehistory

This study follows a hundred-year tradition in which archeologists have focused on the role of food acquisition problems in the cultural dynamics of the Southwest. This tradition began with the integration of two observations. First, early explorers noted the presence of puebloan ruins in areas without modern pueblos, so that it was clear some regions had been abandoned. Second, pioneering research with tree-rings and alluvial deposits showed that there was substantial variation in basic environmental factors critical to indigenous agriculture. It was logical, then, to view regional abandonments as a result of environmental changes that affected the variability of crop harvests. The logic of a clear relation between environmental changes and cultural dynamics in the Southwest is compelling; the Southwest is generally marginal for maize-based horticulture, and even minor changes in precipitation could substantially affect food production systems. Furthermore, the Southwest does not have particularly high biomass edible by humans, and with the lack of a widespread river network and lack of beasts of burden, transportation was inefficient. Therefore, native populations with relatively low population densities may have been more vulnerable to fluctuations in food supply, and the range of responses available may have been more limited that in many other regions.

However, too often these environmental fluctuation/culture change relationships are modeled as a simple correlation between tree-ring, palynological, or geological evidence of environmental change and a change in the archeological record, and too often they are viewed as a natural environmental problem. Much of this can be explained by the presence of well documented tree-ring sequences as measures of precipitation variation. However, as emphasized in this study and others, food stress/culture change associations are primarily sociocultural phenomena. Human groups are not passive players on an environmental stage. Unfortunately, our understanding of social responses to food stress is not as well documented as paleoenvironmental change.

The specific mechanisms or links between environmental variation and cultural processes in the prehistoric Southwest may vary widely. As related to regional abandonment, many environmental factors have been posited as important, including drought or precipitation fluctuation or both (Cordell 1975; Douglass 1929; Jorde 1977), changes in the seasonal pattern of rainfall (Schoenwetter 1962; Schoenwetter and Dittert 1968), arroyo cutting (Fisher 1934), and exhaustion of field fertility (Stiger 1977). Most of these factors are interrelated, and they all may contribute to an increased chance of crop failure.

The interpretive theme of correlating environmental factors and the culture history of an area takes two forms, depending on the data base used. The most common form uses site survey information as an indicator of population movement or regional abandonment. Numerous studies fall within this category (e.g., Cordell 1975; Washburn 1974; Gumerman 1971; Euler and Gumerman 1978; Martin and Plog 1973; Irwin-Williams 1968; Schoenwetter and Dittert 1968; Berry 1982).

The second form of research on human responses to environmental fluctuations in the Southwest is less common than the first. Rather than relying on survey information, this type of analysis depends on excavation data. Using this form, archeologists suggest that differences in artifact assemblages between two occupations of a single site or between two sites is a function of differential food stress. Examples include Bronitsky (1977), Hill (1970, n.d.), Cutler (1952), Gerald (1976), Hanson (1975), Reid (1978), Holbrook and Mackey (1976), and Mackey and Holbrook (1978).

How does this study of the prehistory of the Rio Mimbres region articulate with the study of the general southwestern prehistory? The Mimbres region has a definite mystique. Who devised and executed the usually sophisticated painted pottery and why? From a holistic perspective of the study area archeology, one is stuck by the typicalness of the Mimbreños compared with their contemporaries in other southwestern areas. At about the same time in other regions of the Southwest, similar archeological patterns in settlement distribution and social integration occurred (e.g., the "Pueblo II expansion"). Only in their pottery did the Classic Mimbres population express a unique dimension. There were other groups in the Southwest like the Classic Mimbres population that exhibited similar problems with food stress and attempted similar responses, and many also failed. In five or six areas of the Southwest, it appears that there occurred regional systems with a greater degree of integration than was represented in the study area. The Chacoan phenomenon, Casas Grandes, the Classic Hohokam,

Rio Grandes Pueblo IV, "Western Pueblo", and perhaps a few other populations became complex cultural systems. It often has been suggested that this complexity may have been the responses to food provisioning problems. If so, then we see a step in response inclusiveness beyond what occurred in the Rio Mimbres region. These systems also failed to maintain their complexity. Much of the prehistory of the Southwest may be a study of groups attempting the deal with changes in population size and changing climatic fortunes. In numerous cases, these attempts ended in failure for the cultural systems but not necessarily for the population. The Rio Mimbres region is just one small part of this story. Unfortunately, owing to the extensive vandalism, the Mimbres chapter of southwestern prehistory may never be satisfactorily written.

Food Stress and Culture Change

The relations between food stress and culture change are neither as simple nor as clear as one might first expect. Food stress does not always lead to culture change, and food stress can be a consequence as well as a cause of culture change. Also, food stress can be only one of many indirect and direct processes whose interaction results in culture change. Hence there are no simple formulas to determine the effects of food stress on cultural stability or change. Yet, we can specify conditions that should exacerbate the severity of food acquisition problems and increase the susceptibility of social organization to the effects of food stress. Minimally, these factors include:

1. very high population densities in relation to the productive capacity of an economic system to generate and maintain surpluses;
2. difficulty in storage;
3. large variation in factors that affect the production of food and other commodities;
4. reduction in the economic catchment area of a group;
5. severe environmental alteration, including anthropogenic change;
6. environmental homogeneity;
7. various natural and human-caused disasters (hurricanes, warfare, etc.);
8. recent disruption of traditional patterns of production, distribution, and consumption;
9. endemic chronic malnutrition;

    10. inefficient transportation;
    11. an economy closely tied to a local region.

Each of these factors can be sufficient to increase the severity of
food stress and its effects on human groups, but they are not
necessary causes, and any combination should increase system vulnerability. Also, several characteristics of these factors can
intensify the effects of food stress. The most obvious characteristic is the severity of the perturbation. Severity can involve
intensity, areal extent, frequency, and duration of the food stress
situation. In addition, unexpected or novel perturbations should
magnify the effects of food stress situations on cultural systems.
Intuitively, such unexpected or novel perturbations might have the
greatest effects, because the repertoire of responses used for
previously experienced problems may be less effective for a new
type of problem.

    The model emphasized only one aspect of responses to food
stress, use of socially inclusive responses with increased food
stress severity, but other characteristics can be investigated. As
Sahlin's (1972), Laughlin (1974), and others have pointed out, food
stress, particularly acute starvation, tends to loosen the bonds
between individuals and groups. This research does not discuss the
sequential nature of social dissolution under food stress. Just as
there may be a predictable sequence to the use of more inclusive
food stress responses, cultural systems may well decompose in an
ordered fashion under food stress; after a certain points more
inclusive responses are abandoned before less inclusive responses
ones. This is a testable expectation, though not with the current
Mimbres region data.

    Is food stress an important factor in increasing integration of
human sociopolitical relationships? Most researchers have emphasized the decaying effect of food stress on social organization.
No doubt this is the case, especially with very severe stresses.
However, as Braun and Plog (1980) and others have suggested, food
stress, as broadly defined here, logically can lead to increased
social integration. This probably happens through manipulation of
relationships by participants to provide a varied and secure food
supply (e.g., the hxaro system), rather than occurring during
immediately devastating food shortages, again emphasizing the
anticipatory nature of human adaptation. Thus food stress
indirectly contributes to the formation of alliances, which then
form the basis for further social, political, economic, and cul-

tural integration. With stratified societies food stress probably has a more direct role in enlarging states and other complex polities by increasing the domination of weaker groups by more powerful ones, either by various coercive actions or by offering food supplies to less complex societies that are stressed. Since the vast majority of modern human societies are part of or closely interactive with states, archeological analysis provides one of the few avenues to investigate the role of food stress in the formation of these complex cultural systems. Food stress, then, can have direct and indirect roles in the organization of human society, and archeological research is necessary for understanding the relation between food stress and culture change.

If anthropologists are not in a position to fully understand, let alone predict, the complex relations between food stress and culture change, we are in an excellent position to gather data and formulate cross-cultural models of these relations. The model proposed here, that there are sequential, hierarchically organized responses that involve more inclusive social integration, is one. Dirks's (1980) and Hill's (n.d.) use of Seyles' general stress syndrome is another. The practical value of greater anthropological attention to food stress is clear. As Waddell (1977) pointed out, relief efforts are often insensitive to the local cultural context of the problem. Increased awareness of traditional patterns of response can only make relief efforts more efficient, more effective, and less disruptive to indigenous cultures.

Appendix: Plant Names

Common Name	Scientific Name
Acacia	Acacia spp.
Agave	Agave spp.
Alder	Alnus oblongifolia Torr.
Alkali sacaton	Sporobolus airoides (Torr.) Torr.
Alligator-bark juniper	Juniperus deppeana Steud.
Amaranth family	Amaranthaceae
Apache plume	Fallugia paradoxa (D. Don) Endl.
Ash	Fraxinus velutina Torr.
Banana yucca	Yucca baccata Torr.
Bean family	Leguminosae
Bear grass	Nolina sp.
Beeweed	Cleome serrulata Pursh.
Box elder	Acer negundo L.
Bristle grass	Setaria spp.
Buckthorn	Rhamnus betulaefolia Greene
Buffalo gourd	Cucurbita foetidissima H. B. K.
Bugseed	Corispermum sp.
Bulrush	Cyperus sp.
Cactus family	Cactaceae
Canyon grape	Vitis arizonica Engelm.
Cattail	Typha spp.
Century plant	Agave parryi Engelm.
Chenopod family	Chenopodiaceae
Chokecherry	Prunus serotia Ehrh.
Cholla	Opuntia spp.
Cliff rose	Cowania mexicana D. Don
Common bean	Phaseolus vulgaris L.
Common reed	Phragmitis communis Trin.

Cotton	Gossypium hirsutum L.
Cottonwood	Populus spp.
Coyote melon	Apodanthera undulata Gray
Creosote bush	Larrea tridentata (DC.) Coville
Crucifixion thorn	Koeberlinia spinosa Zucc.
Desert hackberry	Celtis reticulata Torr.
Desert willow	Chilopsis linearis (Cav.) Sweet
Douglas fir	Pseudotsuga taxifolia (Poir.) Britton
Dropseed	Sporobolus spp.
Elderberry	Sambucus sp.
Fir	Abies spp.
Gambel oak	Quercus gambelii Torr.
Giant ragweed	Ambrosia trifida L.
Goosefoot	Chenopodium spp.
Gourd	Lagenaria siceraria L.
Grama grass	Bouteloua spp.
Grass family	Gramineae
Groundcherry	Physalis spp.
Hedgehog cactus	Echinocereus triglochidiatus Engelm.
Juniper	Juniperus spp.
Knotweed	Polygonum spp.
Littleleaf sumac	Rhus microphylla Engelm.
Love grass	Eragrostis spp.
Maize	Zea mays L.
Malva family	Malvaceae
Marsh elder	Iva spp.
Mesquite	Prosopis juliflora (Swartz) DC.M
Mormon tea	Ephedra trifurca Torr.
Morning glory family	Convolvulaceae
Mountain mahogany	Cercocarpus breviflorus Gray
Nightshade	Solanum spp.
Nut grass	Cyperus esculentus L.
Oak	Quercus spp.
One-seed juniper	Juniperus monosperma (Engelm.) Sarg.
Onion	Allium spp.
Peppergrass	Lepidium sp.
Pigweed	Amaranthus spp.
Piñon	Pinus edulis Engelm.

Ponderosa pine	Pinus ponderosa Lawson
Prickly pear	Opuntia spp.
	(generally O. phaeacantha Engelm.)
Purslane	Portulaca spp.
Rabbit brush	Chrysothamnus spp.
Ragweed	Ambrosia spp.
Red sage	Kochia americana Wats.
Ricegrass	Oryzopis cf. micrantha (Trin. & Rupr.)
	or bloomeri (Boland.) Ricker
Rose	Rosa spp.
Sagebrush	Artemisia spp.
Saltbush	Atriplex canescens (Pursh.) Nutt.
Sorghum	Sorghum vulgare Pers.
Sotol	Dasylirion wheeleri Wats.
Spanish bayonet	Yucca elata Engelm.
Squash	Cucurbita spp.
Squawbush	Rhus trilobata Nutt.
Stickleaf	Mentzelia pumila (Nutt.) Torr. & Gray
Sunflower	Helianthus spp.
Sunflower family	Compositae
Sycamore	Platanus wrightii Wats.
Tansy mustard	Descurainia pinnata (Wats.) Britton
Tepary bean	Phaseolus acutifolius
	var. latifolius Freem.
Tobosa grass	Hilaria spp.
Unicorn plant	Proboscidea arenaria (Engelm.) Decne.
Walnut	Juglans major (Torr.) Heller
Wild currant	Ribes spp.
Willow	Salix spp.
Yucca	Yucca spp.

Latin binomials follow Kearney and Peebles (1960), Vines (1960),
Martin and Hutchins (1980), and Terrell (1977).

References

Agency for International Development. 1980. The socio-economic context of fuelwood use in small rural communities. Evaluation Special Study no. 1. Washington, D.C.: Agency for International Development.

Aginsky, Burt W. 1939. Population control in the Shanel (Pomo) tribe. American Sociological Review 4:209-16.

Alland, Alexander, Jr. 1973. Evolution and human behavior. Garden City, N.Y.: Anchor Press.

Annegars, John F. 1973. Seasonal food shortages in West Africa. Ecology of Food and Nutrition 2:251-57.

Anyon, Roger. 1980. The Late Pithouse period. In An archaeological synthesis of southcentral and southwestern . New Mexico, ed. S. LeBlanc and M. Whalen, pp. 142-204. Albuquerque: University of New Mexico, Office of Contract Archaeology.

——. 1982. The Galaz site: Results of the 1929-1931 and 1975-1976 excavations. Paper presented at the Mogollon Conference, Las Cruces.

Anyon, Roger, Patricia A. Gilman, and Steven A. LeBlanc. 1981. A reevaluation of the Mogollon-Mimbres archaeological sequence. Kiva 46:209-25.

Anyon, Roger, and Steven A. LeBlanc. 1980. The architectural evolution of Mogollon-Mimbres communal structures. Kiva 45:253-77.

Arnon, I. 1975. Mineral nutrition of maize. Bern: International Potash Institute.

Bailey, Vernon. 1913. Life zones and crop zones of New Mexico. North American Fauna no. 35. Washington, D.C.: U.S. Department of Agriculture, Bureau of Biological Survey.

——. 1932. Mammals of New Mexico. North American Fauna no. 53. Washington, D.C.: U.S. Department of Agriculture, Bureau of Biological Survey.

Bang, Frederik B. 1978. Famine symposium: The role of disease in the ecology of famine. Ecology of Food and Nutrition 7:1–15.

Barlett, Peggy F. 1980. Agricultural decision making: Anthropological contributions to rural development. New York: Academic Press.

Bartlett, John R. 1854. Personal narrative of explorations and incidents in Texas, New Mexico, California, Sonora, and Chihuahua, vol. 1. New York: D. Appleton.

Bates, Marston. 1962. The human environment. Horace M. Albright Conservation Lectureship. Berkeley: School of Forestry, University of California.

Bateson, Gregory. 1963. The role of somatic change in evolution. Evolution 17:529–39.

Bayham, Frank E. 1976. Faunal exploitation. In Desert resources and Hohokam subsistence: The Conoco Florence Project, ed. W. Doelle, pp. 110–22. Archaeological Series no. 103. Tucson: Arizona State Museum.

Bazilevich, N. I., A. V. Drozdov, and L. E. Rodin. 1971. World forest productivity, its basic regularities and relationship with climatic factors. In Productivity of forest ecosystems, ed. P. Duvigneaud, pp. 345–52. Paris: UNESCO.

Benfer, Robert A., Jr. 1968. An analysis of a prehistoric skeletal population, Casas Grandes, Chihuahua, Mexico. Ph.D. dissertation, Department of Anthropology, University of Texas at Austin.

Bennett, John W. 1976a. Anticipation, adaptation, and the concept of culture in anthropology. Science 192:847–53.

_____. 1976b. The ecological transition. New York: Pergamon.

Bennett, Wendell C., and Robert M. Zingg. 1935. The Tarahumara: An Indian tribe of northern Mexico. Chicago: University of Chicago Press.

Berman, Mary Jane. 1979. Cultural resources overview: Socorro area, New Mexico. Washington, D.C.: U.S. Government Printing Office.

Berry, Michael S. 1982. Time, space, and transition in Anasazi prehistory. Salt Lake City: University of Utah Press.

Bhatia, B. M. 1963. Famines in India, 1860–1965. Bombay: Asia Publishing House.

Binford, Lewis R. 1968. Post-Pleistocene adaptations. In New perspectives in archaeology, ed. L. Binford and S. Binford, pp. 313–41. New York: Academic Press.

_____. 1977. General Introduction. In For theory building in

archaeology, ed. L. R. Binford, pp. 1-10. New York: Academic
Press.

Blake, Michael. 1979. Relative population changes in the central
Mimbres Valley from A.D. 1 to A.D. 1425. Manuscript on file
with the Mimbres Foundation, University of New Mexico,
Albuquerque.

Blake, Michael, and Susan Narod. 1977. Archaeological survey and
analysis in the Deming region, southwestern New Mexico. Paper
presented at the forty-second Annual Meeting of the Society
for American Archaeology, New Orleans.

Blake, Michael, Steven A. LeBlanc, and Paul E. Minnis. 1983.
Archaeological survey of the Mimbres Valley, New Mexico.
Manuscript on file with the Mimbres Foundation, University of
New Mexico, Albuquerque.

Blaney, H. F., and E. G. Hanson. 1965. Consumptive use and water
requirements in New Mexico. Santa Fe: New Mexico State
Engineer Office.

Bluhm, Elaine A. 1960. Mogollon settlement patterns in the Pine
Lawn Valley, New Mexico. American Antiquity 25:538-46.

Bohannon, Laura, and Paul Bohannon. 1953. The Tiv of central
Nigeria. London: International Africa Institute.

Bohrer, Vorsila L. 1976. Peer review. In Desert resources and
Hohokam subsistence: The Conoco Florence Project, ed. W.
Doelle, pp. 245-50. Archaeological Series no. 103. Tucson:
Arizona State Museum.

Boles, Patrick H., and William A. Dick-Peddie. 1983. Woody
riparian vegetation patterns on a segment of the Mimbres River
in southwestern New Mexico. Southwestern Naturalist 28:81-7.

Boserup, Ester. 1965. The conditions of agricultural growth.
Chicago: Aldine.

Bouroncle Carreon, Alfonso. 1964. Contribución al estudio de Los
Aymaras. American Indígena 24:129-69, 233-69.

Bowie, James E., and William Kam. 1968. The use of water by
riparian vegetation, Cottonwood Wash, Arizona. Water Supply
Paper no. 1858. Washington, D.C.: U.S. Geological Survey.

Bradfield, Maitland. 1971. The changing pattern of Hopi agriculture. Occasional Papers no. 30. London: Royal Anthropological Institute of Great Britan and Ireland.

Bradfield, Wesley. 1929. Cameron Creek Village: A site in the
Mimbres area in Grant County, New Mexico. Santa Fe: School
of American Research.

Braudel, Fernand. 1967. Capitalism and material life, 1400-1800.

New York: Harper and Row.

Braun, David P.   1979.   Illinois Hopewell burial practices and
social organization: A reexamination of the Klunk-Gibson mound
group.   In Hopewell archaeology: The Chillicothe Conference,
ed. D. Brose and N. Greber, pp. 66-79.   Kent, Ohio: Kent State
University Press.

Braun, David P., and Stephen Plog.   1982.   Evolution of "tribal"
social networks: Theory and prehistoric North American
evidence.   American Antiquity 47:504-25.

Bray, J. R.   1963.   Root production and the estimate of net
productivity.   Canadian Journal of Botany 41:65-72.

Breternitz, David A.   1959.   Excavations at Nantack Village, Point
of Pines, Arizona.   Anthropological Paper no. 1.   Tucson:
University of Arizona.

————.   1966.   An appraisal of tree-ring dated pottery in the
Southwest.   Anthropological Paper   no. 10.   Tucson: University
of Arizona.

Brody, J. J.   1977.   Mimbres painted pottery.   Albuquerque: University of New Mexico Press.

Bronitsky, Gordon.   1977.   An ecological model of trade: Economic
change in the northern Rio Grande region of New Mexico.   Ph.D.
dissertation, Department of Anthropology, University of
Arizona, Tucson.

Brush, Stephen B.   1977.   Farming the edge of the Andes.   Natural
History 86:32-41.

Buikstra, Jane E.   1977.   Biocultural dimensions of archaeological
study: A regional perspective.   In Biocultural adaptation in
prehistoric America, ed. R. Blakely, pp. 67-84.   Proceedings
no. 11. Southern Anthropological Society.   Athens: University of
Georgia Press.

Burkham, D. E.   1972.   Channel changes of the Gila River in Safford
Valley, Arizona.   Professional Papers no. 655-G.   Washington,
D.C.: U.S. Geological Survey.

————.   1976.   Effects of changes in an alluvial channel on the
timing, magnitude, and transformation of flood waves, southeastern Arizona.   Professional Papers no. 655-K.   Washington,
D.C.: U.S. Geological Survey.

Burnham, Philip.   1973.   The explanatory value of the concept of
adaptation in studies of culture change.   In The explanation
of culture change: Models in prehistory, ed. C. Renfrew,
pp. 93-102.   Pittsburgh: University of Pittsburgh Press.

Burton, Ian, Robert W. Kates, and Gilbert F. White.   1978.   The environment as hazard. Oxford: Oxford University Press.

Buskirk, Winfred. 1949. Western Apache subsistence economy. Ph.D. dissertation, Department of Anthropology, University of New Mexico, Albuquerque.

Bye, Robert A., Jr. 1979. Incipient domestication of mustards in northwest Mexico. Kiva 44:237–56.

Cancian, Frank. 1972. Change and uncertainty in a peasant economy. Palo Alto: Stanford University Press.

Casselbury, Samuel E. 1974. Further refinement of formulas for determining population from floor area. World Archaeology 6:117–22.

Castetter, E. F. 1956. The vegetation of New Mexico. New Mexico Quarterly 26:257–88.

Castetter, Edward F., and Willis H. Bell. 1942. Pima and Papago Indian agriculture. Albuquerque: University of New Mexico Press.

_____. 1952. Yuma Indian agriculture. Albuquerque: University of New Mexico Press.

Castetter, Edward F., Willis H. Bell, and Alvin R. Grove. 1938. The early utilization of agave in the American Southwest. Bulletin 5(4). Albuquerque: University of New Mexico Press.

Cawte, John. 1978. Gross stress in small islands: A study in macropsychiatry. In Extinction and survival in human populations, ed. C. Laughlin and I. Brady, pp. 95–121. New York: Columbia University Press.

Cerulli, Enrico. 1964. Nuove note Sull'Islām in Somalia. Ministero Degli Affari Esteri, Somalia, Scritti Vari Editi ed Inediti (Rome) 3:153–77.

Classen, M. M., and R. H. Shaw. 1970. Water deficit effects on corn, II, grain component. Agronomy Journal 62:652–55.

Cohen, Mark Nathan. 1977. The food crisis in prehistory. New Haven: Yale University Press.

Collier, George A. 1975. Fields of the Tzotzil. Austin: University of Texas Press.

Colson, Elizabeth. 1960. Kariba studies: The social organization of the Gwembe Tonga. Manchester: Manchester University Press.

_____. 1979. In good years and in bad: Food strategies of self-reliant societies. Journal of Anthropological Research 35:18–29.

Cone, L. Winston, and J. F. Lipscomb. 1972. The history of Kenya agriculture. Nairobi: University Press of Africa.

Cordell, Linda S. 1975. Predicting site abandonment at Wetherill

Mesa. _Kiva_ 40:189-202.

Cosgrove, H. S., and C. B. Cosgrove. 1932. _The Swarts Ruin, a typical Mimbres site in southwestern New Mexico._ Papers of the Peabody Museum of American Archaeology and Ethnology, Harvard University, 15(1). Cambridge: Peabody Museum.

Cove, John J. 1978. Survival or extinction: Reflections on the problems of famine in Tsimshian and Kaguru mythology. In _Extinction and survival in human populations,_ ed. C. Laughlin and I. Brady, pp. 231-44. New York: Columbia University Press.

Cowan, C. Wesley, Josselyn F. Moore, Richard I. Ford, and Michael T. Samuels. 1977. _A preliminary analysis of paleoethno-botanical remains from Black Mesa, Arizona: 1977 season._ Ethnobotanical Report no. 504. Ann Arbor: University of Michigan, Museum of Anthropology.

Cowgill, George. 1975. On the causes and consequences of ancient and modern population changes. _American Anthropologist_ 77:505-25.

Cox, George W. 1978. Famine symposium-the ecology of famine: An overview. _Ecology of Food and Nutrition_ 6:207-20.

Cushing, Frank H. 1920. _Zuni Breadstuff._ Indian Notes and Monographs vol. 8. New York: Heye Foundation Museum of the American Indian.

Cutler, Hugh C. 1952. A preliminary survey of plant remains of Tularosa Cave. In _Mogollon culture continuity and change,_ ed. P. Martin, pp. 461-79. Fieldiana: Anthropology vol. 40. Chicago: Field Museum.

————. 1965. Plant materials from the Joyce Well site (29 HISAR 63-16), Hidalgo County, New Mexico. In The excavation of the Joyce Well site, Hidalgo County, New Mexico, ed. E. McCluney, pp. 100-106. Manuscript on file with the Mimbres Foundation, University of New Mexico, Albuquerque.

Dalton, George. 1971. The subject of economic anthropology. In _Studies in economic anthropology,_ ed. G. Dalton, pp. 1-15. Anthropological Studies no. 7. Washington, D.C.: American Anthropological Association.

Dando, W. A. 1976. Man-made famines: Some geographical insights from an exploratory study of a millennium of Russian famines. _Ecology of Food and Nutrition_ 4:219-34.

Darton, N. H. 1916. _Geology and underground water of Luna County, New Mexico._ Bulletin no. 618. Washington, D.C.: U.S. Geological Survey.

_____. 1917. Deming folio, New Mexico. Geologic atlas of the
    United States, folio no. 207. Washington, D.C.: U.S.
    Geological Survey.

Davidson, Sir Stanley, and R. Passmore. 1969. Human nutrition and
    dietetics. Edinburgh: E. and S. Livingstone.

Dean, Jeffrey S., and William J. Robinson. 1978. Expanded tree-
    ring chronology for the southwestern United States. Chronology
    Series 3. Tucson: University of Arizona, Laboratory of Tree-
    Ring Research.

DeAtley, Suzanne P. 1980. Regional integration of Animas phase
    settlements on the northern Casas Grandes frontier. Ph.D.
    dissertation, Department of Anthropology, University of
    California, Los Angeles.

De Castro, Josue. 1952. The geography of hunger. Boston:
    Little, Brown.

Demead, O. T., and R. H. Shaw. 1960. The effects of soil moisture
    stress at different stages of growth on the development and
    yield of corn. Agronomy Journal 52:272-74.

Demerath, Nicholas J. 1957. Some general propositions: An inter-
    pretative summary. Human Organization 16:28-29.

Demerath, Nicholas J., and Anthony F. C. Wallace. 1957. Human
    adaptation to disaster. Human Organization 16:1-2.

Dempsey, James. 1955. Mission on the Nile. London: Burns and
    Oates.

Derman, Bill. 1978. Pastoralism, the Sahelian drought, and
    famine: Anthropology and response to a crisis. Reviews in
    Anthropology 5:89-99.

Dick, Herbert W. 1965. Bat Cave. Monograph no. 27. Santa Fe:
    School of American Research.

Dick-Peddie, William A. 1975. Vegetation of southern New Mexico.
    New Mexico Geological Society Guidebook 26:81-84.

Dim Delobsom, A. A. 1932. L'empire du Mogho-Naba: Coutumes des
    Mossi de la Haute-Volta. Paris: Domat-Montchrestien.

DiPeso, Charles C. 1956. The Upper Pima of San Cayetano del
    Tumacacori: An archaeo-historical reconstruction of the Ootam
    of Pimeria Alta. Publication no. 8. Dragoon, Ariz.: Amerind
    Foundation.

_____. 1974. Casas Grandes: A fallen trading center of the Gran
    Chichimeca. Publication no. 9. Dragoon, Ariz.: Amerind
    Foundation.

Dirks, Robert. 1980. Social responses during severe food
    shortages and famine. Current Anthropology 21:21-44.

Dobzhansky, Theodosius. 1958. Evolution and work. Science 127:1091-99.

Donald, Leland. 1970. Food production by the Yalunka household, Sierra Leone. In African food producton systems: Cases and theory, ed. P. McLoughlin, pp. 165-92. Baltimore: Johns Hopkins University Press.

Donkin, R. A. 1979. Agricultural terracing in the aboriginal New World. Viking Fund Publications in Anthropology 56. Tucson: University of Arizona Press.

Douglass, A. E. 1929. The secrets of the Southwest solved by talkative tree rings. National Geographic 56:736-70.

_____. 1935. The dating of Pueblo Bonito and other ruins of the Southwest. Contributed Technical Papers, Pueblo Bonito Series no. 1. Washington, D.C.: National Geographic Society.

Doyel, David E., and Emil W. Haury, eds. 1976. The 1976 Salado conference. Kiva 42(1).

Dozier, Edward P. 1970. The Pueblo Indians of North America. New York: Holt, Rinehart, and Winston.

Dregne, H. E. 1959. The crop moisture index. Research Report no. 22. Las Cruces: New Mexico State University, Agricultural Experiment Station.

_____. 1960. Soil problems in irrigated agriculture. In Agricultural problems in arid and semiarid environments, ed. A. Beetle, pp. 3-10. Bulletin no 367. Laramie: University of Wyoming, Agricultural Experiment Station.

Drucker, Philip. 1951. The Northern and Central Nootkin tribes. Washington, D.C.: U.S. Government Printing Office.

Dumond, Don E. 1976a. Review of prehistoric carrying capacity: A model. American Anthropologist 78:710-11.

_____. 1976b. Response to Zubrow. American Anthropologist 78:896.

Dundas, K. R. 1908. Notes on the origin and history of the Kikuyu and Dorobo tribes. Man 8:136-39.

Dunnell, Robert C. 1982. Science, social science, and common sense: The agonizing dilemma of modern archaeology. Journal of Anthropological Research 38:1-26.

Eggan, Fred. 1950. Social organization of the Western Pueblos. Chicago: University of Chicago Press.

El-Najjar, Mahmoud Y., Dennis J. Ryan, Christy G. Turner II, and Betsy Lozoff. 1976. The etiology of porotic hyperostosis among the prehistoric Anasazi Indians of southwestern United States. American Journal of Physical Anthropology 44:477-88.

Emerson, R. A., and Harold H. Smith. 1950. Inheritance of number
of kernal rows in maize. Memoir no. 296. Ithaca: Cornell
University, Agricultural Experiment Station.

Euler, Robert C. 1954. Environmental adaptation at Sia Pueblo.
Human Organization 12:27–30.

Euler, Robert C., and George J. Gumerman, eds. 1978. Investigations of the Southwestern Anthropological Research Group: An
experiment in archaeological cooperation. Flagstaff: Museum
of Northern Arizona.

Evans-Pritchard, E. E. 1940. The Nuer. Oxford: University of
Oxford Press.

Faron, Louis G. 1964. Hawks of the sun: Mapuche morality and its
ritual attributes. Pittsburgh: University of Pittsburgh
Press.

Faulkingham, R. H., and P. F. Thorbahn. 1975. Population dynamics
and drought: A village in Niger. Population Studies
29:463–77.

Findley, James S., Arthur H. Harris, Don E. Wilson, and Clyde
Janes. 1975. Mammals of New Mexico. Albuquerque:
University of New Mexico Press.

Findlow, Frank J. 1979. A catchment analysis of certain
prehistoric settlements in southwestern New Mexico. Journal
of New World Archaeology 3:1–15.

Firth, Raymond. 1936. We, the Tikopia: Kinship in primitive
Polynesia. London: George Allen and Unwin.

_____. 1939. Primitive Polynesian economy. London: Routledge and
Kegan Paul.

-----. 1959. Social change in Tikopia. London: George Allen and
Unwin.

Fisher, Reginald. 1934. Some geographic factors that influenced
the ancient populations of the Chaco Canyon, New Mexico.
Bulletin Anthropology Series 3(1). Albuquerque: University of
New Mexico.

Fitting, James E. 1971. The Hermanas Ruin, Luna County, New
Mexico. Southwestern New Mexico Research Reports no. 3.
Cleveland: Case Western Reserve University.

Fitting, James E., and Theron D. Price. 1968. Two Late Paleo-
Indian sites in southwestern New Mexico. Kiva 34:1–8.

Flannery, Kent V. 1968. Archaeological systems theory and early
Mesoamerica. In Anthropological archaeology in the Americas,
ed. B. Meggars, pp. 67–87. Washington, D.C.: The Anthropological Society of Washington.

Forbes, Jack D. 1957. The Janos, Jacomes, Mansos, and Sumas
    Indians. New Mexico Historical Review 32:319-34.
Ford, Richard I. 1968. An ecological analysis involving the
    population of San Juan Pueblo, New Mexico. Ph.D. dis-
    sertation, Department of Anthropology, University of Michigan,
    Ann Arbor.
_____. 1972a. An ecological perspective on the Eastern Pueblos.
    In New perspectives on the Pueblos, ed. A. Ortiz, pp. 1-18.
    Albuquerque: University of New Mexico Press.
_____. 1972b. Barter, gift, or violence: An analysis of Tewa
    intertribal exchange. In Social exchange and interaction, ed.
    E. Wilmsen, pp. 21-46. Anthropological Papers no. 46.
    Ann Arbor: University of Michigan, Museum of Anthropology.
Franke, Paul R., and Don Watson. 1936. An experimental corn field
    in Mesa Verde National Park. In Symposium on prehistoric
    agriculture, ed. D. Brand, pp. 35-41. Bulletin no. 296.
    Albuquerque: University of New Mexico.
French, James A. 1917. Surface water supply of New Mexico, 1916.
    Santa Fe: New Mexico State Engineer Office.
Fried, Morton H. 1970. The evolution of political society. New
    York: Random House.
Fritts, H. C. 1976. Tree rings and climate. New York: Academic
    Press.
Fritts, Harold C., James E. Mosimann, and Christine P. Bottorff.
    1969. A revised computer program for standardizing tree-ring
    series. Tree-Ring Bulletin 29:15-20.
Fuller, Wallace H. 1975a. Soils of the desert Southwest. Tucson:
    University of Arizona Press.
_____. 1975b. Management of southwestern desert soils. Tucson:
    University of Arizona Press.
Galt, Anthony H., and Janice W. Galt. 1979. Peasant use of some
    wild plants on the island of Pantelleria, Sicily. Economic
    Botany 32:20-26.
Garn, Stanley M., and Walter D. Block. 1970. The limited
    nutritional value of cannibalism. American Anthropologist
    72:352.
Gasser, Robert. 1978. Cibola-Anasazi diet: The evidence from the
    Coronado Project. Paper presented at the forty-third Annual
    Meeting of the Society for American Archaeology, Tucson.
Gerald, Rex E. 1976. Drought correlated changes in two prehis-
    toric Pueblo communities in southeastern Arizona. Ph.D.
    dissertation, Department of Anthropology, University of

Chicago, Chicago.

Gilman, Patricia A. 1980. The early Pueblo period: Mimbres Classic. In An archaeological synthesis of southcentral and
southwestern New Mexico, ed. S. LeBlanc and M. Whalen, pp.
205-70. Albuquerque: University of New Mexico, Office
Contract Archaeology,

_____. 1983. Changing architectural forms in the prehistoric
Southwest. Ph.D. dissertation, Department of Anthropology,
University of New Mexico, Albuquerque.

Gladwin, Harold S. 1940. Tree-rings and drought. Medallion
Papers no. 37. Globe, Ariz.: Gila Pueblo.

Glassow, Michael A. 1978. The concept of carrying capacity in the
study of culture process. In Advances in archaeological
method and theory 1:32-48.

Glover, Charles R., Ricardo Gomez, R. D. Baker, and Larry Cihacek.
1980. Fertilizer guide for New Mexico. Circular no. 478.
Las Cruces: New Mexico State University, Cooperative Extension
Service.

Gould, Stephen Jay. 1977. Ever since Darwin. New York: W. W.
Norton.

Grayhill, Donald A. 1973. Prehistoric settlement pattern analysis
in the Mimbres region, New Mexico. Ph.D. dissertation,
Department of Anthropology, University of Arizona, Tucson.

_____. 1974. Measurement of the amount and rate of site
destruction in southwestern New Mexico. Paper presented at
the thirty-ninth Annual Meeting of the Society of American
Archaeology, San Francisco.

_____. 1975. Mimbres-Mogollon adaptations in the Gila National
Forest, Mimbres district, New Mexico. Archaeological Report
no. 9. Albuquerque: U. S. Forest Service Southwest Region.

Green, Dee, and Steven A. LeBlanc, eds. 1979. Vandalism of
cultural resources: The growing threat to our nation's
heritage. Cultural Resource Report no. 28. Albuquerque: U.S.
Forest Service Southwest Region.

Gumerman, George J., ed. 1971. The distribution of prehistoric
population aggregates. Anthropological Reports no. 1.
Prescott, Ariz.: Prescott College.

Hack, John T. 1942. The changing physical environment of the Hopi
Indians of Arizona. Papers of the Peabody Museum of American
Archaeology and Ethnology, Harvard University 31(1).
Cambridge: Peabody Museum.

Hallowell, A. Irving. 1955. Culture and experience. Philadelphia: University of Pennsylvania Press.

Hanson, John A. 1975. Stress response in cultural systems: A prehistoric example from east-central Arizona. In Chapters in the prehistory of Arizona, IV, ed. P. Martin, E. Zubrow, D. Bowman, D. Gregory, J. Hanson, M. Schiffer, and D. Wilcox, pp. 92–102, Fieldiana: Anthropology, vol. 65. Chicago: Field Museum.

Hantman, Jeffrey L. 1978. Models for the explanation of changing settlement on the Little Colorado Planning Unit. In An analytical approach to cultural resource management: The Little Colorado Planning Unit, ed. F. Plog, pp. 169–87. Anthropological Research Papers no. 13. Tempe: Arizona State University.

Hara, Hiroko S. 1976. Hare Indians and their world. Ph.D. dissertation, Department of Anthropology, Bryn Mawr College.

Hargrave, Lyndon L. 1970. Mexican macaws: Comparative osteology and survey of remains from the Southwest. Anthropological Papers no. 20. Tucson: University of Arizona.

Haslam, S. M. 1978. River plants: The macrophytic vegetation of water courses. Cambridge: Cambridge University Press.

Hassan, Fekri A. 1981. Demographic archaeology. New York: Academic Press.

Hastings, James R., and Raymond M. Turner. 1965. The changing mile. Tucson: University of Arizona Press.

Hastorf, Christine A. 1977. A predictive model for changing food resources in the prehistoric Mimbres Valley, New Mexico. M.A. thesis, Department of Anthropology, University of California, Los Angeles.

———. 1980. Changing resource use in subsistence agricultural groups of the prehistoric Mimbres River Valley, New Mexico. In Modeling change in prehistoric subsistence economies, ed. T. Earle and A. Christenson, pp. 79–120. New York: Academic Press.

Haury, Emil W. 1936. The Mogollon culture of southwestern New Mexico. Medallion Papers no. 20. Globe, Ariz.: Gila Pueblo.

———. 1957. An alluvial site on the San Carlos Indian Reservation, Arizona. American Antiquity 23:2–27.

———. 1976. The Hohokam: Desert farmers and craftsmen. Tucson: University of Arizona Press.

Hayden, Brian. 1975. The carrying capacity dilemma: An alternative approach. In Population studies in archaeology and biological anthropology: A symposium, ed. A. C. Swedlund, pp. 11-21. Memoir no. 30. Austin, Tex.: Society for American Archeology.

Heller, Maurice M. 1976. Zooarchaeology of Tularosa Cave, Catron County, New Mexico. M. A. thesis, Department of Biological Sciences, University of Texas at El Paso.

Henderson, D. C., and E. F. Sorenson. 1968. Consumptive irrigation requirements of selected irrigated areas in New Mexico. Bulletin no. 531. Las Cruces: New Mexico State University, Agricultural Experiment Station.

Herold, Laurance. 1965. Trincheras and physical environment along the Rio Gavilan, Chihuahua, Mexico. Technical Paper no. 65-1. Denver: University of Denver, Department of Geography.

Herrington, LaVerne C. 1977. Prehistoric field and irrigation systems of the Rio de Arenas and Cameron Creek drainages, Grant County, New Mexico. Paper presented at the forty-second Annual Meeting of the Society for American Archaeology, New Orleans.

_____. 1979. Settlement patterns and water control systems of the Mimbres Classic phase, Grant County, New Mexico. Ph.D. dissertation, Department of Anthropology, University of Texas at Austin.

Hill, James N. 1970. Broken K Pueblo: Prehistoric social organization in the American Southwest. Anthropological Papers no. 18. Tucson: University of Arizona.

_____. n.d. Research design, Pajarito Archaeological Research Project. Manuscript on file with the U.S. Forest Service Southwest Region, Albuquerque.

Hitchcock, R. K. 1978. The traditional response to drought in Botswana. In Proceedings of the symposium on the drought in Botswana, ed. M. Hinchey, pp. 91-97. Worchester, Mass.: Clark University Press.

Holbrook, Sally J., and James C. Mackey. 1976. Prehistoric environmental change in northern New Mexico: Evidence from a Gallina phase archaeological site. Kiva 41:309-17.

Honigmann, John J. 1954. The Kaska Indians: An ethnographic reconstruction. New Haven: Yale University Press.

Hooten, Earnest A. 1930. Indians of Pecos Pueblo. New Haven: Yale University Press.

Horowitz, Michael M., ed. 1976. Colloquium on the effect of drought on the productive strategies of Sudano-Sahelian herdsmen and farmers. Binghamton, N.Y.: Institute for Development Anthropology.

Hough, Walter. 1898. Environmental interrelations in Arizona. American Anthropologist 11:133-55.

Howard, William A., and Thomas M. Griffiths. 1966. Trinchera distribution in the Sierra Madre Occidental, Mexico. Technical Paper no. 66-1. Denver: University of Denver, Department of Geography.

Howell, William W. 1932. The skeletal remains. In The Swarts Ruin, a typical Mimbres site in southwestern New Mexico, ed. H. S. and C. B. Cosgrove, pp. 115-70. Peabody Museum of American Archaeology and Ethnology, Harvard University, Papers 15(1). Cambridge: Peabody Museum.

Huss-Ashmore, Rebecca, Alan H. Goodman, and George J. Armelagos. 1982. Nutritional inference from paleopathology. Advances in archaeological method and theory 5:395-474.

Irwin-Williams, Cynthia. 1967. Picosa: The elementary southwestern culture. American Antiquity 32:441-56.

_____. 1968. The reconstruction of archaic culture history in the southwestern United States. Contributions in Anthropology 1:19-23. Portales, N.M.: Eastern New Mexico University.

Jelliffe, Derrick B., and E. F. P Jelliffe. 1971. The effects of starvation on the function of the family and of society. In Famine: A symposium dealing with nutrition and relief operations in times of disaster, ed. G. Blix, pp. 54-62. Stockholm: Swedish Nutrition Foundation.

Jensen, M. E. 1968. Water consumption by agricultural plants. In Water deficits and plant growth, ed. T. T. Kozlowski, pp. 1-22. New York: Academic Press.

Jernigan, E. Wesley. 1978. Jewelry of the prehistoric Southwest. Albuquerque: University of New Mexico Press and School of American Research.

Jodha, N. S. 1978. Effectiveness of farmers' adjustments to risk. Economic and Political Weekly 13:A38-48.

Jorde, L. B. 1977. Precipitation cycles and cultural buffering in the prehistoric Southwest. In For theory building in archaeology: Essays on faunal analysis, aquatic resources, spatial analysis, and systemic modeling, ed. L. Binford, pp. 385-96. New York: Academic Press.

Judd, Neil M. 1954. The material culture of Pueblo Bonito. Miscellaneous Collections vol. 124. Washington, D.C.: Smithsonian Institution.

Judge, James W. 1973. Paleo-Indian occupation in the central Rio Grande Valley in New Mexico. Albuquerque: University of New

Mexico Press.

Judge, J. W., W. B. Gillespie, S. H. Lekson, and H. W. Toll. 1981.
Tenth century developments in Chaco Canyon. Anthropological
Papers 6:65-98. Santa Fe: Archaeological Society of New
Mexico.

Kagwa, Apolo. 1934. The customs of the Baganda. New York:
Columbia University Press.

Kearney, Thomas H., and Robert H. Peebles. 1960. Arizona Flora.
Berkeley: University of California Press.

Kelly, J. Charles, and Ellen Abbott Kelly. 1975. An alternative
hypothesis for the explanation of Anasazi culture history. In
Collected papers in honor of Florence Hawley Ellis, ed. T.
Frisbie, pp. 178-223. Papers no. 2. Santa Fe: Archaeological
Society of New Mexico.

Kelso, Gerald K. 1980. Palynology and human paleoecology in Dead
Valley. In Prehistory in Dead Valley, east-central Arizona:
The TG&E Springerville Project, ed. D. Doyel and S. Debowski,
pp. 349-70. Archaeological Series no. 144. Tucson: Arizona
State Museum.

Kendeigh, S. Charles, and George C. West. 1965. Caloric values of
plant seeds eaten by birds. Ecology 46:553-55.

Kennedy, Michele R. 1982a. Mortuary practices and social status
at two Mogollon sites in New Mexico. In NAN Ranch Ruin: A
collection of papers on the archeology of the NAN Ranch Ruin,
Grant County, New Mexico, ed. H. Shafer, pp. III1-6. College
Station: Texas A&M University, Department of Anthropology.

_____. 1982b. Analysis of jewelry from the NAN Ranch Ruin. In
NAN Ranch Ruin: A collection of papers on the archeology of
the NAN Ranch Ruin, Mimbres Valley, Grant County, New Mexico,
ed. H. Shafer, pp. IV1-11. College Station: Texas A&M
University, Department of Anthropology.

Keyes, A., J. Brozek, A. Henschel, O. Michelsen, and H. L. Taylor.
1950. The biology of human starvation. Minneapolis: University of Minnesota Press.

Kirkby, Anne V. T. 1973. The use of land and water resources in
the past and present Valley of Oaxaca, Mexico. Memoir no. 5.
Ann Arbor: University of Michigan, Museum of Anthropology.

_____. 1978. Individual and community responses to rain fall
variability in Oaxaca, Mexico. In Natural hazards: Local,
national, global, ed. G. White, p. 119-28. Oxford: Oxford
University Press.

Kirsch, Patrick V. 1980. The archaeological study of adaptation:

Theoretical and methodological issues. In Advances in
archaeological method and theory 3:101-56.

Kuhnlein, H. V., and D. H. Calloway. 1977. Contemporary Hopi food
intake patterns. Ecology of Food and Nutrition 6:159-73.

Lancaster, Chet S. 1981. The Goba of the Zambezi: Sex roles,
economics, and change. Norman: University of Oklahoma Press.

Lange, Charles H. 1959. Cochiti: A New Mexico Pueblo, past and
present. Carbondale: Southern Illinois University Press.

Langenwalter, Paul. 1979. Prehistoric record of the Muskrat
(Ondatra Ziebethicus) in the Mimbres River drainage, New
Mexico. Journal of Mammalogy 60:431-34.

Larson, W. E., and J. J. Hanway. 1977. Corn production. In Corn
and corn improvement, ed. G. Sprague, pp. 625-69. Agronomy
Series no. 18. Madison, Wisc.: American Society of Agronomy.

Laughlin, Charles D., Jr. 1974. Deprivation and reciprocity. Man
9:380-96.

Laughlin, Charles D., and Ivan A. Brady, eds. 1978. Extinction
and survival in human populations. New York: Columbia
University Press.

Leakey, Louis S. B. 1953. Mau Mau and the Kikuyu. London:
Methuen.

LeBlanc, Catherine J. 1977. Design analysis of Mimbres pottery.
Paper presented at the forty-second Annual Meeting of the
Society for American Archaeology, New Orleans.

LeBlanc, Steven A. 1976. Mimbres Archaeological Center:
Preliminary report of the second season of excavation, 1975.
Journal of New World Archaeology 1:1-23.

_____. 1980a. The Early Pithouse period. In An archaeological
synthesis of southcentral and southwestern New Mexico, ed. S.
LeBlanc and M. Whalen, pp. 119-41. Albuquerque: University of
New Mexico, Office of Contract Archaeology.

_____. 1980b. The terminal Pueblo period: Salado. In An
archaeological synthesis of southcentral and southwestern New
Mexico, ed. S. LeBlanc and M. Whalen, pp. 290-316.
Albuquerque: University of New Mexico, Office of Contract
Archaeology.

_____. 1980c. The dating of Casas Grandes. American Antiquity
45:799-805.

_____. 1983. The Mimbres people: Ancient Pueblo painters of the
American Southwest. London: Thames and Hudson.

LeBlanc, Steven A., and Ben A. Nelson. 1976. The question of
Salado in Southwestern New Mexico. Kiva 42:71-79.

LeBlanc, Steven A., and Dale Rugge. 1980. The late Pueblo period: Animas and Black Mountain. In An archaeological synthesis of southcentral and southwestern New Mexico, ed. S. LeBlanc and M. Whalen, pp. 271–90. Albuquerque: University of New Mexico, Office of Contract Archaeology.

LeBlanc, Steven A., and Michael E. Whalen, eds. 1980. An archaeological synthesis of southcentral and southwestern New Mexico. Albuquerque: University of New Mexico, Office of Contract Archaeology.

Lee, Richard B. 1968. What hunters do for a living or how to make out on scarce resources. In Man the hunter, ed. R. Lee and I. Devore, pp. 30–48. Chicago: Aldine.

_____. 1979. The !Kung San: Men, women and work in a foraging society. Cambridge: Cambridge University Press.

Lee, Richard B., and Irvin Devore, eds. 1968. Man the hunter. Chicago: Aldine.

Lehmer, Donald J. 1948. The Jornada ranch of the Mogollon. Bulletin 19(2). Tucson: University of Arizona.

Leighton, Dorothea C., and John Adair. 1963. People of the middle place: A study of the Zuni Indians. New Haven: Human Relations Area Files.

Lessa, William A. 1964. The social effects of Typhoon Ophelia (1960) on Ulithi. Micronesia 1:1–47.

Leven, A. A., and H. E. Dregne. 1963. Productivity of Zuni Mountain forest soils. Bulletin no 469. Las Cruces: New Mexico State University, Agricultural Experiment Station.

Lewontin, Richard C. 1978. Adaptation. Scientific American 239:212–30.

Lightfoot, Kent G. 1979. Food redistribution among prehistoric Pueblo groups. Kiva 44:319–40.

Lightfoot, Kent G., and Gary M. Feinman. 1980. Social differentiation and leadership development in Early Pithouse villages in the Mogollon region of the American Southwest. American Antiquity 47:64–86.

Longacre, William A. 1970. Archaeology as anthropology: A case study. Anthropological Papers no. 17. Tucson: University of Arizona.

Lowe, Charles H. 1964. Arizona's natural environment. Tucson: University of Arizona Press.

Lyman, R. Lee. 1979. Available meat from faunal remains: A consideration of techniques. American Antiquity 44:545–66.

Lytle-Webb, Jamie. 1978. Pollen analysis in southwestern archaeology. In Discovering past behaviors: Experiments in the archaeology of the American Southwest, ed. P. Grebinger, pp. 13-28. New York: Gordon and Breach.

McCluney, Eugene B. 1968. A Mimbres shrine at the West Baker site. Archaeology 21: 196-205.

Macfarlane, Alan. 1976. Resources and population: A study of the Gurungs of Nepal. Cambridge: Cambridge University Press.

McGuire, Randall H. 1980. The Mesoamerican connection in the Southwest. Kiva 46:3-38.

Mackey, James C., and Sally J. Holbrook. 1978. Environmental reconstuction and the abandonment of the Largo-Gallina area, New Mexico. Journal of Field Archaeology 5:29-50.

McKim, Fred. 1947. San Blas: An account of the Cuna Indians. In The forbidden land: Reconnaissance of the Upper Bayano River, ed. H. Wassen, pp. 1-186. Goteberg: Etnografiska Museet.

Maclachlan, Morgan D. 1983. Why they did not starve: Biocultural adaptations in a South Indian village. Philadelphia: Institute for the Study of Human Issues.

McNeill, William H. 1976. Plagues and Peoples. Garden City, N.Y.: Anchor/Doubleday.

McQueen, I. S., and R. F. Miller. 1972. Soil moisture and energy relationships associated with riparian vegetation near San Carlos, Arizona. Professional Papers no. 655-E. Washington, D.C.: U.S. Geological Survey.

Maker, H. J., O. F. Bailey, and J. U. Anderson. 1970. Soil associations and land classification for irrigation, Luna County. Research Report no. 176. Las Cruces: New Mexico State University, Agricultural Experiment Station.

Maker, H. J., R. E. Neher, and J. U. Anderson. 1971. Soil associations and land classification for irrigation, Grant County. Research Report no. 200. Las Cruces: New Mexico State University, Agricultural Experiment Station.

Malinowski, Bronislaw. 1935. Coral gardens and their magic. New York: American Book.

Margalef, Ramon. 1968. Perspectives in ecological theory. Chicago: University of Chicago Press.

Marshall, Michael P., John R. Stein, Richard W. Loose, and Judith E. Novotny. 1979. Anasazi communities of the San Juan Basin. Santa Fe: New Mexico Historic Preservation Bureau.

Martin, Paul Schultz. 1963. The last 10,000 years: A fossil pollen record of the American Southwest. Tucson: University of Arizona Press.

Martin, Paul Schultz, and William Byer. 1965. Pollen and archae-
    ology at Wetherill Mesa. In Contributions of the Wetherill
    Mesa Archaeological Project, ed. D. Osborne, pp. 122-35.
    Memoir no. 19. Salt Lake City: Society for American
    Archaeology.
Martin, Paul Sidney. 1950. Conjectures concerning the social
    organization of the Mogollon Indians. In Sites of the Reserve
    phase, Pine Lawn Valley, western New Mexico, ed. P. Martin and
    J. Rinaldo, pp. 556-69. Fieldiana: Anthropology 38(3).
    Chicago: Field Museum.
Martin, Paul Sidney, and Fred Plog. 1973. The archaeology of
    Arizona. Garden City, N.Y.: Doubleday/Natural History Press.
Martin, Paul Sidney, and John B. Rinaldo. 1950. Sites of the
    Reserve phase, Pine Lawn Valley, western New Mexico.
    Fieldiana: Anthropology 38(3). Chicago: Field Museum.
Martin, Paul Sidney, John R. Rinaldo, and Ernst Antevs. 1949.
    Cochise and Mogollon sites, Pine Law Valley, western New
    Mexico. Fieldiana: Anthropology 38(1). Chicago: Field
    Museum.
Martin, William C., and Charles R. Hutchins. 1980. A flora of New
    Mexico. Vaduz, West Germany: J. Cramer.
Mauss, Marcel. 1967. The gift: Forms and functions of exchange in
    archaic societies. New York: W. W. Norton.
Mayer, Jean. 1975. Management of famine relief. Science
    188:571-77.
Meinzer, Oscar E. 1927. Plants as indicators of ground water.
    Water Supply Papers no. 577. Washington, D.C.: U.S. Geological
    Survey.
Merker, Meritz. 1910. Die Masai: Ethnographische Monographie
    verbesserte Ostafrikanischen Semitenvolkes. Berlin: Ernst
    Vohsen.
Merrill, William L. 1978. Thinking and drinking: A Raramuri
    interpretation. In The nature and status of ethnobotany, ed.
    R. Ford, pp. 101-17. Anthropological Papers no. 67. Ann
    Arbor: University of Michigan, Museum of Anthropology.
Miller, Robert R. 1961. Man and the changing fish fauna of the
    American Southwest. Papers of the Michigan Academy of
    Science, Arts, and Letters 46:365-404.
Minnis, Paul E. 1978. Paleoethnobotanical indicators of
    prehistoric environmental disturbance: A case study. In The
    nature and status of ethnobotany, ed. R. Ford, pp. 347-66.
    Anthropological Papers no. 67. Ann Arbor: University of

Michigan, Museum of Anthropology.

———. 1979. Plant remains from the Bradsby site. Manuscript on file with the Mimbres Foundation, University of New Mexico, Albuquerque.

———. 1980a. The Archaic. In An archaeological synthesis of southcentral and southwestern New Mexico, ed. S. LeBlanc and M. Whalen, pp. 63–102. Albuquerque: University of New Mexico, Office of Contract Archaeology.

———. 1980b Population size and settlement configuration in southwestern New Mexico. In An archaeological synthesis of southcentral and southwestern New Mexico, ed. S. LeBlanc and M. Whalen, pp. 460–503. Albuquerque: University of New Mexico Office of Contract Archaeology.

———. 1980c. Domesticating plants and people in the Greater Southwest. Paper presented at the School of American Reseach Advanced Seminar, The Origins of Plant Husbandry in North America, Santa Fe.

———. 1981a. Seeds in archaeological sites: Sources and some interpretive problems. American Antiquity 46:145–52.

———. 1981b. Economic and organizational responses to food stress by non-stratified societies: A case from prehistoric New Mexico. Ph.D. dissertation, Department of Anthropology, University of Michigan, Ann Arbor.

———. n.d. Prehistoric ethnobotany of the Rio Mimbres Salado. Manuscript on file with the Mimbres Foundation, University of New Mexico, Albuquerque.

———. n.d. Prehistoric ethnobotany of the northwestern Chihuahuan Desert. Manuscript on file with the Mimbres Foundation, University of New Mexico, Albuquerque.

Minnis, Paul E., and Richard I. Ford. 1977. Analysis of plant remains from Chimney Rock Mesa. In Archaeological investigations at Chimney Rock Mesa: 1970-72, ed. F. Eddy, pp. 81-91. Memoir no 1. Boulder: Colorado Archaeological Society.

Minnis, Paul E., and Steven A. LeBlanc. 1979. The destruction of three sites in southwestern New Mexico. In Vandalism of cultural resources: The growing threat to our nation's heritage, ed. D. Green and S. LeBlanc, pp. 69-78. Cultural Resources Report no. 28. Albuquerque: U.S. Forest Service Southwest Region.

Minnis, Paul E., Margaret C. Nelson, Michael Blake, and Steven A. LeBlanc. n.d. Effects of prehistoric population increase on

the environment and economy in the Rio Mimbres drainage, New
Mexico. Manuscript on file with the Mimbres Foundation,
University of New Mexico, Albuqueque.

Minnis, Paul E., and Alan J. Wormser. 1982. Late Pithouse period
occupation in the Deming region: Preliminary report of
excavations at the Florida Mountain site. Paper presented at
the Mogollon Conference, Las Cruces.

Mohr, P. J., and E. P. Dickinson. 1979. Mineral nutrition in
maize. In Maize, ed. E. Haflinger, pp. 26-32. Basle: CIBA-
GEIGY.

Morgan, Lewis H. 1877. Ancient Society. New York: Holt.

_____. 1901. League of the Ho-de-no-sau-nee or Iroquois. New York:
Dodd and Mead.

Munson, Patrick J., Paul W. Parmalee, and Richard A. Yarnell.
1971. Subsistence ecology of Scovill, a Terminal Middle Woodland village. American Antiquity 36:410-31.

Nagata, Shuichi. 1970. Modern transformations of Moenkopi Pueblo.
Illinois Studies in Anthropology no. 6. Urbana: University of
Illinois Press.

Nash, June C. 1970, In the eyes of the ancestors: Belief and
behavior in a Maya community. New Haven: Yale University
Press.

National Institute for Arthritis and Metabolic Diseases. 1961.
Tabla de composición de alimentos para uso en America
Latina. Bethesda, Md.: National Institutes of Health.

Naylor, Thomas H. 1969. The extinct Suma of northern Chihuahua:
Their origin, cultural identity, and disappearance. Artifact
7:1-13.

Nelson, Ben A., Magaret C. Rugge, and Steven A. LeBlanc. 1979. LA
12109: A small Classic Mimbres ruin in the Mimbres Valley. In
Limited activity and occupation sites, ed. A. Ward, pp.
191-296. Contributions to Anthropological Studies no. 1.
Albuquerque: Center for Anthropological Studies.

Nelson, Margaret C. 1980. The Paleo-Indian period. In An
archaeological synthesis of southcentral and southwestern New
Mexico, ed. S. LeBlanc and M. Whalen, pp. 38-62. Albuquerque:
University of New Mexico, Office of Contract Archaeology.

_____. 1981. Chipped stone analysis in the reconstruction of
prehistoric subsistence practices: An example from southwestern New Mexico. Ph.D. dissertation, Department of Anthropology, University of California, Santa Barbara.

Nesbitt, Paul H. 1931. The ancient Mimbreños, based on investi-

gations at the Mattocks Ruin, Mimbres Valley, New Mexico.
Logan Museum Bulletin no. 4. Beloit, Wisc.: Beloit College.

Newman, James L. 1970. The ecological basis for subsistence
change among the Sandawe of Tanzania. Washington, D.C.:
National Academy of Sciences.

_____. 1975. Dimensions of Sandawe diet. Ecology of Food and
Nutrition 4:33–39.

New Mexico State Engineers Office. 1975. Grant County, water
resource assessment for planning purposes. Santa Fe: New
Mexico State Engineers Office.

Nino, Bernardino. 1912. Etnografía Chiriguano. La Paz:
Tipografía Comercial de Ismael Argote.

Odum, Eugene P. 1959. Fundamentals of ecology. Philadelphia: W.
B. Saunders.

Orians, Gordon H. 1980. Micro and macro in ecological theory.
BioScience 30:79.

Ortiz, Alfonso. 1969. The Tewa world. Chicago: University of
Chicago Press.

_____, ed. 1979. Handbook of North American Indians, vol. 9,
Southwest. Washington, D.C.: Smithsonian Institution.

Ovington, J. D., Dale Heitkamp, and Donald B. Lawrence. 1963.
Plant biomass and productivity of prairie, savanna, oakwood,
and maize field ecosystems in central Minnesota. Ecology
44:52–63.

Page, Gordon B. 1940. Hopi agricultural notes. Mimeographed
manuscript in author's possession.

Palkovich, Ann M. 1980. Pueblo population and society: The Arroyo
Hondo skeletal and mortuary remains. Arroyo Hondo Archae-
ological Series vol. 3. Santa Fe: School of American
Research.

Pendergast, David M. 1962. Metal artifacts in prehispanic Meso-
America. American Antiquity 27:520–45.

Pendleton, J. W. 1979. Cropping practices. In Maize, ed. E.
Haflinger, ed., pp. 18–21. Basle: CIBY-GEIGY.

Pennington, Campbell W. 1969. The Tepehuan of Chihuahua: Their
material culture. Salt Lake City: University of Utah Press.

Pepper, George H. 1920. Pueblo Bonito. Anthropological Papers
vol. 24. New York: American Museum of Natural History.

Phillipson, John. 1966. Ecological Energetics. London: Edward
Arnold.

Plog, Fred. 1974. The study of prehistoric change. New York:
Academic Press.

_____. 1978. An analytical approach to cultural resource
management: The Little Colorado Planning Unit. Anthropological Research Papers no. 13. Tempe: Arizona State
University.

Plog, Stephen E. 1980. Stylistic variation in prehistoric
ceramics. Cambridge: Cambridge University Press.

Powell, Susan. 1977. Changing subsistence patterns as reflected
in faunal remains from the Mimbres River area, New Mexico.
M.A. thesis, Department of Anthropology, University of
California, Los Angeles.

Powell, Susan, and Paul Langenwalter. 1977. Changes in
prehistoric hunting practices in the Mimbres River Valley.
Paper presented at the forty-second Annual Meeting of the
Society for American Archaeology, New Orleans.

Prindle, Peter H. 1979. Peasant society and famine: A Nepalese
example. Ethnology 18:49-60.

Provinzano, James. 1968. The osteological remains of the Galaz
Mimbres Amerinds. M.A. thesis, Department of Anthropology,
University of Minnesota, Minneapolis.

Rahaman, M. Mujibur. 1978. The cause and effect of famine in
rural and populations. Ecology of Food and Nutrition 7:99-102.

Rappaport, Roy A. 1968. Pigs for the ancestors: Ritual in the
ecology of a New Guinea people. New Haven: Yale University
Press.

_____. 1971. The sacred in human evolution. Annual Review of
Ecology and Systematics 2:23-44.

Rayner, Jeanette F. 1957. Studies of disasters and other extreme
situations--An annotated selected bibliography. Human Organization 16:30-40.

Redfield, Robert. 1950. A village that chose progress. Chicago:
University of Chicago Press.

Reed, Howard S. 1942. A short history of the plant sciences.
Waltham, Mass.: Chronica Botanica.

Reichel-Dolmatoff, Gerardo. 1949-50. Los Kogi: Una tribu de la
Sierra Nevada de Santa Marta, Columbia. Instituto Etnológico
Nacional Revista Columbia 1:1-319.

Reichman, Harold C. 1976. Relationships between dimensions,
weights, volumes, and calories of some Sonoran seeds.
Southwestern Naturalist 20:573-86.

Reid, J. Jefferson. 1978. Response to stress at Grasshopper
Pueblo, Arizona. In Discovering past behavior: Experiments in
the archaeology of the American Southwest, ed. Paul Grebinger,

pp. 195–214. New York: Gordon and Breach.

Reining, Conrad C. 1970. Zande subsistence and food production. In African food production systems: Cases and theory, ed. P. McLoughlin, pp. 125–64. Baltimore: Johns Hopkins University Press.

Rice, Glen E. 1975. A systemic explanation of a change in Mogollon settlement patterns. Ph.D. dissertation, Department of Anthropology, University of Washington, Seattle.

Richards, Audrey I. 1939. Land, labour, and diet in northern Rhodesia: An economic study of the Bemba. Oxford: University of Oxford Press.

Robbins, Richard G., Jr. 1975. Famines in Russia: 1891–1892. New York: Columbia University Press.

Robins, J. S., and C. E. Domingo. 1953. Some effects of severe soil moisture deficits at specific growth stages in corn. Agronomy Journal 45:618–25.

Robson, J. R. K., and G. R. Wadsworth. 1977. The health and nutritional status of primitive populations. Ecology of Food and Nutrition 6:187–202.

Rodin, L. E., and N. I. Bazilevich. 1965. Production and mineral cycling in terrestrial vegetation. Edinburgh: Oliver and Boyd.

Rodin, L. E., N. I. Bazilevich, and N. N. Rozov. 1975. Productivity of the world's main ecosystems. In Productivity of world ecosystems, ed. D. Reichle, J. Franklin, and D. Goodall, pp. 13–26. Washington, D.C.: National Academy of Sciences.

Romer, Alfred S. 1933. Vertebrate paleontology. Chicago: University of Chicago Press.

Rosenzweig, Michael L. 1968. Net primary productivity of terrestrial communities: Prediction from climatological data. American Naturalist 102:67–74.

Rudel, Thomas K. 1980. Social responses to commodity shortages: The 1973–1974 gasoline crisis. Human Ecology 8:193–212.

Rugge, Dale. 1975. A petrographic study of ceramics from the Mimbres River Valley, New Mexico. Manuscript on file with the Mimbres Foundation, University of New Mexico, Albuquerque.

Sabels, Brun E. n.d. Manganese and phosphorus abundances in Wetherill Mesa feces and soils with some implications concerning the prehistory of Mesa Verde. Manuscript on file with the Mesa Verde National Park Museum, Mesa Verde.

Sahlins, Marshall D. 1968. Tribesmen. Englewood Cliffs, N.J.: Prentice-Hall.

_____. 1972. Stone age economics. Chicago: Aldine.

Sahlins, Marshall D., and Elman R. Service, eds. 1960. Evolution and culture. Ann Arbor: University of Michigan Press.

Sandor, Jonathan A. 1983. Soils at prehistoric agricultural terracing sites in New Mexico. Ph.D. dissertation, Department of Soil Sciences, University of Califiornia, Berkeley.

Sauer, Carl O. 1934. The distribution of aboriginal tribes and languages in northwestern Mexico. Ibero-Americana no. 5.

Saxe, Arthur A. 1970. Social dimensions of mortuary practices. Ph.D. dissertation, Department of Anthropology, University of Michigan, Ann Arbor.

Sayles, E. B., and Ernest Antevs. 1941. The Cochise culture. Medallion Papers no. 29. Globe, Ariz.: Gila Pueblo.

Schellberg, John D. 1982. The development of social complexity in Chaco Canyon. New Mexico Archaeological Council Newsletter 4(5&6):15-20.

Schneider, David M. 1957. Typhoons on Yap. Human Organization 16:10-15.

Schoenwetter, James. 1962. The pollen analysis of eighteen archaeological sites in Arizona and New Mexico. In Chapters in the prehistory of eastern Arizona, I, ed. P. Martin, J. Rinaldo, W. Longacre, C. Cronin, L. Freeman, and J. Schoenwetter, pp. 168-209. Fieldiana: Anthropology, vol. 53. Chicago: Field Museum.

Schoenwetter, James, and Alfred E. Dittert, Jr. 1968. An ecological interpretation of Anasazi settlement patterns. In Anthropological archaeology in the Americas, ed. B. Meggars, ed., pp. 41-66. Washington, D.C.: Anthropological Society of Washington.

Scott, Linda J. 1979. Dietary inferences from Hoy House coprolites: A palynological interpretation. Kiva 44:257-81.

Scott, Stuart. 1966. Dendrochronology in Mexico. Research Papers no. 2. Tucson: University of Arizona, Laboratory of Tree-Ring Research..

Scudder, Thayer. 1962. The ecology of the Gwembe Tonga. Manchester: Manchester University Press.

_____. 1971. Gathering among African woodland savannah cultivators, a case study: The Gwembe Tonga. University of Zambia, Institute of African Studies Zambian Papers no. 5. Manchester: Manchester University Press.

Segraves, B. Abbott. 1974. Ecological generalization and structural transformation in sociocultural systems. American

Anthropologist 76:53-52.

_____. 1977. The Malthusian proposition and nutritional stress: Differing implications for man and society. In *Malnutrition, behavior, and social organization*, ed. L. Greene, pp. 173-218. New York: Academic Press.

Service, Elman R. 1962. *Primitive social organization: An evolutionary perspective.* New York: Random House.

Seyles, Hans. 1956. *The stress of life.* New York: McGraw-Hill.

Shafer, Harry J. 1982a. *NAN Ranch Ruin: A collection of papers on the archeology of the NAN Ranch Ruin, Mimbres Valley, Grant County, New Mexico.* College Station: Texas A&M University, Department of Anthropology.

_____. 1982b. Classic Mimbres phase households and room use patterns. In *NAN Ranch Ruin: A collection of papers on the archeology of the NAN Ranch Ruin, Mimbres Valley, Grant County, New Mexico*, pp. 11-35. College Station: Texas A&M University, Department of Anthropology.

_____. 1983. *The NAN Ranch Archaeological Project, 1982 season.* Special Series no. 5. College Station: Texas A&M University, Anthropology Laboratory.

Shafer, Harry J., A. J. Taylor, and Steve J. Usrey. 1979. *Archaeology of the NAN Ranch Ruin, Grant County, New Mexico: A preliminary report.* Special Series no. 3. College Station: Texas A&M University, Anthropology Laboratory.

Shaw, Robert H. 1977. Climatic requirements. In *Corn and corn improvement*, ed. G. Sprague, pp. 591-623. Agronomy Series no. 18. Madison, Wisc.: American Society of Agronomy.

Sigleo, A. C. 1975. Turquoise mine and artifact correlation for the Snaketown site, Arizona. *Science* 189:459-60.

Silva, Alcionilio B. A. 1962. *A civilização indígena do Uaupés.* Saõ Paulo: Centro de Pesquisas de Iauareté.

Simmons, James S. 1954. *Global epidemiology: A geography of disease and sanitation.* Philadelphia: Lippincott.

Singh, K. Suresh. 1975. *The Indian famine, 1967.* New Delhi: People's Publishing.

Skidmore, E. L., and N. P. Woodruff. 1968. *Wind erosion forces in the United States and their use in predicting soil loss.* Agricultural Handbook no. 346. Washington, D.C.: U.S. Department of Agriculture.

Skiner, Elliott P. 1964. *The Mossi of the Upper Volta: The political development of a Sudanese people.* Palo Alto:

Stanford University Press.

Slobodkin, Lawrence B. 1964. The strategy of evolution. American Scientist 52:342-57.

_____. 1968. Toward a predictive theory of evolution. In Population biology and evolution, ed. R. Lewontin, pp. 187-205, Syracuse: Syracuse University Press.

Slobodkin, Lawrence B., and Anatol Rapoport. 1974. An optimal strategy of evolution. Quarterly Review of Biology 49:181-200.

Slovic, Paul, Baruch Fischoff, and Sarah Lichtenstein. 1979. Rating the Risks. Environment 21:14-20.

Smith, Watson, and John M. Roberts. 1954. Zuni law: A field of values. Cambride: Harvard University Press.

Snow, David H. 1973. Prehistoric southwestern turquoise industry. El Palacio 79:33-51.

Snow, Edgar. 1961. Red star over China. New York: Grove Press.

Sorokin, Pitirim A. 1975. Hunger as a factor in human affairs. Gainesville: University of Florida Press.

Spencer, Herbert. 1871. Synthetic philosophy: Principles of psychology. New York: D. Appleton.

Spooner, Brian. 1972. Population growth: Anthropological implications. Cambridge: M.I.T. Press.

Sprague, Roderick, and Aldo Signori. 1963. Inventory of prehistoric southwestern copper bells. Kiva 28:1-20.

Stailey, David. n.d. Tabulation of mineral artifacts. Manuscript on file with the Mimbres Foundation, University of New Mexico, Albuquerque.

Staten, Glen, D. R. Burnham, and John Carter, Jr. 1939. Corn investigations in New Mexico. Bulletin no. 260. Las Cruces: New Mexico State University, Agricultural Experiment Station.

Stefansson, Vilhjalmur. 1913. My life with the Eskimo. New York: Macmillan.

Stein, Zena, and Mervyn Susser. 1975. Fertility, fecundity, famine: Food rations in the Dutch famine 1944/45 have a causal relation to fertility and probably fecundity. Human Biology 47:131-54.

Steinbock, R. T. 1979. Paleopathological diagnosis and interpretation: Bone diseases in ancient human populations. Springfield, Ill.: Charlies C. Thomas.

Stephens, Alexander M. 1936. Hopi journal. ed. E. Parsons. Contributions to Anthropology no. 23. New York: Columbia University.

Stevenson, Matilda Cox. 1904. The Zuni Indians: Their mythology,
    esoteric fraternities, and ceremonies. Annual Report no. 23.
    Washington, D.C.: Bureau of American Ethnology.
Steward, Julian H. 1937. Ecological aspects of southwestern
    society. Anthropos 32:87-104.
_____. 1938. Basin-plateau aboriginal sociopolitical groups.
    Bulletin no. 120. Washington, D.C.: Bureau of American
    Ethnology.
Stewart, Frances L., and Peter W. Stahl. 1977. Cautionary note on
    edible meat poundage figures. American Antiquity 42:267-69.
Stiger, Mark A. 1977. Anasazi diet: The coprolite evidence.
    M.A. thesis, Department of Anthropology, University of
    Colorado, Boulder.
Stockton, Charles W. 1975. Long-term streamflow records
    reconstucted from tree-rings. Research Paper no. 5. Tucson:
    University of Arizona, Laboratory of Tree-Ring Research.
Stokes, Marvin A. 1968. An introduction to tree-ring dating.
    Chicago: University of Chicago Press.
Street, John M. 1969. An evaluation of the concept of carrying
    capacity. Professional Geographer 21:104-7.
Struever, Mary B. 1977. Relation of pollen and flotation analyses
    to archaeological excavations, Chaco Canyon (flotation
    component). M.A. thesis, Department of Biology, University of
    New Mexico, Albuquerque.
Swindale, L. D., S. M. Virmani, and M. V. K. Sivakumar. 1981.
    Climatic variability and crop yields in semi-arid tropics. In
    Food-climate interactions, ed. W. Bach, J. Pankrath, and S.
    Schnieder, pp. 139-16. Dordrecht, Holland: D. Reidel.
Taylor, Anne J. 1982. Analysis of ceramics from the NAN Ranch
    Ruin, Grant County, New Mexico. In NAN Ranch Ruin: A
    collection of papers on the archeology of the NAN Ranch Ruin,
    Grant County, New Mexico, ed. H. Shafer, pp. V1-13. College
    Station: Texas A&M University, Department of Anthropology.
Talayesva, Don C. 1942. Sun Chief: The autobiography of a Hopi
    Indian. ed. L. Simmons. New Haven: Yale University Press.
Terrell, Edward E. 1977. A checklist of names of 3,000 vascular
    plants of economic importance. Agriculture Handbook no. 505.
    Washington, D.C.: U.S. Department of Anthropology.
Thomas, Alfred B. 1932. Forgotten frontiers. Norman: University
    of Oklahoma Press.
Thornthwaite, C. W. 1933. The climates of the earth. Geo-
    graphical Review 23:433-40.

229   References

Tindale, Norman. 1962   Some population changes among the Kaiadilt
    people of Bentinck Island, Queensland. Record of the South
    Australian Museum 14:259-96.
Torry, William I. 1979. Anthropological studies in hazardous
    environments: Past trends and new horizons. Current Anthro-
    pology 20:517-540.
Tuan, Yi-Fu, Cyril E. Everard, Jerold G. Widdison, and Iven
Bennett. 1973. The climate of New Mexico. Santa Fe: New Mexico
    State Planning Office.
Turnbull, Colin M. 1972. The mountain people. New York: Simon
    and Schuster.
_____. 1978. Rethinking the Ik: A functional non-social system.
    In Extinction and survival in human populations, ed. C.
    McLaughlin and I. Brady, pp. 49-75. New York: Columbia
    University Press.
Turner, Raymond M. 1974. Quantitative and historical evidence of
    vegetation changes along the upper Gila River, Arizona.
    Professional Papers no. 655-H. Washington, D.C.: U.S.
    Geological Survey.
United States Geological Survey. 1974. Water Supply Paper no.
    2133. Washington, D.C.: U.S. Geological Survey.
Van Devender, Thomas R., and Geoffrey Spaulding. 1979. Develop-
    ment of vegetation and climate in the southwestern United
    States. Science 204:701-10.
Van Devender, Thomas R., and Richard D. Worthington. 1977. The
    herpetofauna of Howell's Ridge Cave and the paleoecology
    of the northwestern Chihuahuan desert. In Transactions of the
    symposium on the biological resources of the Chihuahuan desert
    region, United States and Mexico, ed. R. Waver and D. Riskind,
    pp. 85-106. Transactions and Proceedings Series no. 3.
    Washington, D.C.: National Park Service.
Vayda, Andrew P., and Bonnie J. McCay. 1975. New directions in
    ecology and ecological anthropology. Annual Review of Anthro-
    pology 4:293-306.
Vines, Robert A. 1960. Trees, shrubs and woody vines of the
    Southwest. Austin: University of Texas Press.
Von Endt, David W., and Donald J. Ortner. 1982. Amino acid
    analysis of bone from a possible case of prehistoric iron
    deficiency from the American Southwest. American Journal of
    Physical Anthropology 59:377-85.
Waddell, Eric. 1972. The mound builders: Agricultural practices,
    environment, and society in the Central Highlands of New

Guinea. Seattle: University of Washington Press.

_____. 1975. How the Enga cope with frost: Response to climatic perturbations in the Central Highlands of New Guinea. Human Ecology 3:249-73.

_____. 1977. The hazards of scientism: A review article. Human Ecology 5:69-76.

Waddington, C. H. 1974. A catastrophe theory of evolution. New York Academy of Sciences Journal 231:32-42.

Walter, H. 1954. Le facteur eau dans les régions arides et sa signification pour l'organization de la végétation dans les contrées sub-tropicales. Paris: Centre National de la Recherche Scientifique.

Washburn, Dorothy K. 1974. Nearest neighbor analysis of Pueblo I-III settlement patterns along the Rio Puerco in eastern New Mexico. American Antiquity 39:315-35.

Weaver, Donald E. 1978. Prehistoric population dynamics and environmental exploitation in the Manuelito Canyon district, northwestern New Mexico. Ph.D. dissertation, Department of Anthropology, Arizona State University, Tempe.

Weigand, Phil C., Garman Harbottle, and Edward V. Sayre. 1977. Turquoise sources and source analysis: Mesoamerica and the southwestern U.S.A. In Exchange systems in prehistory, ed. T. Earle and J. Ericson, pp. 15-34. New York: Academic Press.

Wendorf, Fred. 1959. Folsom points from Deming, New Mexico. El Palacio 66:109.

Werge, Robert W. 1979. Potato processing in the Central Highlands of Peru. Ecology of Food and Nutrition 7:229-34.

Westman, Walter E. 1978. Measuring the inertia and resilience of ecosystems. BioScience 28:705-10.

Wetterstrom, Wilma E. 1976. The effects of nutrition on population size at Pueblo Arroyo Hondo, New Mexico. Ph.D. dissertation, Department of Anthropology, University of Michigan, Ann Arbor.

Whalen, Michael E. 1980. The Pueblo periods of southcentral New Mexico. In An archaeological synthesis of southcentral and southwestern New Mexico, ed. S. LeBlanc and M. Whalen, pp. 387-448. Albuquerque: University of New Mexico, Office of Contract Archaeology.

Whalen, Norman. 1971. Cochise culture in the central San Pedro drainage. Ph.D. dissertation, Department of Anthropology, Unviersity of Arizona, Tucson.

Wheat, Joe Ben. 1955. Mogollon culture prior to A.D. 1000.

American Anthropologist, Memoir no. 82.

White, Gilbert F., ed. 1974. *Natural hazards: Local, national, global*. Oxford: Oxford University Press.

White, Theodore E. 1953a. A method of calculating the dietary percentage of various food animals uilized by aboriginal peoples. *American Antiquity* 18:396-98.

_____. 1953b. Observations on the butchering technique of some aboriginal peoples. *American Antiquity* 19:160-64.

White, Walter N. 1934. Progress report on the ground-water supply of the Mimbres River, New Mexico. In *New Mexico State Engineer eleventh biennial report, 1932-1934*, pp. 109-25. Santa Fe: New Mexico State Engineer Office.

Whittaker, Robert H. 1970. *Communities and ecosystems*. New York: Macmillan.

_____. 1975. *Communities and ecosystems*, 2d ed. New York: Macmillan.

Whittaker, R. H., and W. A. Niering. 1975. Vegetation of the Santa Catalina Mountains, Arizona, V: Biomass, productivity, and diversity along the elevation gradient. *Ecology* 56:771-90.

Whittaker, R. H., and G. M. Woodwell. 1971. Measurement of net primary production of forests. In *Productivity of forest ecosystems*, ed. P. Duvigneaud, pp. 159-75. Paris: UNESCO.

Whittaker, R. H., Nel Cohen, and Jerry S. Olson. 1963. Net production relations of three tree species at Oak Ridge, Tennessee. *Ecology* 44:806-10.

Whyte, Ann. 1977. Systems as perceived: A discussion of "maladaptation in social systems." In *The evolution of social systems*, ed. J. Friedman and M. J. Rowland, pp. 73-78. London: Duckworth.

Wiessner, Polly. 1982. Risk, reciprocity, and social influences on !Kung San economics. In *Politics and history in band society*, ed. E. Leacock and R. Lee, pp. 61-84. Cambridge: Cambridge University Press.

Wilkes, H. G. 1977. Hybridization of maize and teosintle in Mexico and Guatemala and the improvement of maize. *Economic Botany* 31:254-63.

Wilmsen, Edwin N. 1970. *Lithic analysis and cultural inference: A Paleo-Indian case*. Anthropological Papers no. 16. Tucson: University of Arizona.

_____. 1978. Seasonal effects of dietary intake on Kalahari San. *Federation of American Societies for Experimental Biology*

Proceedings 37:65-72.

Wilson, Arnold T. 1932. Persia. London: E. Benn.

Wilson Gilbert L. 1934. The Hidatsa earthlodge. Anthropological
    Papers 33:340-420. New York: American Museum of Natural
    History.

Wilson, Monica H. 1959. Communal rituals of the Nyakyusa.
    Oxford: Oxford University Press.

Wing, Elizabeth S., and Antoinette B. Brown. 1979. Paleo-
    nutrition: Method and theory in prehistoric foodways. New
    York: Academic Press.

Winter, Joseph C. 1977. Hovenweep 1976. Archaeological Report
    no. 3. San Jose: San Jose State University.

Wood, John J., and R. G. Matson. 1973. Two models of socio-
    cultural systems and their implication for the archaeological
    study of change. In The explanation of culture change:
    Models in prehistory, ed. C. Renfrew, pp. 663-72. Pittsburgh:
    University of Pittsburgh Press.

Woodall, J. Ned. 1968. Growth arrest lines in long bones of the
    Casas Grandes population. Plains Anthropologist 13:152-60.

Woodbury, Richard B. 1961. Prehistoric agriculture at Point of
    Pines, Arizona. Society for American Archaeology Memoir
    No. 17. Salt Lake City: University of Utah Press.

Woodham-Smith, Cecil. 1962. The great hunger. New York: Harper
    and Row.

Wyckoff, Don G. 1977. Secondary forest succession following
    abandonment of Mesa Verde. Kiva 42:215-32.

York, John C., and William A. Dick-Peddie. 1969. Vegetation
    changes in southern New Mexico during the past hundred years.
    In Arid lands in perspective, ed. W. McGinnies and B. Goldman,
    pp. 157-66. Tucson: University of Arizona Press.

Young, John A. 1978. Conservative, liberal, and radical view-
    points on the world food problem. Reviews in Anthropology
    5:513-28.

Zaino, Edward C. 1968. Elemental bone iron in the Anasazi
    Indians. American Journal of Physical Anthropology 29:433-36.

Zubrow, Ezra B. W. 1971. Carrying capacity and dynamic
    equilibrium in the prehistoric Southwest. American Antiquity
    36:127-38.

_____. 1975a. Ecological perspectives in the Hay Hollow Valley.
    In Chapters in the prehistory of eastern Arizona, IV, ed. P.
    Martin, E. Zubrow, D. Bowman, D. Gregory, J. Hanson, M.
    Schiffer, and D. Wilcox, pp. 17-39. Fieldiana: Anthropology,

vol. 65. Chicago: Field Museum.

_____. 1975b. Prehistoric carrying capacity: A model. Menlo
Park: Cummings.

Index